George A. Talley

A History of the Talley Family on the Delaware and their

Descendants

George A. Talley

A History of the Talley Family on the Delaware and their Descendants

ISBN/EAN: 9783337098513

Printed in Europe, USA, Canada, Australia, Japan

Cover: Foto ©ninafisch / pixelio.de

More available books at **www.hansebooks.com**

A

HISTORY

OF

The Talley Family

ON THE DELAWARE

AND THEIR DESCENDANTS;

INCLUDING A

GENEALOGICAL REGISTER, MODERN BIOGRAPHY

AND

MISCELLANY.

Early History and Genealogy From

1686.

By

GEORGE A. TALLEY.

PHILADELPHIA,
MOYER & LESHER, PRINTERS,
223 East Girard Avenue.

1899.

INTRODUCTION.

WHY write a history of the Talley family? Who were they and what have they accomplished? Those who ask these questions need have the means of answering themselves. This reason is a sufficient justification for the issue of this book.

No claim will we make that all of the Talleys were great and noble. Where will you find a crop of fruit or grain entirely free from blight or chaff? In searching out this record many extensive fields have been gleaned; and in the subsequent processes of threshing and winnowing, we have secured an abundant yield of well-formed, full-weight, golden grain.

Why should I assume the task and the responsibility of gathering up and preserving this record? The answer may be found in the fact that it has never heretofore been done, though highly important that it should have been.

When I began this work, I, like many others, simply knew my ancestry back to my grandfather. I knew that Thomas Talley was my grandfather, merely because I had in childhood played around his knees, in front of the blazing hearth.

We were then too young to further scan the past. Youth lives only for the future, and in hope of the coming manhood. After maturity our minds are more given to retrospection, and Inquiry will then often ask, "Who were our ancestors?" Alas, how often no response is heard! Many times have we asked this question without receiving a satisfying answer.

Through perseverence, however, the question has been solved so far as it relates to America. These revealed matters must not be kept a secret for one alone, but must be for all. By this publication it is brought within the reach of every one.

That I have been able to devote the time necessary to accomplish this task, arises from the fact that my health gave way, at three different times, under too intense application to my profession—the law—in the active, bustling city of Chicago. On this account, alone, I was forced to leave the city, and to seek retirement and rest in the country, amidst green fields and shady trees.

While thus resting, the Talley genealogy has been gradually unfolded, and made ready for publication. The earnest desire and hope is, that it may prove satisfactory to the most critical, and of lasting benefit to this numerous family.

Mr. O. B. Talley, of Sioux City, Iowa, has been most active, earnest, and successful in gathering up matters connected with the family genealogy, and has most generously given his services in aid of the work. We take pleasure in introducing this distant Talley to the consideration of his many relatives in other parts of our country. He is entitled to sit around the family board without other credentials than the record just made. He is a worshiper of our ancestral name, and delights to honor it.

William A. Talley, of Brandywine Hundred, has firmly and heroically stood by me in this work. He has labored most effectively in the matter of procuring subscribers and thereby producing the motive power, which is, after all, the one thing necessary to start the wheels of any large enterprise. May he always remember with pleasure our many consultations about this work, at his home on the Naaman's Creek Road. We must feel under great obligations to Mrs. Elizabeth A. Talley, widow of Samuel Talley, Mrs. Mary Johnson, Curtis M. Talley, Isaac N. Grubb, J. Henderson Talley, Amos C. Brinton, Lewis F. Talley, Henry I. Talley of Philadelphia, and a host of others, who kindly gave time, furnished papers, and records of many kinds, all of which aided in solving the difficult problem.

When judging of the merits of our work, kind reader,

view it not in the light of its present *development*, but consider the conditions existing a year ago, when all were content with tracing back only to the grandparents. Standing now at the close of the book, with its leaves thrown open, you may conclude that the task had been easy. Perhaps, your opinion may be modified by viewing the book from the front, with its leaves securely sealed against you.

A certain family record was thirty years in preparation. If this work had required so long a time for its completion, some one other than a Talley must have done it. No one of our name could have patience to engage in so long a term of service. The material for this book has been procured in a comparatively short time, although attended with most trying difficulties.

Many times in our searching did the way grow dark with discouragements. Occasionally would we catch the faintest glimmer of the guiding Star of Hope ; then would it fade and disappear ; again would it return more bright than before ; until at last it shone forth as the perpetual Polar Star, which most kindly led us into the great highway of certainty and success. May you all share with us the *pleasures* of our fortunate discoveries.

In the future let us not sit quietly down, but let us note *all* matters relating to our genealogy, whether in America or in Europe. This being done, may we not hope that our history in the " old country " shall yet be unfolded ?

Bright Star of Hope ! *still* lead us on.

G. A. T.

Sept. 14, 1899.

CHAPTER I.

OUR NAME—ITS ORIGIN.

That every person should have a name appears to be an indispensable requisite. The reason for the adoption of a personal name is, that one person may be distinguished from all others, and thereby become identified.

Some bear long and illustrious ancestral names, won by noble deeds on the field of battle, or in halls of state. Such a name should be prized by all and disparaged by none. However, the blind worship of a noble name, which causes one to live in listless idleness, and to feed himself upon the glory of a renowned ancestry, is anything but commendable. Every one should strive to add new lustre to his family name ; for it is aptly said :

> " By birth the name alone descends,
> Your honor on yourself depends."

Family names often originate from some office, occupation or color ; as, Smith, Miller, King, Black, Brown, etc. Our name is most positively " Talley," and not " Tally." It is spelled " Talley " the first place we find it written in this country. It is spelled the same in England to-day, and was thus written on the Swedish list of 1693. This very old name in Virginia is also spelled " Talley." Throughout the early deed of Mary Campbell to William Talley, it is written " Talley." Let us not deviate from the old, well-beaten path, but always write it " Talley."

The name is of very ancient origin. From the Latin adjective *talis*, meaning like or similar, we get the genitive case *tale*, pronounced " Talley." From this Latin word comes the French infinitive *tailler*, to cut, or to make like by cutting, also comes the participle *taille*, a cutting. These words are pronounced as if spelled *tahl-yai*, with the "l" almost silent.

All the Latin countries, as Italy, Spain, Portugal, and France, have a similar word ; but it is not found in Germany, Holland or Sweden, because their language comes almost wholly from the old German or Teutonic. There is still another Latin word that may have much to do with our name. *Talea* means a shoot, sprig, scion or stock. Thus the stock or stump of a tree. The French have formed from this word their word *talle*, pronounced exactly as if spelled "Talley." The meaning is, the stump or trunk after cutting away the branches ; hence throwing out shoots or new branches.

Either of the words *tailler* or *talle* may have been the origin of the name Talley, or perhaps both combined may have been. In either case the name would be of Latin–French origin.

The word *stille*, from which the name Stilley came, is of old German origin, and is found almost wholly with the nations which sprang from the Teutonic race. It is thus shown that certain names are local to a class of nations, and not general among all.

Some persons suppose that the word *tally* is used only to express the number *five*. A *tally* in counting does express five, but this is only one of several ways of using the word. This meaning grew up from the custom of counting by cutting notches on a stick, or making strokes with a pencil ; thus four notches or strokes and one for tally. Counting by this method was not by units, but by *fives* or *tallies*, and was both speedy and accurate.

In France a sort of tax was levied, called the *taille* tax. A tax cut out or taken on a like ratio from all persons of a certain class. It was levied upon land, and arbitrarily, whenever it might be needed by the government. Here again is our name found in the language of France. (See *Victor Duruy's* History of France.)

In England, when two things were cut to match, they were said to *tally*. In this way the English words, tally, tally-man and tally-shop, originated. A tally-man was the keeper of a tally-shop. A tally-shop was a place where goods were sold on credit, and the accounts were kept by notches cut on sticks, each party holding one of the sticks, which were carefully compared on final settlement.

It is stated by Wagner in his book entitled, "Names and Their Meaning," printed in London in 1891, that prior to 1782, when the British Government accepted money upon loan, the acknowledgment was written on both sides of a broad, flat stick, which was cut into two parts ; one piece, called the stock, was given to the lender, and the other piece, called the counter-stock, was deposited in a government room called the tally-office. This instrument of reckoning was called the *tally*, from the French verb *tailler*, to cut. When the stock and the counter-stock matched, they were said to *tally*, and settlements were made accordingly.

There are other ways in which our name may have originated, but they all run back in the direction of France. There was born in England, in 1515, a certain Thomas Tallis, who was justly styled the father of English Cathedral music. This name is of French construction, but Tallis wrote his name simply "Thomas Tallys." He was the author of such high-class music as the *Te Deum, Nicene Creed, Gloria in Excelsis, Nunc Demitis*, and many others.

Tallis and his pupil, William Byrd, obtained from Queen Elizabeth a royal grant for the exclusive right to print music in England for twenty-five years. Tallis died in 1585, and was buried in the church at Greenwich. We have not had the means to follow this family farther, but if Tallis left descendants, they may have come down the long centuries since his death as the modernized Talley.

There was in Wales as far back as the eighth or ninth century a renowned bard named Taliesen — one who thrilled the patriotic hearts of ancient Wales by his poetry and national song, and caused these hardy western mountaineers to gain the mastery over all eastern England. We are told that this illustrious songster was so much revered by the Welsh people that to this day many youths are given the Christian name of Taliesen ; also in southern Wales there are people surnamed Talley, whose names may have originated from Taliesen, they being called Talley for short. As an illustration, we state the fact that a noted singer attended the Ocean Grove Camp Meeting this year (1899) whose name is Taliesen Morgan. Those who knew him, simply called him Talley Morgan.

Then, again, we have the name of Talleyrand, illustrious in France centuries before the birth of the brilliant diplomat of the Napoleonic *regime*.

Hence we have here clustered together many signboards pointing to the probable origin of our name. Perhaps, were we to follow all of the windings of these devious paths, we might converge at last in that land of the vine, and of beautiful flowers, and of national greatness, just across the English Channel.

CHAPTER II.

OUR NATIONALITY.

Perhaps one of the most interesting questions to us, and the one most difficult of absolute and correct solution, is, What is our nationality? Or from what country did our ancestors emigrate, when they sailed for America?

The search on this line has been both prolonged and earnest. Old and new books have been bought, borrowed and hired, with the hope of finding a faint trace of how our common ancestors first landed on the shores of the Delaware. All known Swedish and Dutch histories of our early colonies have been ransacked from preface to index, with the view of finding, if possible, somewhere hidden away among the Petersons, Stidhams, Neilsons, Springers, Jaquettes, Alrichs, and Vandeveers, one stray name of Talley.

He does not materialize either as Governor, Legislator, Surveyor, Tax-Collector, Land-owner, Wolf-catcher, or even as Dust-sweeper in the church.

If we search all of the petitions, presented in the early days on many different occasions (and their number was legion), we may not find the name of Talley thereon.

We have been unable to find a single deed with the name Talley therein, prior to the first coming of William Penn. Even in the "Long Finn's Rebellion" in 1669, in which nearly all of the Swedes on the Delaware were implicated, we do not find the name Talley among them, nor in any manner connected with the trial.

The Talleys have in most things been considered modest, but not in the matter of acquiring and holding lands. They have been accredited with knowing a good thing at sight. Had they been here with the early Swedes, they, without doubt, would have owned some of the fine lands that lay adjacent to the Delaware River, when they could have procured them almost for the asking.

The spirit which induced people to emigrate to this new country was that of liberty and acquisition. What was there here to acquire but lands and Indian scalps? Our family were never known to glory in the latter, and where was the land that they acquired in the Swedish days?

It not appearing definitely what our nationality is we must claim our birthright with some of the nations which have treasured our name and preserved it in history. We find no trace of our name in either the Swedish or the German language ; but, finding it in France, England and Wales, we are forced to the conclusion, that some one of these is the place of our origin.

In Southwestern France, near the ocean, we find the town of Taillebourg, where the British were defeated in battle about 1242. Somewhat to the southeast of this city is the province of Perigord, a district centuries ago conferred upon the Talleyrand family for meritorious services.

In the list of eminent names of the Talleyrand family we find—Elie Talleyrand, an eminent cardinal, born at Perigord, 1301 and died 1364 ; Henri Talleyrand, Comte de Chalois, a courtier to the king, born 1599 ; Gabriel Marie Talleyrand, Comte de Perigord, a French general, born 1726, uncle to the great diplomat, fought at Hastenbeck and Crefeld, and died 1795 ; Louis Augusti Talleyrand, a diplomat, was born in 1770 ; and Charles Maurice Talleyrand de Perigord, born at Paris, February 2d, 1754.

The last named, the meteoric diplomat of Europe, eclipsed all his compeers, and for his brilliancy procured the denunciation of the bookmakers of the age in which he lived. If he was devoid of honor, it may have resulted from the teachings and examples set him, in the days of intrigue in which he lived. Napoleon conceived that he was most valuable to him, or he (Talleyrand) would not have filled the offices that he did. Poor Talleyrand could practice artifice on other nations for the benefit of his master, but not upon

Napoleon. Not living in that day, we can only hope that
Talleyrand was not so black as he has been painted.

The last Talleyrand lived up to the year 1838, and
died at the age of eighty-four. It is not claimed that we
are descended from this Talleyrand. It is, however, interesting to search out the origin of the early Talleyrand name.
The name undoubtedly was Talley before it became Talleyrand. Rand means an edge or a border. May not the word
have been formed by bringing into one word the phrase
talle y rand? *Talle* is a perfect French word, as shown in
Chapter I.

We wish to record some facts here that may or may
not in the future aid in solving the nationality problem.
James Le Fevre came to America in the early Swedish days
and settled about New Castle. He had two brothers, John
and Hypolite ; all were French Huguenots. John and Hypolite settled in England. We find that in 1698 a Hypolitus
Le Fevre made a deed as the husband of Katharine Johnson, daughter of John Johnson, who lived just north of
Marcus Hook. William Talley also joined in the same deed
as the husband of Elinor, the late widow Johnson and
mother of Katharine Le Fevre. William Talley may have
also been a Huguenot, and came from England with Hypolitus Le Fevre. This is only the merest supposition, however.

We now turn in our search to the British Isles, and
here we find Tallis (Thomas Tallys) the great composer of
church melody. *Tallis* is in form French, but as spelled by
himself "Tallys," using a "y," would indicate a Welsh
derivation. However, there was about ten years ago a lawyer
in England named William Talley.

In the rugged and romantic hills of Wales, in Car-
marthenshire, we discover the full-fledged town of "Talley ;"
and down the highway, about five miles southward, we find
at the Railroad Crossing the "Talley road-station." For a
moment's delight procure a large Atlas and view for the first
time your own name written on the map of Europe.

After months of research, it was as refreshing as a
spring in a desert to find what might tend to cast some

light upon the subject so earnestly sought and longingly desired.

Another adventure, almost as thrilling, was the finding of the name of William Talley on the records of Probate at Philadelphia as early as February 17th, 1686. On this date he was appointed joint administrator with Elinor, widow of Jan Jansen. He afterwards married the widow.

He is shown on a tax list in 1693, on the Swedish church list of 1693, and joins in a deed of the Jansen land in 1698. The Talley has at last crawled from his hiding-place. It is no longer a matter of conjecture.

A list of Swedes, and those affiliating with the Swedish churches here, was sent to the mother country in 1693. On this list William Talley was placed as the head of a family of seven. The purpose of this list was to induce the sending of ministers and some religious books to the colony. Now, it cannot be claimed that all on the list were Swedes, as several thereon were known to be of different nationalities. Elias Toy and Thomas Dennis were surely from the Emerald Isle ; Cornelius, Jacob and William Vandeveer were well-known Hollanders ; Isaac Savoy may have been French ; Robert Longhorn and William Talley were from England or Wales, no doubt. The reliability of this list, being wholly Swedish, is thus completely destroyed. William Talley's name is on the list because he had become the husband of the widow Jansen, who perhaps was a Swede or a Hollander ; although she may have been French.

This family of seven was no doubt composed largely of the minor children of the late Jan Jansen, who were known to have been in existence at that time, and who no doubt gathered around the family board, after William came to preside as the adopted father.

The tax list of Chichester, then of Chester County, Pennsylvania, for 1693 shows the name of "William Talle" among many other old and familiar names. As the Jansen name does not appear on the list, it may be that Talley was assessed as representing the Jansen land, or he may have been assessed for his own land in the upper part of Rockland Manor.

William Talley was contemporary with such men as
William Clayton, William Cloud, John Grubb, Philip Roman
and Francis Chadsey. Some of the important names on this
tax list were—

Jeremiah Collet,	Phillip Rumen,
John Kingsman,	Richd. Buffinton,
Wm. Clayton,	Wm. Talle,
Jas. Browne,	Rogger Smith,
Wm. Flower,	Henery Hasteings,
Jos. Chandler,	Wm. Thomas,
Jas. Whitaker,	Chas. Rawson,
ffrancis Chadsey,	Wm. Hues.

There is some bad spelling in making up this list. An assessor's orthography is not always to be followed. The following names are misspelled on this list, viz: Roman, Buffington,
Talley, Henry Hastings, Hewes and Roger Smith.

These men were assessed, several at 8s. 4d. ; others at
6s. 0d. ; and some at 2s. 6d. William Talley is assessed 6s. 0d.
He was not the highest nor the lowest on the list. This list
shows that nearly all on it were of British descent.

Now, in closing this chapter, we may safely claim,
until the contrary is shown, that we belong to the Gaelic or
French race, which inhabited ancient France or Gaul, and
centuries ago, perhaps, passed over into England or Wales,
and from there found our way to America, about the time of
William Penn.

It has been stated in a humorous though truthful way,
that the Talleys, although of Gaelic origin, have in changing
from France into the British Isles, and from Britain to the
Rocky Hills of Brandywine Hundred, lost probably from association some of their " _Gaul_," and have become modest and
unostentatious Americans.

A quiet vote was taken on the question of our nationality, as the canvass was being made for the information
necessary for this book. The majority was overwhelming in
favor of England being the place from which our ancestors
migrated to America. This will we ever claim until some
sure foundation is laid for a different local habitation for our
emigrant ancestors.

Without question there has been an intermixture by marriage with other nations since coming to America ; but this cannot change the nationality of the first Talley who landed here. This man's nationality must ever be considered as determining that of the Talley family in America.

We find not the usual German and Swedish Christian names among the Talleys of the early day. We find only such English names as Thomas, John, William, Samuel, David, Mary, Charity, Hannah, Sarah, and Rachel. Even the name on the Swedish list of 1693 is written in clear English, " William Talley."

Historians out of the family may without much thought class us with other nations, but we of the family know some things by *intuition* and *instinct*, as well as by *tradition*. These constrain us to believe that the Talleys are British, except so far as intermarriage may have wrought changes.

No matter what the nationality of our mothers may have been, we are Talleys, all of one family and bound together by the strong ties of flesh and blood. We are without doubt all good and true American citizens, and proud of our country. May nothing ever arise to destroy our patriotism, or to estrange us from one another !

CHAPTER III.

THE LANDING IN AMERICA—THE PROCURING OF THE FIRST TRACT OF LAND.

Certain it is that some one by the name of Talley landed in America from some European port, but the time and place of landing is involved in much doubt. The date has been placed by some as early as 1648, by some as 1664, and by others as 1668. Dr. Reuben Allmond, of Illinois, who made quite a study of the matter, places the date at 1675.

There is nothing of record to show the exact date, so far as has yet been discovered. We can neither find the vessel which carried this precious freight to the shores of America, nor the foreign port of embarkation. If they came in 1648, they must have landed at Christiana, now Wilmington, and should have been found in the territory either north or south of the Christiana Creek. We find no mention of the Talleys in or about this region in the early Swedish or Dutch times. They held no land there, nor did they hold any office, or take any part in the affairs of the Swedish churches at Cranehook, Tinicum, Wicacoe, or Christiana.

We frequently find lists of church officers, pew-holders, and donors to the church fund, as well as names of soldiers about the forts ; even laborers are often mentioned. Among all of these we find no name of Talley, until after the first arrival of William Penn. After this date it is not difficult to find the name, if we make the proper research, and have the endurance to continue to the end.

The needle may be *known* to be in the haystack, and still may not be found. It is *not* known that the man Talley was in these vast colonial forests prior to the time of Penn. If it is difficult to find the needle, how much more so to find the man in the woods, when perhaps he never was there. Chasing myths through the jungle may be very amusing, but otherwise not a very profitable occupation.

We have but one tradition as to the *place* of landing in America. Mr. J. Henderson Talley, son of John Talley, the Methodist minister, informs us that he has often heard his father, and a very old man who lived in their family named James Zebley, speak of the Talley landing-place, and that it was at Upland, now Chester. Later revelations have tended to confirm this tradition.

William Talley, our common ancestor, was here in 1686, and was on February 17th, 1686, at Philadelphia, appointed joint administrator with Elinor Jansen, of the estate of Jan Jansen, her deceased husband. Jan Jansen at the time of his death resided on the east side of Chichester Creek. William Talley is also named on the Swedish Church list of 1693. The same year he is placed on the tax list of Chichester Township, then of Chester County, Pennsylvania. He married widow Jansen sometime between 1686 and 1693. Jan Jansen was an extensive land-owner along the river, east of the location of the Trainor Cotton Mills.

William Talley about this time purchased a tract of land down in Rockland Manor. There he made his abode, among rocks, swamps, large trees, wolves and Indians, and was the first settler at Foulk's Corner. Thus was founded the first Talley settlement in Brandywine Hundred. From this wilderness home, whether it was the open woods, a cave, or a log hut, sprang the great Talley family, which afterwards swept over the whole north and northwestern portions of Rockland Manor, from Naaman's Creek to the Brandywine.

We find that Isaac Warner, of Philadelphia, procured a warrant on the 2d mo., 12th day, 1682, from William Penn, for a tract of land called the "Partner's Adventure," situate on the west branch of Naaman's Creek and extending for nearly a mile on each side of the creek. The tract contained four hundred acres, and was thus bounded : "Beginning at a corner marked poplar standing by the south side of said branch and running by a line of marked trees northeast 267

perches to a corner marked white oak standing by the head of
a small run ; thence by a line of marked trees northwest 120
per. to a black oak ; thence by a line of marked trees southwest 534 per. to a corner white oak standing by a swamp ;
thence along a line of marked trees southeast 170 per. to a
corner poplar ; thence by a line of marked trees northeast 267
per., crossing to the first named poplar."

It may be that William Talley was the silent partner in
this "adventure." It will be noticed that although this land
extended from near the Siloam Church to the Thomas Vance
place on the Foulk Road, not a road, house, or other artificial
structure, is mentioned, nor does it appear that any neighbor's
land bounded this tract. Neighbors were scarce, no doubt,
in that day and territory. All of the boundary lines ran
along by " marked trees," thus proving that the whole tract
was carved out of a dense woods.

Think of living and feeding a family in such a place,
and possibly without funds, horses, cattle, or implements of
agriculture. It was truly hewing out a home in the wilds of
America. No doubt the old " flint lock " was the means of
procuring meat for the family, which, with johnny cake, was
the staple diet.

On the 16th day of March, 1695, William Talley procured from Isaac Warner a deed for all of said tract of land
lying on the westerly side of the creek, which deed was on
March 17th thereafter acknowledged in open court at New
Castle. This deed conveyed the legal title to the first tract
of land owned by the Talleys in Rockland Manor.

William Talley did not survive long to enjoy the liber-
ties acquired in his new domain, for he died some time
between 1698 and 1702. He joined with his wife and the
heirs of Jan Jansen, in 1698, in conveying one tract of the
Chichester lands to Robert Langham. In 1702, when the remaining tract was sold to Philip Roman, Mrs. Elinor Talley
made the deed as the widow of William Talley.

In the interim between these two deeds, William Talley
passed away, and no stone or monument marks the place of
his interment. He, like many of the early settlers, sleeps in
an unknown grave, " unwept, unhonored and unsung."

CHAPTER IV.

DEATH OF THE FIRST WILLIAM TALLEY—HIS CHILDREN—
DESCENT OF HIS LANDS.

William Talley the first died about 1700, the exact date not being known. It is supposed that his two children, Thomas and Mary, were born of the marriage with Elinor Jansen. These children may have been born not later than 1690. They would be old enough to marry by 1711. It is known that Thomas had a son William, born in 1714. This would indicate that Thomas married some time between 1711 and 1713.

As William had only two children, and he and Elinor were married sufficiently long before his death to allow of the birth of these, we may well conclude, in the absence of other proof, that Elinor was the mother of these children. Still it may have been that William had a prior wife, and that the two children were born of such marriage, and that no children were born of the last marriage.

Let this be as it may, it is clear that Thomas and Mary were the children and only heirs-at-law of William Talley the first, and inherited the land, consisting of two hundred acres, which William purchased from Isaac Warner in 1695. William, it seems, added nothing more to his land holdings, as he lived only about five years after receiving the Warner deed.

Thomas Talley married, but no record has been found of the marriage, nor has the name of his wife been discovered. Her name has not been mentioned in any deed, family Bible, or other found record. Thomas was not an extensive land-owner, or his wife's name would have been shown in some deed of conveyance.

Thomas lived to a great age. He, from all accounts, may have been the oldest Talley known to have lived on this

continent, and may be entitled to be styled the Patriarch.
His death occurred in 1781, as is recited in a deed by and between his three sons, William, Samuel and David, which is
recorded at Wilmington in Deed Record E, vol. 2, pg. 426.

The son William being born in 1714, the father must
have been born as early as 1690. This would make him 91
years old in 1781. If his mother was not Elinor, then he was
born of a prior marriage, and may have been more than 100
years old at his death in 1781. A tradition is recorded by
John Foulk Talley, of Ohio (son of Harmon), that an ancestor, Thomas, lived to be 115 years old, and that he was a
great violinist and played all night for a party when he was
111 years old. The number of years mentioned here may be
a little excessive.

Thomas was the man who erected the first saw-mill on
Naaman's Creek, at Foulk's Corner. It was in operation
long prior to 1771. As the mill sawed slowly at the early
day, Thomas had abundant time to tune the violin, and
amuse himself and his helpers, as the huge logs jogged
their weary way through the mill. We may in our fancy
imagine the beautiful harmony in the lonely woods of the
jog ! jog ! jog ! of the mill, keeping time to the sweet strains
of the violin.

This life in the woods was wild, romantic and musical,
if not entirely one of ease and comfort. Thomas Talley was,
in life, full of music, at his death full of years, and in early
manhood he was the pioneer manufacturer on the headwaters
of Naaman's Creek. This was perhaps honor enough for the
day in which he lived.

The deed mentioned herein shows that Thomas had six
children, named as follows : William, David, Samuel, Mary,
Susanna, and Hannah. The parents who gave names to these
children were surely descended from the English race, and
must have been people of strong character ; for several of the
children became able men and women, and a power in the
community.

Mary, the only sister of Thomas, married Peter Campbell, of Salem County, New Jersey. Peter and Mary, on
September 28th, 1738, by deed conveyed their share of their

father's land to William (son of Thomas), who was their nephew. William then became tenant in common with his father in the original Talley tract of two hundred acres. This deed from Campbell is the earliest deed known to be in existence, to-day, which conveyed land to the Talleys in Brandywine Hundred. The deed from Warner to William Talley is of earlier date ; but who now has it in keeping? We know nothing farther of the Campbell family. May some enthusiastic Talley youth take up this thread and follow it to the end.

The original Campbell deed is in the possession of John Booth's family. It is written on paper, not on parchment, and is well preserved. Its preservation is surely a wonder. The deed is here given in full, as copied from the original :

TO ALL PEOPLE TO WHOM these presents shall come greeting; Know ye, That we Mary Talley alias Mary Campbell and Peter Campbell of Salem County in the West Jersey. That for and in consideration of the sum of ten pounds to us in hand paid before the ensealing hereof well and truly paid by William Talley Jr., of Brandywine Hundred in the County of New Castle on Delaware Husbandman the receipt whereof we do hereby acknowledge and ourselves therewith fully satisfied and contented and thereof and of every part and parcel thereof Do exonerate acquit and discharge the said William Talley his heirs, executors and administrators forever by these presents, have given, granted, bargained, sold, aliened, conveyed and confirmed, and by these presents, Do freely, fully and absolutely give, grant, bargain, sell, alien, convey and confirm unto him the said William Talley, his heirs and assigns forever, one third part of the messuage or tract of land whereon Thomas Talley now dwells ; situate lying and being in Brandywine Hundred County of New Castle on Delaware, containing by estimation two hundred acres be it more or less butted and bounded viz., joining upon Joseph Cloud's land on the east end and joining upon the west side of the west branch of Naaman's Creek ; and also joining to John Grubb's land on the North West side To have and to hold the said granted and bargained premises with all the appurtenances, priviliges, commodities to the same belonging or in any wise appurtaining to him the said William Talley his heirs and assigns forever. To his only and there proper use benefit behoof forever and we the said Mary Talley alias Mary Campbell and Peter Campbell for us our heirs, executors and administrators do covenant promise and grant to and with the said William Talley his heirs and assigns that before the ensealing hereof that we are the true, just and lawful owners of the above granted premises and have in ourselves good right, full power and lawful authority to grant, bargain, sell, convey and confirm said bargained premises in manner as above said. And that the said William Talley his heirs and assigns shall and may from time to time and at all times forever hereafter by force and virtue of these presents lawfully, peaceably and quietly have, hold, use, occupy, possess and enjoy the said demised and bargained premises with all the appurtenances free and clear and freely and clearly acquited exonerated and discharged of from all and all manner of bargains formerly or gifts, grants, bargains, sales, leases, mortgages, wills, entails, jointures, dow-ries, judgements, executions, incumbrances and extents. Further more We the said Mary Talley alias Mary Campbell and Peter Campbell for ourselves our heirs, executors and administrators Do covenant and engage the above demised premises to him the said William Talley his heirs and assigns against the lawful claims or demands of any person or persons whatsoever forever hereafter to warrent secure and defend, the Lord of the soile only excepted. In witness whereof we have hereunto put our hands and seals this twenty-eighth day of September Anno Domini 1738.

Signed, sealed and delivered in the presence of us:

JOSEPH HINCHLOW,

JOSEPH ┼ CLOUD,
mark
his

WILLIAM W. C. CAMPBELL.
mark
his

PETER X CAMPBELL. { SEAL }
his
mark

MARY M CAMPBELL. { SEAL }
her
mark

New Castle County ye fourth of December seventeen and forty-five.

Then appeared Joseph Cloud of Brandywine Hundred in the County of New Castle personally before me one of His Majesties Justices of the Peace for the County of New Castle and on his solam affirmation saith that he was personally present and saw Peter Campbell and Mary Campbell, his wife, sign, seal and deliver the within deed to William Talley and that he signed as an evidence taken before me the day and year above said.

ADAM BUCKLEY.   JOSEPH ┼ CLOUD.
his
mark

Acknowledged in the Court of Common Pleas held at New Castle for the County of New Castle in August term 1759. Witness my hand and seal of the County aforesaid.

JAMES BOGGS, d'ty Prothy.

Recorded in the Rolls Office at New Castle in Book T, page 74.

Given under my hand and seal this third day of September, 1760.

R. W. WILLIAMS, Recorder of Deeds.

NOTE.—By the statute of Charles II, (1683) governing Delaware, the eldest son inherited a double share. Hence Thomas owned ⅔ and Mary ⅓. William by this deed only acquired ⅓ of the original tract.

CHAPTER V.

THE FIRST TRACT OF LAND — ITS CORRECT LOCATION —
ITS USE—THE TALLEY SAW-MILL.

The tract of land conveyed by Isaac Warner in 1695
to William Talley contained much more than two hundred
acres. The surveys made by these early surveyors were
scarcely more than walks through the woods.

This tract of Talley land, whatever it contained, was
bounded to the northeast by the branch of Naaman's Creek,
and extended westerly on both sides of *what is now* the Foulk
Road, and beyond Lonkum Run, just west of the present
house of Thomas Vance. The tract included all of the
Foulk farm, those of Adam Pierce and James Wilkinson,
and the farm now occupied by Wesley Beeson, the Foulk
Road frontage of the farms of Uriel Pierce and Robert
Casey, nearly all of the Vance farm on both sides of the
road, and the tract southeast of Edmund Mousley's house.
The creek boundary on the northeast is a crooked line, but
the side lines are practically parallel, and the west end line
is straight and nearly right angle to the sides. The northwesterly abuttal is a part of a straight line which extends
from near Zebley's corner almost to Shellpot Creek. A part
of the southeasterly boundary is the line between the Adam
Pierce and Casey farms. The entire southeasterly line is
made by protracting this Pierce–Casey line easterly to Naaman's Creek and westerly across the Casey and Uriel Pierce
farms, and across the Grubb Road, through the Vance farm
and across Lonkum Run. The strip on the southeasterly side
of the Foulk Road is about 22 rods deep. It is about 37½
rods from Foulk's Cross-Roads to the Pierce–Casey line. See
map on another page.

What was the inducement to take up this home in the
wilderness? It was not to hunt wolves nor to catch fish.
The overtowering timber, the "forest primeval," was the
magnet which drew the Talley family to this tract of land.
Historians tell us that the hunting of timber in the back
country, miles from the river, indicated the nationality of the
settler there ; it being as natural for the British settler to go
to the timber as it is for the proverbial duck to seek the
water. The Dutch and Swedish settlers remained close to
the rivers and the rich pasture lands.

By a search among some ancient deeds we soon find
where the Talley saw-mill was located, and what *kind of crops*
were harvested from this tract. The exact date of the start-
ing of this mill is not known. It was, however, in operation
on the creek, just above the residence of the late John Foulk,
prior to 1771. By a recital in a deed made by Samuel Talley
(son of Thomas) to John Foulk, dated in 1787, it appears that
"Thomas Talley, Sr., deceased, father of Samuel, did in
"writing, dated March 26th, 1779, convey to John Foulk a
"lot or tract of land on the westerly branch of Naaman's
"Creek, on which there *was* and *now is* a saw-mill." It thus
appears that Thomas Talley, son of the first William, had a
saw-mill at this place at a very early period.

The saw-mill tract can be readily found at this day by
running the following lines : Beginning at a corner stone by
the side of the great road leading to Wilmington, on the
lower edge of the creek ; thence south 55° west 6 per. to a
corner stone ; thence north 35° west 25 per. along a road that
leads to Gibson's mill ; thence north 55° east 10 per. to the
creek ; thence along the creek southeasterly and along Robert
Cloud's land 35½ per. to the place of beginning, containing
1¼ acres.

The great Wilmington Road was the Foulk Road, and
the road to Gibson's mill was a road that ran somewhere
near the present Foulk farm lane, and passed on to Beaver
Valley, where the Gibson mill was located. Robert Cloud's
land lay just across Naaman's Creek, and was the northeast-
erly portion of the Isaac Warner tract, and included more
than two hundred acres. Mr. Cloud did not purchase this

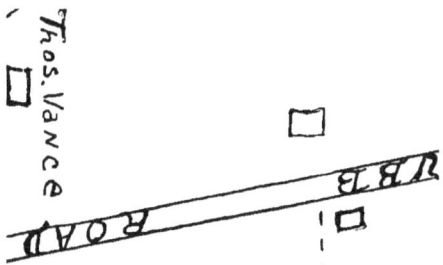

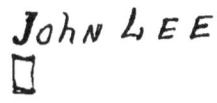

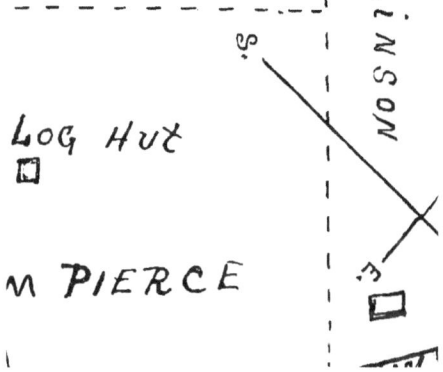

tract until after 1700. The saw-mill deed is recorded in Book "I," vol. 2, page 90, in the Recorder's Office at Wilmington. The saw-mill is again mentioned in a deed recorded in Book "E," vol. 2, page 426. The recital being that "Thomas "Talley conveyed to John Foulk, Samuel Talley and David "Talley a small tract or piece of land to build a saw-mill "upon." The date is not recited, but it says it was prior to 1780.

In an old account book, belonging to William Talley, who was born in 1714, we find a charge under the date 1771 against Samuel Talley for "one day hauling logs to the saw-"mill," and "to hauling one load of scantling to Marshall's "house." The charge for the day's hauling was £1, and for the scantling 14 shillings. This mill was in operation, then, before 1771, and no doubt did a flourishing business, and was the first manufactory in that neighborhood. Some of the lumber run out may have been used in that vicinity, but no doubt large quantities were hauled to Marcus Hook and Grubb's Landing, and shipped to foreign parts. Fine white oak abounded in that country, and large quantities were hauled away for ship building.

The mill kept in operation until nearly all of the valuable timber was cleared away. The grubbing business then began along the Foulk Road district, and to quote the complaining farmer there, it has been grub! grub! ever since. But, then, where is the man who does not grub for what he gets in this world?

He either grubs to get it, or grubs to hold what has generously been given him by some kind ancestor. Let us, then, all take courage and heroically *grub* and tally!, and *tally* and grub! until our purpose in life has been accomplished.

CHAPTER VI.

THOMAS TALLEY—HIS FAMILY—HIS LANDS—AN ALL IMPORTANT DEED.

Thomas Talley and his son William continued to hold the Warner Tract, west of the creek, as tenants in common until May 6th, 1758. As before stated, this tract extended from Naaman's Creek to the west of Loukum Run, beyond the house of Thomas Vance ; and from the northerly line of the Wilkinson land to the Adam Pierce and Casey line.

At the date last mentioned Thomas Talley and his son William made a division of this tract, and Thomas conveyed to William the westerly end of this land, containing 96¼ acres. This deed made by Thomas to William was handed down by William, so it came to the hands of his son Elihu. Elihu passed it to Nathaniel Booth, Sr. It has been protected for years by the Booth family, and is now guarded by the family of John Booth, who is son of Nathaniel.

The preserving of this deed and its discovery were almost miraculous. This deed with other valuable historical papers had occupied a corn crib for a considerable time, and were much damaged by rain, and might have been eaten by rats. For some reason they were gathered up by Mrs. Booth and taken to the house. After this chapter had been written for this book, the author stopped at the house of John Booth, near Booth's Corner, Pa., to see if another name might not be added to the subscriber's list. While talking of this history, the question was asked if they did not have somewhere preserved a paper that might give some explanation about the log hut, at the end of Casey's lane on the Foulk Road, and how it came to be moved there.

All the old family papers were brought forth by Mrs. Booth. No one but the author understood what a world of history was that day unfolded. The discovery was rich, a veritable Klondike. The deed of Thomas Talley to William is now given in full in these words. Copied from the original :

THIS INDENTURE Made the sixth day of May in the year of Our Lord One thousand seven Hundred and fifty eight Between Thomas Tally of Brandywine Hundred in the County of New Castle on Delaware Yeoman on the one part and William Tally son of the said Thomas on the other part, Whereas Isaac Warner by virtue of a Warrent from William Penn Esq., Proprietor and Commander in Chief of the Counties on Delaware and Province of Pennsylvania bearing date the 22d 12th mo. Anno Domini 1682 : became lawfully possessed of a certain tract of land called " the partners Adventure " situate lying and being on the West side of Delaware and on boath sides of a branch of Naaman's Creek and Beginning at a Corner marked popler standing on the South side of the said branch and Running from thence by a line of marked trees North East Two hundred and sixty seven perches to a corner marked white Oak standing by the head of a Small run, and from thence by a line of marked trees North West One hundred and twenty perches to a Corner marked Black Oak, thence by a line of marked trees South West five hundred and thirty-four perches to a marked Corner White Oak standing in a Swamp, then by a line of marked trees South East One hundred and twenty perches to a Corner marked popler, from thence by a line of marked trees North East, Two Hundred and sixty seven perches Crossing to the first mentioned popler, Containing and laid out for four Hundred Acres of land Surveyed the 28th day of October Ano. Domo. 1683 : Who by his Indenture of Bargain and Sale dated the 16th of March Ano. Domo. 1695 : and acknowledged in open Court at New Castle the 17th of the same month Sold and Conveyed unto William Tally all that part of the said tract which was on the South West side of the said branch and to hold to him his heirs and Assigns forever as by the said Indenture may appear Who afterwards died Intestate leaving to Survive him two Children (viz) the above named Thomas and Mary who Intermarried, with Peter Camble of the County of Salem in the Province of West Jersey Yeoman Who together with the said Mary his wife by their Deed Poll dated the 28th of September Ano. Domo. 1738 Sold and Conveyed all their undivided Right, of the above tract unto the above named William Tally to hold to him his Heirs and Assigns forever as by the said Deed may appear and the said Thomas Tally and William Tally being desirrous to make and Establish a division thereof between them THEREFORE this INDENTURE WITNESSETH that the said Thomas Tally for and in Consideration of the sum of five shillings Currentmoney to him in hand paid by the said William Tally the receipt whereof is hereby Acknowledged and the said Thomas Tally doth hereby

Release and discharge the said William Tally his heirs and assigns by
these presents HATH Promised, Released and forever Quit Claimed and by
these presents for himself his Heirs, Executors, Administrators and Assigns DOTH fully Clearly and Absolutely Remise, Release and forever
Quit Claim unto the said William Tally in his peaceable possession and
Seizen being and to his Heirs and Assigns forever all the Estate, Right,
Title, Interest, Claim and demand which I the said Thomas Tally now
have, or which I or my Heirs at any time hereafter may or ought to have of,
in or to all that part of the above Recited tract of land which is butted and
Bounded as followeth (viz) BEGINNING at a new marked Corner white
Oak Bush from thence along the old line South West One hundred and
Seven perches to the above mentioned Corner White Oak then South East
One hundred and forty four perches to a Corner Stone where an old Corner
popler formerly stood, from thence North East One hundred and Seven
perches to a new Corner white Oak, from thence along a new line dividing this from the said Thomas Tally's part North fifty One degrees
and a half west One hundred and forty four perches to the place of Beginning Containing Ninety six Acres and a quarter be the same more or
less TO HAVE AND TO HOLD all and singular the said peice or parcel
of Land and every part thereof with the appurtenances unto the said
William Tally his Heirs and Assigns forever, So that neither I the said
Thomas Tally nor my Heirs or any other person or persons for me or
them or in mine or their Names, Right, Title or Stead, Shall or may by
any ways or means hereafter have, Claim, Challenge or Demand any
Estate, or Interest of, in, or to the same premisses or any part thereof,
But from all Action, Right, Estate, Title, Interest and Demand of in and
to the same premisses and Every part there of Shall and will utterly excluded and debarred forever by these presents AND I the said Thomas
Tally and my Heirs the said piece or parcel of Land and premisses and
Every part thereof with the appurtenances unto the said William Tally
his Heirs and Assigns to his and their proper use and uses against me
the said Thomas Tally and my Heirs and all and every other person or
persons Lawfully claiming the same or any part thereof by from or
under me the said Thomas Tally shall and will warrent and forever defend by these presents.

　　In witness whereof I have hereunto put my hand and seal and dated
the day and year first above written.

his
THOMAS T.T. TALLY.　｛ SEAL ｝
mark

Seald and delivered in the presence of
　　ROBERT CLOUD,
　　NATHANIEL CLOUD.

　　JHN. STAPLER
　　　　proved the execution of this deed in open Court at the August
　　　　term 1759, and it was recorded in the Rolls Office at New Castle
　　　　in Book T at page 484, on the 13th day of Feb'y, 1762.

The spelling of proper names in this deed is most inaccurate. Campbell is spelled "Camble," and Talley is spelled "Tally." Thomas Talley's wife did not join in the execution of this deed ; perhaps she was not then living. The discovery of the deed caused the re-writing of this chapter, which was gladly done.

This deed shows the genealogy from William, who married Mrs. Jansen, down to William his grandson, and is the connecting link between the past and the present of the Talley family. Without this deed the record of our family at the beginning would be entirely lost. It is the bridge that has carried us safely and surely over, what had appeared before to be the impassable gulf. It deserves to be printed in letters of gold. It should be carefully read and studied by every one who cares at all for the line of our family descent.

This deed had been recorded at Wilmington, but how much better to see and read the original deed, as it was written in "ye olden days." The making and recording of the deed shows the vast importance attached to the holding of lands. If we have lost trace of any of our early relatives, it has been caused by their want of prosperity, and their failure to procure land, and record the deed of the same. It cannot be too strongly urged that every one should hold a deed for some tract of land. Our children should be taught this around the fireside, and later when they have grown up. Land is a safe bank of deposit, free from the ravages of speculating officials.

As already stated, Thomas by his marriage to a yet undisclosed wife, became the father of six children, viz : William married to Hannah Grubb, Samuel married to Margaret Cloud, David married to Catharine, her maiden name not now known, Mary married to John Worrough (possibly an attempt to spell John Worrall), Hannah married to William Smith, (to find this William would be as difficult as it would be to find a particular blackbird in a flock), and Susanna married to Nathaniel Ring, brother of Benjamin who owned the house occupied by Washington as his headquarters at the battle of Brandywine.

Benjamin's house and farm lay directly in front of

Chads' Ford, while his brother Nathaniel's lay adjoining, and to the southeast of Benjamin's. Susanna was a widow at the time of this battle, and resided on the farm. We have no tradition that she was molested, but no doubt she was overrun by both armies at that eventful period.

Mr. Amos C. Brinton, the octogenarian and historian of Birmingham, was reared on the farm adjoining Nathaniel's, to the southeast. He remembers having eaten fruit from "Granny Ring's Field," and in 1832, when a young man, he stuck down a buttonwood stake in a swamp in the Ring line fence, and the stake took root and grew, and now stands a huge tree, several feet in girth. He also says that Susan Ring lived nearly one hundred years, and at the age of ninety, took a sickle and reaped wheat in the field. He also states that the history of Susan (Talley) Ring and the struggles at the battle of Brandywine, were topics talked of around the fireside, morning, noon and night, when he was a boy, and were most firmly impressed on his mind.

It is pleasant to know that Thomas Talley, while not sawing at the mill, nor tenderly trilling on the strings of the violin, was engaged in preserving family history, to be afterwards recorded in this deed to his son William, which has so fortunately become the connecting link of our genealogy. Can we ever forget Thomas Talley, his saw-mill, his violin, and this deed?

CHAPTER VII.

WILLIAM TALLEY "THE GREAT"—HIS FAMILY—HIS
LANDS—HIS LIFE.

Some men are born great, others have greatness thrust
upon them. William Talley, the son of Thomas the patriarchal musician, was born in 1714; and if he is compared
with others of his day, he may very justly be styled William
Talley "the Great." He was not great in battle, but in
enterprise, character and good-citizenship.

Born in a country affording but few educational advantages, he learned to "read, write and cipher," and has
handed down the only account book known to have been kept
by the early Talleys. This book is 12 inches long and 1¼
inches thick, with sheepskin binding. The penmanship is
fair, and all accounts therein are kept, up to the time of his
death, in pounds, shillings and pence. He was exceedingly
careful in business, and all matters of account were accurately
recorded.

This book shows how luxuriously the laborer kept the
Christmas festival in the early day. We find a charge against
John Stilley and James Wood, each dated December 23d, 1767,
of "three shillings" for "Syder and a goose."

William Talley had in his library such books as "a
large Bible," "Ambrose Looking," "Self Denial," "Prayer
Book," "Young Man's Companion" and a "Horse Farrier's
Book". His desk was appraised at £3. We find the following on the appraisement list : Saddle-bags, case and bottles,
mortar and pestle, tea table, walnut table, coffee mill and
toaster, two large pewter dishes, delft bowl and six wine
glasses, brass kettle, churn, wool, new spinning wheel, side

saddle, check reel and candlestick, feather beds, nine head of
cows, unrotted flax in the old barn, still and worm, seventeen
hogs, cross-cut saw, cobbling tools, blacksmith tools, carpenter's tools, horses and colts, sheep, cider-mill, old corn, rotted
flax, hay in the barns and in stacks, hay in the swamp
meadow, wheat and rye, cutting box, six hives of bees, flax
brake, and lastly, negroes, "Nan" and "Baltis," each appraised at £30.

This appraisement shows that William was a veterina-
rian, as well as a farmer, and that his home on the Foulk
Road was a veritable hive of manufacturing industry. There
was spinning of flax and of wool, blacksmithing, shoemaking,
and carpentry, all, at times, going on at this home. William
also kept nearly all kinds of domestic animals, even down to
the "busy little bee." There can be no doubt but that every-
body about this William was busy, even to "Nan" and
"Baltis." Perhaps they were most busy.

The extent of William's business can be judged of by
examining the long list of creditors whose claims were paid
by the administrators, Thomas and William Talley, in course
of settlement. These claims number sixty-eight, and the list
now in the hands of Lewis F. Talley is almost a complete
directory of the people of Brandywine Hundred for the year
1790.

William was 76 years old when he died, and *must* have
been active in business until his death, as is proven by this
list. The creditors were as follows, to wit:

Parker Askew,	Ziba Ferris,
Garrett Lawrence,	Peter Bryanburg,
Bryanburg & Andrews,	Wm. Sharpley,
George Righter,	Francis Day,
Thos. Newlin,	John Stapler,
John Huron,	Henry Webster,
Wm. Cloud,	John Ferris,
Zach. Ferris,	John Bird,
John Reese,	Jos. James,
Wm. Forwood,	Jos. Day,
Samson Babb,	Jacob Hewes,

Isaac Starr,	Hezekiah Niles,
Appolo Moore,	Chas. Afflick,
James McClintock,	Benj. Elliott,
Richard McMeneman,	Regina Mortenson,
Philip Bonsall,	Richard Lampley,
Richard Hanby,	Jos. Pierce,
Emanuel Grubb,	Jas. Council,
Jos. Tatnall,	Geo. Davis,
John Grubb,	Isaac Grubb,
Wm. Ford,	Moses Martin,
Nich. Robinson,	John Jarvis,
Jos. Gorby,	Thos. Smith,
Thos. Hollingsworth,	Samuel Talley,
John Harmon,	Parker Askew,
Benj. Grubb,	Wm. Canby,
Isaac Lawrence,	Sarah Hooten,
Thos. Ford,	Wm. Smith,
John Stidham,	Amor Chandler,
Jas. Broome,	Jos. Cloud,
Nicholas Way,	Gunning Bedford, Esq.,
Isaac Stevenson,	Thos. Talley,
Edward Talley,	Jas. Booth,
Wm. Talley,	Elihu Talley.

The personal property of this estate sold for £273. The cash demands due the estate raised the total receipts of the personal estate to £322, which balanced the list of small debts above, and discharged the administrators' commissions. The large landed estate was left to be divided among the heirs-at-law.

William probably built and occupied the commodious log house (being two and a half stories high) which stood along the Foulk Road, east of Lonkum Run, and was taken down by Thomas Vance. This was a *house* and not a *hut*, and was finely paneled inside. William married about 1735, and probably built the house about 1738, the date he obtained a deed for this tract.

Perhaps, the most valuable papers in this estate are the guardianship papers relating to the estates of William, Thomas,

Sarah and Charity, the children of William and his deceased
wife, Hannah (Grubb) Talley. Hannah died before her
father, Joseph Grubb. Her share of her father's estate then
descended to her four children. They being under age at the
date of their grandfather's death, it became necessary for the
father to become guardian. He was appointed such on April
17th, 1753, at New Castle, and then received the estate
coming to the four children from their grandfather, Joseph
Grubb.

As William was a stirring man and a great land-buyer,
he invested the guardianship funds by common consent, and
the money was left in his hands at six per cent. interest for
about forty years, or until the settlement of his estate in 1793.
Upon settlement with the wards, after William's death, interest was computed for thirty years, only. The receipts
given by the wards stated on their face that ten years' interest was abated on account of the hardships produced by
the War for Independence.

Several matters of doubt are removed by the fortunate
discovery of these guardianship papers. It is proven that
Hannah Talley, wife of William, died prior to 1753. It re-
moves a doubt, heretofore raised, as to whether William,
Thomas, Charity and Sarah were brothers and sisters or not.
It proves that William and Hannah (Grubb) Talley were the
parents of the last named children. It is firmly established
also that Hannah Grubb was the daughter of Joseph, the son
of the first John Grubb. It seems that William, like his
patriarchal father, Thomas Talley, has also made a "golden
record" for us.

These papers, and others most valuable, were carefully
preserved and handed down from *Adam* — that is, Adam
Talley—to Lewis, and from Lewis to Lewis F. Talley, his
son. Up to this date we were compelled in searching our
ancestry to grope our way through what appeared at one time
as midnight darkness and uncertainty. The flood light at
last has been thrown in, and we walk no more by faith, but
by fact and by well established landmarks.

That which caused William Talley to become "Great,"
more than any other one thing, was his insatiable desire to

acquire and hold lands. His first tract he purchased from his aunt, Mary Campbell, of Salem, N. J., in 1738. He was then only twenty-four years old. No aid from his father in this boy's start in life! Upon the death of Thomas (his father), William even consented that his share of his father's land might pass to his (William's) son Edward.

He fortunately inherited from some remote ancestor, across the Atlantic, the *genius* of carrying on large undertakings, and of pushing on far in advance of those who started in life's race with him. The spirit of acquisition was so marvelously developed in him that it can truly be said that it was *born* in him.

> " Time, place and action may with pains be wrought,
> But genius must be born and never can be taught."

William received no parental aid, and held at one time about six hundred acres of land. As stated, his first purchase was the ninety-six acres from his Aunt Mary. This tract began somewhere near the house of Uriel Pierce, and extended westward beyond Lonkum Run. From this time on, William advanced by regular strides until he owned all of the lands on both sides of the Foulk Road, westward to Talley's corner, and on the northerly side of the said road to the line of Isaac Webster's land.

Still these did not not satisfy his ambition. He purchased other tracts in the swamp meadow adjoining him on the northwest, and also owned a tract near where the Valentine Forwood farm is located. For a little diversion in 1758, he cast his eyes towards Cherry Island Marsh, and then became the first Talley owner there. We find him there in 1762, taking active part in erecting the first permanent embankment, which enclosed the whole of the one thousand acre tract.

We identify him in the marsh by an account in his book, where Isaac Grubb is charged for "cow paster in the mash," as well as by his signature on the old marsh book which is now in existence. This being identical with known signatures on deeds, and his signature on the church records of St. Martin's Episcopal Church, at Marcus Hook.

He was no one-sided man ; he seemed to be every place, where a good work was going on. In 1745, when the first brick church was erected upon the grounds of St. Martin's Church, we find William Talley a substantial donor to the building fund. He about this time became an official member, and remained such until his death in 1790. His pew rent for 1790 was paid by his administrators in due course, as shown by the receipt among the papers in Lewis F. Talley's hands. Richard Hanby was the Collector.

This little church society was composed almost entirely of the yeomanry of Brandywine Hundred. The descendants of these people have in recent years nearly all allied themselves with the Methodist Church. Some of the Talleys also attended at an early day the St. John's Church at Concord.

William not only attended church himself, but also took his children with him. Thomas and William (his sons) were on the official board for a number of years at St. Martin's. They all withdrew from this church in 1793, the date of the settlement of their father's estate. William's brother Samuel was a warden in this church in 1758, but afterwards held his connection with St. John's.

William was great in matrimony, as in all other undertakings. He was married three times. Hannah Grubb became his first wife prior to 1736, as Sarah, the first child, was born that year. Hannah died between 1747, the date of her son William's birth, and 1753, the date of the guardian's appointment.

William married his second wife, whose name was Rebecca, prior to 1754, as Elihu, a son, was born in that year. The record in the Swedes Church at Wilmington shows the birth of Elihu, a son of William and Rebecca Talley, March 25th, 1754. Rebecca probably died about 1766, as we find an entry in 1766 on the old account book of William in favor of William H. Askew, an undertaker, "By wife's coffin, £3."

William married his third wife (Magdalena) prior to 1768, as we find her joining in a deed, recorded in Book "Y," page 658 (1768), of a marsh lot to Joseph Cloud, and in another deed, recorded in Book "I," vol. 2, page 158 (1774), to

William, son of William Talley. We find by some recently discovered deeds that Magdalena survived her husband.

William and Hannah had the four children mentioned herein. William and Rebecca had also four children, viz: Elihu, Edward, Rebecca, wife of Thomas Smith, and Esther, wife of James Council. William conveyed to his sons at different times large tracts of his lands, but still had at his death 253 acres. This tract of 253 acres was on October 11th, 1790, conveyed by seven of William's heirs to the other heir, Elihu, for the purpose of making a division thereof. This original deed is on parchment, being 2½ feet long and 2 feet wide; not much left of the sheep's hide that made this deed. The deed is in the possession of John Booth's family, and as good as new, notwithstanding its term in the corn crib. This deed is most carefully drawn, and shows the whole genealogy of William Talley's family. It sets at rest many questions which were debatable before its discovery. It is recorded in Book "H," vol. 3, page 97, at Wilmington.

No children were born of the third marriage. The last deed mentioned states that Magdalena survived her husband. William died in August, 1790, after a most remarkable career, and without a stain upon his character. It is a fact to be noted that his grave in St. Martin's Church-yard is the first American Talley grave to be marked with a marble slab, or to have an engraved or written record of identification over it. There is quite a space to the right of his grave, and who knows but that here he and his three wives are quietly resting, unmindful of the heat of summer, or winter's withering blasts.

CHAPTER VIII.

SAMUEL TALLEY—HIS LAND—HIS FAMILY.

Samuel Talley, son of Thomas the first and brother of William and David, was born in 1726, and was twelve years younger than William.   He married in 1758 Margaretta Cloud, and in 1760 purchased from the Pennsylvania Land Company a large tract of land in Rockland Manor, containing 175 acres.   This land was located near the circular line and became at that time, the frontier Talley settlement.

This tract comprised the present home of Zach. Ebright and the farm of Wm. Wier, also about 84 acres of the farm now owned by W. W. Talley, late the home of Thos. Lea Talley, Sr.   It seems that 50 acres, of this 84-acre tract, were purchased from Samuel by Eli Baldwin, the grandfather of Eli Baldwin Talley.

Samuel at a very early day owned a share in the Talley saw-mill at Foulk's Creek.   He also acquired at his father's death a share in the original Talley land, and upon a division procured about 48 acres across the northwesterly side, extending from Naaman's Creek almost to the Grubb Road.   This tract was 33 rods wide and of about the same width as the present Wilkinson farm, and included most of it.   It included also a part of the Foulk farm, extending from the creek to the Naaman's Creek Road.   The deed to Samuel for this tract was dated about 1789.   He later sold this land to John Foulk.

Samuel died in 1802, and was buried in the Talley–Foulk burying ground on the original Talley land.   His grave is marked with a marble slab.   He made a will, and devised his lands to his four sons, Thomas, Joseph, Jehu and Samuel, they to pay certain legacies to his daughters, or their representatives. His daughters were : Phebe, married to John Zebley ; Susanna, married to Jeffrey Frame ; Hannah, wife of James Smith ; Margaret Fields ; and Elizabeth, who had died leaving six children. Elizabeth may have been the wife of Edward Talley, although this is only conjecture, from the fact that her father did not mention her husband's name in the will ; and from the further fact that Edward Talley's wife had died prior to Samuel's death, leaving about the corresponding number of children.

The reason that we are not able to give more of the history of Samuel, is because very few records have been found with his descendants. Once more the record of deeds and of wills comes to our rescue and furnishes what little we are able to give concerning Samuel and his family. It is an interesting fact to state that of this large family of Samuel and Margaretta Talley, only a few remain in Brandywine Hundred. They have mostly gone to seek their fortunes in other territory, and have become very respectable citizens. We know but little about the qualifications, character and wealth of Samuel. He was first a warden at St. Martin's Church in 1758, and after, held his relationship with St. John's Church at Concord.

We find his descendants to be able, just and prosperous. As the stream has been found to be good, the fountain must of necessity have been pure. It is a coincidence that he and his brother William each died at the age of 76 years.

CHAPTER IX.

DAVID TALLEY.

David Talley, the son of Thomas and brother of Samuel and William, has unfortunately left no record or paper to show the day of his birth, marriage, or death, or the place of his burial. We find that his wife was Catharine, because she joined in some deeds with her husband, David Talley, about 1790 to 1792.

He purchased thirty-four acres of the Pennsylvania
Land Company in 1760. This land lay to the southeast of
the farm buildings on the Uriel Pierce farm, and extended
to the Samuel Grubb line, and back to the line of the Casey
land. David, on May 5th, 1788, conveyed this tract to his
brother William. David also held quite a tract in the original
Talley land, which was inherited from his father, Thomas.
He also at one time held an interest in the Talley saw-mill.
David may have emigrated to some other State upon the
sale of his lands here, and may have died there. His known
children were, Susanna, wife of (tall) Thomas Cartmell ;
Martha, wife of John Marshall ; and Priscilla, wife of Thomas
Thompson. Mrs. Mary Ann Burke, grand-daughter of David
Talley, says that he may have had a son George, and one
David. She has a slight remembrance of these names in
the family.

There is in this branch an almost total loss of records,
if indeed any ever existed. We can find no will of David,
nor any settlement of his estate. The few deeds made by and
to him are the Alpha and the Omega of his history. Even
the family of John and Martha Marshall are not known to
the other descendants of David Talley. The known representatives of David Talley are confined to the heirs of
Susanna Cartmell and Priscilla Thompson. How fortunate
to secure the testimony of Mrs. Burke and her brother, Stephen H. Thompson, as to who was their grandfather, and
thus preserve some record of David Talley's family !

There may be others living to-day who are of this
family and bearing the name of Talley, having come down by
the paternal line, but who, where, or what, we are not able
to conjecture. Sad, is it not, for a Talley to lose himself in
the midst of a forest of Talleys? Talleys to the right of
him, Talleys to the left, and Talleys all around him, and
still he is lost. May he yet discover himself, and then assume
his proper place in the ranks of the great Talley army !

CHAPTER X.

THOMAS TALLEY.

Thomas Talley, son of William Talley the "Great," was born sometime about 1744, and died in 1818. The place of his burial is not known. He married Hannah Grubb November 4th, 1766. Hannah Grubb was the daughter of Richard Grubb, Richard was the son of John Grubb, and John was the second son of John Grubb, the emigrant who settled first at Upland, and later at Grubb's Landing. The mother of Thomas was also Hannah Grubb the daughter of Joseph, a brother of John second. Thomas Talley and his wife Hannah were second cousins.

Thomas Talley acquired from his father a deed of one hundred acres of land in 1775. This extended from Isaac Webster's land on the Foulk Road eastward to the cross-roads at Talley's Corner, and was later owned by Penrose R. Talley, and on which he made his home. Thomas filed for record the deed so obtained from his father, William. The deed and the record were carried away or destroyed by the British army after the battle of Brandywine, in September, 1777.

William Talley, on March 6th, 1786, made a confirmatory deed to Thomas for the same land, the deed reciting on its face that it was made to replace a deed made in 1775 and which was carried away by the British army in 1777. This historic deed is now in the possession of Penrose Talley, son of Charles Talley. It was signed by William Talley, and witnessed by Emanuel Grubb and John Stapler.

On October 12th, 1790, Thomas Talley purchased of Elihu Talley, his half-brother, a tract of land consisting of

88½ acres, bounded on the southwest by the Kellam Road, on the southeast by land then of Isaac Grubb, and on the northwest partly by the Foulk Road and partly by a narrow strip lying southeast of the Foulk Road and twenty rods deep, which narrow strip extended from the Norris Talley line easterly to the Grubb Road ; and on the northeast by the Grubb Road. This 88-acre tract comprised nearly the whole of the Lewis Talley farm, and all of the Norris Talley farm. Thomas and Hannah Talley, on January 25th, 1794, conveyed this last named tract to their sons William and Adam.

Thomas Talley died in February, 1818, leaving a will and appointing therein his sons Adam and Thomas Talley his executors. His personal estate amounted to £272, and the probated claims amounted to a few dollars more. Thomas was a member and a pew-holder at St. Martin's Episcopal Church at Marcus Hook. He was a vestryman as early as 1783. He continued to attend this church until 1793. He then gave up his pew. No records other than the deeds and will made by Thomas Talley have been found ; hence nothing further can be given of his history.

Charity, the daughter of Thomas, has left a record of the births of the children of Thomas and Hannah ; not written with pen and ink, however, but worked with silk and needle, upon and in what was named in olden times a "Sampler." It is given thus on the Sampler : "W. Talley "born May 13, 1768. A. Talley born Feby. 7, 1770. T. "Talley born May 5, 1772. R. Talley born July 12, 1780. "C. Talley born Feby. 19, 1784." This is a record of the children William, Thomas, Adam, Richard, and Charity. The last named never married, but died about 1819. This "Sampler" was worked about 1793 by Charity, she then being nine years old.

It is fortunate that this record has been made in silk, as no Bible entry has been found showing the births of these children. The "Sampler" was handed down by Charity Talley to her niece, Charity Booth, and is now in the possession of Mrs. Margaret Booth. She has also in her possession, having come down the line, from Charity Talley, a corset more than a hundred years old, and which is almost identical in shape with those of the present day, but resembles more an iron casement. This is a genuine curiosity and was surprising, as it was not believed that the ancestors could endure such torturing. She has also a lady's ancient hat, made of fine felt, almost as strong as buckskin, and of dove-gray color. This hat has an immense brim and a crown not over a half-inch in height. The hat measures in diameter about 18½ inches. Surely an umbrella would be useless to a lady who might walk under this hat.

Thomas and Hannah are the ancestors of the Talleys who resided in the Foulk Road district. This branch is quite able and numerous, and many of them to-day are residing in the far West, and are men of action and influence. Thomas Talley was a greater man than we are able to describe him. We know from circumstances that he was the equal of any who lived in his vicinity. He was the ancestor of a very thrifty and religious line of descendants. They have to a large extent comprised the congregation of the Bethel M. E. Church, and have large political influence in the northern part of Brandywine Hundred. The absence of records prevents us from saying more of this noble man. We know this, however, that he was a credit to the family. What more need we know?

CHAPTER XI.

WILLIAM TALLEY ON THE BRANDYWINE.

This William Talley was the son of William and Hannah (Grubb) Talley. He was born in 1747, died May 9th, 1812, and was buried at the Foulk burying ground on the original Talley tract. A marble slab has been erected to his memory. He married, November 5th, 1768, Dinah Stilley, the daughter of Jonathan and Magdalena (Vandever) Stilley. Dinah was born February 27th, 1751, and was baptized March 31st, of the same year, at the Swedes Church at Wilmington.

William Talley attended the St. Martin's P. E. Church at Marcus Hook until 1793. He then joined the Swedes

Church at Wilmington. He and his sons, Amor and Elihu, were pew-holders there in 1806. This is shown by the records of that church. The English had almost sole control of the Church at that date. Among the pew-holders for 1806 we find the following names : Talley, Allmond, Bayard, Weldin, Perkins, Cartmell, Stidham, Derrickson, Elliott, Smith, Vandever, Stilley and many others.

It is supposed that William and Dinah lived on the farm once owned by Lewis Zebley, at Talley's Corner on the Foulk Road. He procured a deed from his father for this land, about the date of his marriage. He sold it to Capt. William Glover about 1794. Captain Glover was the father-in-law of George Clark ; and Mr. Clark was father-in-law of preacher John Talley, Lewis S. Talley and John Clayton of Delaware County, Pa.

William Talley purchased land of Thos. McKim's estate, along the Brandywine, in 1792. This tract contained 300 acres, and extended from a point east of the present site of the "Eight Square" school house to the Brandywine. It was bounded on the northwest by a tract of 196 acres, which William, in 1807, purchased of John Wall, et al. William, after this last purchase, owned 500 acres of land in one tract. The 196-acre tract (except 50 acres which were sold by William in his lifetime) is now the homestead of William T. Talley. It is said that William owned other tracts in addition to the 500 acres. He and his wife moved to the great historic Brandywine, shortly after this purchase from McKim.

William Talley was a remarkable man in business affairs ; and had push, energy and good judgment. He was much like his father, "William Talley the Great." He lived through the whole period of the Revolutionary struggle. It is traditionally told that he took some part in the war, but precisely what, cannot now be stated. He was about thirty years old at the time of the Battle of Brandywine. The history of these times, as they affected Brandywine Hundred, has been almost entirely lost.

William and Dinah left to survive them a family of ten children, who, from what we can learn, were remarkable for their ability, influence and intelligence. Two sons, John and

Lewis, became quite able ministers in the Methodist Church. It is stated that Harmon was a member of the Delaware Legislature in 1828. A great-grandson of this William is the head of a family of twenty-five children. William and his family were of a religious turn of mind. The first Methodist Camp Meeting ever held around or about Wilmington was held in the woods of William Talley near the Brandywine.

No doubt but that many incidents of great interest were connected with William Talley's career. Unfortunately very little has been disclosed to us. Would it not be well to search the many bundles of old and yellow papers lying time worn in garrets of members of this important branch of our family? Do not let the history of this able man fade and vanish. May a wholesome spirit of rivalry be engendered within the families who have descended by this line, to the end that this history may yet be revealed and perpetuated !

CHAPTER XII.

ELIHU TALLEY OF THE FOULK ROAD.

Elihu Talley was the first son of William Talley and his wife Rebecca, and was half-brother to Sarah, Charity, Thomas and William. Elihu resided on the farm afterward owned by Robert Miller, on Lonkum Run. He was born March 25th, 1754, and died January 22d, 1833, at the age of 79 years. He married Lydia, daughter of William Forwood the second. She was aunt of Jehu Forwood of later years, and died in 1795. Elihu married for his second wife, Rachel Robinson, daughter of Charles Robinson, who lived on the Robert Casey farm along the Foulk Road.

Elihu was a man of affairs, and upon his father's death in 1790, the other joint heirs made a conveyance to him of the lands owned by William, the father, at his death. This deed was made for the purpose of making a convenient division of the property. Elihu may have purchased the shares of some of the other heirs, as, in later years, we find him owning a large part of the lands so conveyed to him.

It is stated by those who knew him that he was quite stylish in his early life. When in full dress he was seen with sparrow-tail coat, knee breeches and low shoes with silver buckles. He, like many of his neighbors, wore a cue. He was the head of a large family. Among them were Capt. Amor Talley ; John Forwood Talley, who became wealthy and prominent in Cleremont County, Ohio ; Sarah Talley, who married Major Joseph Grubb ; Mary, who married Harmon Talley, and who married second Thomas Smith ; and Charles Talley, the small but dressy man who " went to war," possibly the Mexican War, and was never heard of again by his relatives.

There is a sword in existence somewhere which was worn by Capt. Amor Talley, who may have been captain of Militia in the 1812 war. In later years he moved to Cleremont County, Ohio, where he resided for a number of years ; and there he died. He lived to a very great age. As an illustration of his courage and endurance it is stated that he accompanied his nephew, John William Talley, from Cleremont County to John's home in Vigo County, Indiana. They arrived at Terre Haute sometime after dark. As John's home was twelve miles in the country, he told his uncle to stay at a hotel over night, and he would call for him in the morning with his team. He was astonished to hear his uncle of eighty years respond : " Guy, John, if you walk it, I guess I can, too," and walk he did ; and arrived at the country home at the same time as did his young nephew.

Elihu Talley's family was known for the number of its handsome women. Mary and Rachel were fine looking ; but it is said of Sarah that she was the " belle of Delaware." If any doubt the truth of the statement let them examine the fine old *silhouette* now in the possession of Mrs. William Goodley, of Bethel Township, Delaware County, Pa. Sarah was the grandmother of Mrs. Goodley. The pictures preserved of these people, of nearly a century ago, demonstrate that they were no " backwoods people," but possessed of taste and refinement. We should feel grateful to Elihu and his family for transmitting to us some facts demonstrating the character and appearance of our people of the olden day.

CHAPTER XIII.

EDWARD TALLEY.

Edward Talley was son of William and Rebecca Talley; and was brother of Elihu, mentioned in the last chapter. We know not the day of Edward's birth, but find that he died about 1800. His first wife was Elizabeth. She may have been the daughter of his uncle Samuel, who lived close against the circular line, dividing Pennsylvania and Delaware. Some circumstances indicate that Elizabeth was both the wife of Edward and the daughter of Samuel.

His second wife was a widow named Christianna Dick. Edward was the owner of a considerable amount of land. He must have parted with the greater portion of it in his lifetime, as we find very little owned by him at his decease. He seems to have had seven children born of the marriage with his first wife, Elizabeth; and possibly none by his last marriage. The Lloyds who lived near the Delaware River are descended from Susanna (Talley) Lloyd, daughter of Edward Talley.

He had some land dealings with William Cloud, in later life. He was half-uncle to William Cloud, being a half-brother to William Cloud's mother, Charity (Talley) Cloud. The descendants of Edward Talley are somewhat scattered; but several may be located in Philadelphia, or in its suburbs. James Talley, the carpenter, known a few years ago in Brandywine Hundred, was a grandson of Edward Talley.

In the old family Bible of Jeremiah and Susanna (Talley) Lloyd is found a full register of the children of Edward Talley and his wife Elizabeth. The finding of this record opened up for investigation a new field. We find in this Bible, for the first time, such names as :   Cyrus, Oliver, Enoch and Orpah Talley.

Should we fail in fully tracing the descendants of these people to the present date, enough is here given to assist in locating the missing ones at some later period. Edward passed away about 1800, as William Cloud was appointed administrator of Edward's estate about this last date. The place of his burial is not known.

***

CHAPTER XIV.

REV. JOHN TALLEY.

John Talley, the seventh son of "William on the Brandywine," was born on his father's farm on the Brandywine. He married Letitia Clark, July 26th, 1812. She died October 2d, 1820. He married for his second wife Ann W. Henderson, of Milford, Delaware, October 7th, 1823. She died December 21st, 1827. Lastly, he married Ann H. Hollingsworth, of Elkton, Maryland, October 11th, 1832. She died March 1st, 1850.

John Talley's Methodism dates back to the time of holding the first Camp Meeting along the Brandywine, in his father's woods. From this time on, until he was received into the Conference as a full-licensed minister, he taught school and preached occasionally to his neighbors. He was thus fitting himself for the more important duties awaiting him.

John Talley has the distinction of being the first Talley who entered the ministry in America. It was so remarkable that, ever afterwards, he was styled, " Preacher John Talley." He was small of stature, clean-shaven and very neat in appearance. His style of oratory was smooth, pathetic and convincing. He, as a minister, took rank with the able ministers of that day. All of the older members of the Methodist Church well remember the preaching of John Talley. He has always been the pride of the *Methodist* Talleys.

We kindly give below the Memoir prepared under the direction of the Philadelphia M. E. Conference, upon his death in 1861 :

Memoir.

Rev. John Talley was born in Brandywine Hundred, New Castle County, Delaware, September 25th, 1791. He was converted to God when about eighteen years of age (the first of his family except his mother), on his way home from a Camp Meeting. He then joined the Methodist Episcopal Church, of which he was a member and minister for over fifty-two years. Immediately after his conversion he began to labor for the salvation of his neighbors, and held meetings in the school houses 'round about, where many of them were converted. After serving the Church as a Local Preacher for several years, he joined the Philadelphia Annual Conference in 1819, being then a married man, and was Ordained a Deacon in 1821, and an Elder in 1823. He traveled the following Circuits, viz: Lancaster in 1819 ; Annamessex in 1820 ; Cambridge in 1821 ; Chester in 1822 ; Milford in 1823 ; Caroline in 1824 ; Cecil in 1825. In 1825 he was made Supernumerary, and continued in that relation until 1861, when he was made Superannuated.

He served the Church with great efficiency after he ceased to travel, and until about three years before his death he preached much in the neighborhood of his birthplace. He was then attacked with paralysis, which enfeebled his mind and greatly impaired his memory. He finally sank under this disease, and died at the residence of his son, J. Henderson Talley, Esq., in East Goshen Township, Chester County, Pa., on Saturday, July 6th, 1861. He was buried at Mt. Lebanon Church, near his birthplace ; and his funeral sermon was preached by Rev. Samuel Hance (whom he had previously selected for that purpose), from Tim., iv., 7, 8.

As a man, Brother Talley was cheerful and amiable in his disposition ; mild and kind in his deportment ; had many friends, but few enemies. As a minister, he was simple, practical, powerful, and many souls were saved through his ministry. Four days before his death another stroke of paralysis deprived him of both speech and reason ; but as he lived right, so he died right, and now sleeps in Jesus to be like Him in the morning of the resurrection.

CHAPTER XV.

LEWIS TALLEY, THE SWEET SINGER.

Lewis Talley, the son of Adam and Rebecca (Day) Talley, was born on his father's farm in 1810, and died in

1890. The children of his parents numbered ten. Lewis had no advantages in early life, except what were common to his brothers and sisters, and perhaps to the other children in the neighborhood. He attended the Forwood District School, this being the beginning and the finishing of his school education.

Lewis, when grown to manhood and installed as the head of a family, followed farming on one of his father's farms. He was quite successful in this line of business, and, at the same time, reared a prosperous and musical family of nine children.

We wish more particularly to record here, what, in Lewis Talley's life, caused him to become famous. He was musical almost from the time of his birth. Music was a passion in him. Genius is always a passion, and is born with its possessor. Lewis Talley could no more resist the passion of music than the "old toper could his cup."

It is said of him that, when a mere lad, he was not charmed so much by farm work as he was by music. He could, without apparent effort, stop his ordinary labors and begin singing and beating time. Even while riding the horses to the run for water, he would forget to hasten back, and would often be found, down by the run, on the horse's back, beating time to the trees, as if they were persons. Lewis should not be censured for this, as *he* could not help it. Music and farming were to this lad absolutely incompatible.

We are told that Lewis could readily see a scrap of printed music even when it might be blowing around in the highway. It was caught on sight, and speedily sung by him. Anything in the shape of a musical staff with notes printed on it was music to him. He was the first one in the upper part of Brandywine Hundred to master the *blind* or *round* note system of music. It is not known that any of his family, from his father down, aided or encouraged him in his singing. Can it be that the musical talent of Thomas Talley, the ancient violinist, has descended in a dormant state, through many generations, and at last burst forth with all its melodious energy and brilliancy in Lewis Talley of 1810?

All persons making any pretensions to music, from the Brandywine Creek to Chelsea, in Delaware County, Pa., and from Elam to the Delaware River (in the days of sixty years ago), received the start under the teaching of Lewis Talley. He was *the* singing teacher until the growing up of a younger generation. The credit belongs to him of being the musical *developer* who first kindled the musical fires all along the Foulk Road District, even into Delaware County, Pa. The light of these fires has not grown dim, but is increasing in brightness, as the younger generations take up the work where it was laid down by this great musical pioneer.

His teaching was methodical, clear and thorough. He, at this early stage of teaching, used a blackboard in demonstrating the rudiments of music to his classes. Lewis found that it required persistent practice to become perfect in singing. He never grew tired in practicing so long as improvement was being made. He was not only a theoretical singer, but his voice was most clear, sweet and effective. He was known throughout his neighborhood as "Singing Lewis Talley;" and to-day, all will agree that this was not a misnomer. His entire family of nine children were musical, also many of his grandchildren.

Lewis Talley was a man of influence, a kind neighbor and a good citizen, as well as a great musician. His name should be cherished and revered, and ever kept green in memory.

> "Music resembles poetry ; in each
> Are numerous graces which no methods teach,
> And which a master-hand alone can reach."
> *Pope.*

CHAPTER XVI.

A PLACE OF SACRED MEMORY.

"The breezy call of incense-breathing morn,
　The swallows twittering from the straw-built shed ;
　The cock's shrill clarion, or the echoing horn,
　No more shall rouse them from their lowly bed."

Gray.

On the original Talley tract in Brandywine Hundred, at Foulk's Corner, is located the Talley-Foulk burying ground. It occupies a small square about 66 by 66 feet. It is a most excellent site for a rural burying ground, being elevated and gently sloping towards the southeast. We have not searched to ascertain the exact date of the *dedication* of this tract to this most sacred and holy use. It is probable that it was dedicated by the Talleys before the conveyance of the title to the Foulks.

The great majority buried there bear the name of Talley. The early ones have no slab to record their birth and death. The first *known* grave is that of Priscilla (Foulk) Talley, wife of Harmon Talley. She died March 3d, 1802, as shown by the tombstone. Then comes the grave of Samuel Talley, brother of William and David Talley, who died December 30th, 1802. Then follow William Talley on the Brandywine, 1812 ; Joseph Talley, son of Samuel, 1815 ; Sarah (Talley) Foulk, daughter of William Talley the Great, and the maternal ancestor of all, who came by the line of John Foulk, 1822 ; Rebecca (Lloyd) Talley, wife of Thomas, 1829 ; Thomas Talley, son of Samuel, 1836 ; Samuel Talley, son of Samuel, 1837 ; Jehu Talley, son of Samuel, 1848 ; Mary

(Russell) Talley, wife of Samuel the second, 1847; Aaron Smith, husband of Margaret (Talley) Smith, 1855; and several others of the younger generation. It is reported that John Foulk the first, who died in 1820; Richard Talley, father of Penrose; and George Talley, son of Richard, are also interred there.

Some years ago the relatives of those resting in this sacred spot, assisted the owner of the farm in placing around the burying ground a rough stone wall, which has since inclosed it; but to-day this wall is in a tumble-down state. Let it be the duty of those who reside adjacent to this ground to care for its preservation. Let this "home of the dead" become the "Mecca" of all who are related to those within the inclosure; and may regular visits be made there, that it may be kept in live, active remembrance, and that its history may never be forgotten. The right to maintain this as a permanent place of holy sepulture is based upon a sure foundation.

1st. It was most solemnly *dedicated*, more than one hundred years ago, by the legal owner of the farm on which it is located. This *dedication* was not for a term of years, but was forever. The interment of a body is not, as a general thing, for a short space of time, but the *intention* is that the body shall remain where it has been placed, forever, or until the Morning of the Resurrection. The body, and the relatives interested therein, are in possession of the tract of ground, which is full notice of all rights therein to any purchaser who may succeed to the property. The remains have possession below the surface, while the tombstones occupy the surface. It is not a hardship to the owner of the farm, for he purchases subject to this right in others, and thereby consents to it.

2d. By the will of John Foulk the first, probated November 14th, 1820, it is provided in words as follow: "And further it is my will that the grave-yard fence be kept "in good repair by my said wife and grandson his *heirs and* "*assigns forever;* also that all my family connections have the "privilege of burying their dead in said family burying "ground on said dwelling plantation and do hereby declare "the same to be devised as aforesaid subject thereto." It thus appears that the farm was by this will devised to the *grandson*, John Foulk. It was subject to the burden of maintaining the fence around the grave-yard in good repair forever. This was a *charge* upon the farm, and bound the lands into whose hands it might pass from grantee to grantee forever. It is thus shown by the will that this ground had been set apart from the farm as a grave-yard and fenced, long prior to the making of the will in 1820. The clause just quoted from the will expressly provides that the devise of the farm is "subject" to the burden of fencing, and to the right of burial therein of all "family connections." The will expressly recognizes the grave-yard as an established and fixed fact. The decision of the Supreme Court of the United States in *Beatty* vs. *Kurtz*, 2 Peters, 566, sets at rest all such questions.

John Foulk, the son of John Foulk, possibly died in 1797, as one John Foulk is buried at Newark Union Cemetery in 1797. As John Foulk the first did not die until 1820, he left the land to the son of John, who died in 1797 ; that is, to the grandson of the devisor.

The right to the permanent maintaining of this grave-yard being undoubted, may it be carefully protected from ruin and dilapidation, and may it be cherished and guarded as a tender ward all along down the coming ages !

> " Yet e'en these bones from insult to protect,
> Some frail memorial still erected nigh,
> With uncouth rhymes and shapeless sculpture deck'd,
> Implores the passing tribute of a sigh."
>
> *Gray.*

CHAPTER XVII.

THE HISTORIC LOG HUT.

We should all desire to learn something of how our forefathers sheltered themselves and their families while subduing the wilderness, and introducing civilization among the savages about the headwaters of Naaman's Creek, in Rockland Manor. The first Talley home in this section may have

GORBY-BOOTH HOUSE.

Photographed by W. Arthur Green.

been a cave, but this is not authenticated. The log house known as the Gorby–Booth house, along the Foulk Road, may have been the early Talley home. It sheltered the important deeds of Campbell to William Talley, and Thomas Talley to William Talley, for many years, while Charity (Talley) Booth resided there. This house was years ago taken down, and moved stick by stick to its present location ; but from where, opinions differ. Some say that it once stood along the Naaman's Creek Road ; others state that it once was located on the easterly side of the Foulk farm lane, in front of the present Foulk farm residence. The best opinion is that it came from the Foulk farm.

Very many years ago two Talley houses were erected on the *original tract*, near the intersection of the creek and the Foulk Road. One was more modern than the other ; it was of frame, and stood west of the lane. The other was of logs, and was more ancient, and was located to the east of the lane. The *Log* house was identical with the Gorby–Booth house, in shape, size and appearance, each being a fair representation of the other. By viewing this Gorby–Booth house, we in our imagination can see the early Talley home, in all its primitive grandeur and cheerfulness. A cave could not compare with this cozy home as a place of permanent residence. This was a *palace* by the side of the neighboring *wigwams*.

No one doubts but what the fires burned as brightly and as *fiercely* in this "old cabin home" as they do now in the home of the nineteenth century *millionaire*. Love and happiness, without doubt, abounded there. Can gilded halls, with "modern conveniences," yield a more genuine article or in larger quantity ? There is a sacredness about the ancient home of the brave pioneer of two hundred years ago. Let us always respect and cherish the "old cabin home."

GENEALOGICAL REGISTER.

It is the purpose in this department of our book to register the names of the Talleys, descending from William Talley, who landed at Upland (now Chester), Pa., just before the coming of William Penn, so far as they have been discovered and disclosed. It cannot be expected that we shall do the impossible thing—i. e., print the names of those who decline to give any information about themselves. Nor will we attempt to print the names of those who have requested to be left out of the book.

We began the work with the intention of making the book as complete as possible, considering the amount of funds in hand and in sight. We hoped and believed that practically all would, gladly, give the needed information to make a complete family register. A few letters sent out soon demonstrated how false the hope, and how ill-founded our opinion. As we progressed, letter after letter was sent, and but few responses came in return. The circular was then resorted to, and a few more responded ; then another circular ; and lastly, a third was issued. Notwithstanding this most importuning method, a number who reside at distant points (and we are sorry to say some who are not so distant), are not recorded in this list.

If the names of yourself and your relatives are not found herein, it is not because an effort was not made to that end. All must know that the larger the book the greater the benefit to the family, and the more credit to the author. We have left out none from choice, nor through the lack of solicitation. Our whole duty in this line has been fully discharged. When we scan this list of names, we wonder how they were all collected in so short a space of time.

There was some hope that we might engage the Southern Talleys in this work, and, especially, those in Virginia. Nothing whatever could be procured by correspondence, although we have been assured that the Delaware and Virginia branches were, in the beginning, as near to each other as "brother to brother." Had there been a fund at hand, some one would have visited the "Old Dominion," and possibly worked out the problem.

We believe that the genealogy of the Talley family on the Delaware is shown in this Register almost to mathematical correctness and certainty. The work has been done in a way that leaves little for conjecture, and that overthrows many former traditions in the family. Our work is almost wholly based upon official records, deeds, etc. The proof of the early genealogy is shown in the deeds and matter set out in the historical part of our work. We now prove the correctness of our former work by resorting to a List of Taxables in Brandywine Hundred for 1787, and to a Voters' List of the same hundred for 1812. On this Tax List we find no Talley names but David, Edward, Elihu, Joseph, Samuel, Thomas, Thomas Jr., William Sr. and William Jr. Every one of these names is fully accounted for in the line of descent from William Talley the first. The Voters' List, made as late as 1812, contains sixteen Talley names, every one of whom is as familiar as the Alphabet to us. We are immovably founded on the bed rock, when we find that the Talleys on these two lists all belong to our line, and that no others are found therein. If William the first had a brother Thomas or a brother John, as tradition claims, why were their descendants *all* excluded from the Tax List, or prevented from appearing on the Voters' List of 1812? If Thomas and John were emigrants, we must look for them in Virginia, or perhaps in South Carolina. They and their descendants did not remain here. All Delaware Talleys owe their allegiance to the standard of William Talley, who landed at Upland, married Elinor Jansen, and dashed through the bramble and settled at Foulk's Corner. "That is certain which has been proved to be such" is a maxim of universal law.

Dates of births and deaths as recorded in this Register

were obtained from tombstones, family Bibles, records, and
many times by word of mouth. Much *data* had to come by
mail ; this of course we had no opportunity to verify. We
have observed the greatest care to have the dates correct, but
in many cases dates on tombstones were different from what
were shown in family Bibles. In some cases Bibles belonging
to different members of a family were at variance. We found
some persons who did not even know the date of their birth.
We have attempted to give a correct record, but if you find
the register of yourself or relatives incorrect, we advise an
immediate correction with pen and ink, as it will not be well
to perpetuate an error.

FIRST GENERATION.

1. WILLIAM TALLEY came to this country prior to
1686, for in this year he was appointed, in Probate at Philadelphia, Pa., joint administrator with the widow Elinor Johnson, of the estate of Jan Jansen (Johnson) deceased. William
must have been here before this date, as the Court would not
be likely to appoint a raw emigrant to fill a position of such
responsibility. William married Elinor sometime between
1686 and 1693. He died between 1698 and 1702.

SECOND GENERATION.

WILLIAM TALLEY, (*1*) married Elinor Jansen, a widow.

Children of William Talley the first.
2. Thomas—birth not known.
3. Mary—birth not known.
> The mother of these children is not now cer-
> tainly known. Elinor may have been the
> mother.

THIRD GENERATION.

THOMAS TALLEY (*2*) married ——— ———
Children.
4. William, b. 1714, d. Aug. 1, 1790.
5. David—birth and death unknown.

6. Mary, m. John Worrough, (Worrall.)
7. Hannah, m. William Smith.
8. Susanna, m. Nathaniel Ring.
9. Samuel, b. April 26, 1726, d. Dec. 30, 1802.

MARY TALLEY (3) married Peter Campbell, of Salem County, N. J. Their children are not known.

FOURTH GENERATION.

WILLIAM TALLEY (4) married about 1735 Hannah Grubb, daughter of Joseph Grubb, and grandchild of John Grubb the emigrant. Hannah died about 1749. William married second, Rebecca ―――― prior to 1754. Rebecca died about 1766. He married third, Magdalena ―――― about 1768. She survived him.

Children of first marriage.

10. Sarah, b. Feb'y, 1736, d. Sept. 6, 1822.
11. Charity, b. ―――― d. ――――
12. Thomas, b. ―――― d. Feb'y 26, 1818.
13. William, b. Jan'y, 1747, d. May 9, 1812.

Children of second marriage.

14. Elihu, b. March 25, 1754, d. Jan'y 22, 1833.
15. Edward, b. ―――― d. about 1800.
16. Esther, m. James Council.
17. Rebecca, m. Thomas Smith, Elam, Pa.

No issue of third marriage.

DAVID TALLEY (5) married Catharine ――――. His wife joined in making several deeds, and in this way her Christian name has been ascertained.

Children.

18. Susanna—birth not known.
19. Martha—birth not known.
20. Priscilla—birth not known.
21. Elizabeth—unmarried.
22. George, (?)
23. David, (?)

SAMUEL TALLEY (*9*) married Margaretta Cloud, April 1, 1758, as shown on Swedes' Church Records, Wilmington, Del. (See sketch.)

Children.

24. Thomas, b. 1759, d. Aug. 19, 1836.
25. Joseph, b. June 4, 1764, d. Sept. 7, 1815.
26. Jehu, b. 1765, d. May 7, 1848.
27. Samuel, b. 1777, d. July 8, 1837.
28. Phebe, m. John Zebley.
29. Susanna, m. Jeffrey Frame.
30. Hannah, m. James Smith.
31. Elizabeth, m. possibly Edward Talley.
32. Margaret, m. ———— Fields.

FIFTH GENERATION.

SARAH TALLEY (*10*) married John Foulk the first. He was the ancestor of all the Foulks who lived about Foulk's Corner, Brandywine Hundred, Del. He was born April 22, 1735, and died November 8, 1820. She died 1822. Both were buried in the Talley–Foulk burying ground. John and Sarah were married October 12, 1756.

Children.

33. John, b. July 14, 1765, d. Feb'y 12, 1797.
34. Esther, b. Dec. 23, 1769, d. Oct. 27, 1855.
35. Hannah, b. Oct. 21, 1761.
36. Priscilla, b. March 3, 1775, d. March 3, 1802.
37. Sarah, b. Oct. 24, 1763.
38. William, b. Sept. 15, 1757.
— Elizabeth, b. July 26, 1759.
— Stephen, b. Dec. 28, 1767.

The old Foulk Bible was found in the possession of Mrs. Susanna Pierce, at Wilmington, Del. Numbers could not be given to the last two names without renumbering the whole genealogy through, numbers having been given to the other names before the Foulk Bible was discovered.

CHARITY TALLEY (*11*) married Joseph Cloud, May 9, 1760. He may have been a grandson of Wm. Cloud, the emigrant.

Children.

39. William.
40. Charity.

THOMAS TALLEY (*12*) married Hannah Grubb, daughter of Richard, November 4, 1766. Richard was the son of John and Rachel (Buckley) Grubb. John was the son of John the first.

Children.

41. Willlam, b. May 13, 1768, d. 1839.
42. Adam, b. Feb'y 7, 1770, d. July 28, 1844.
43. Thomas, b. May 5, 1772, d. Jan'y 9, 1859.
44. Richard, b. July 12, 1780, d. about 1826.
45. Charity, b. Feb'y 19, 1784, d. about 1819.
    These births were taken from a sampler worked by the hands of Charity, No. 45, about 1793. This sampler is now in possession of John Booth's family. It was handed down by Charity (Talley) Booth.

WILLIAM TALLEY (*13*) married Dinah (Diana) Stilley, November 5, 1768. (See sketch of "William on the Brandywine.") They lived at Talley's Corner when first married. This place derived its name from the fact, that William lived on one corner, his brother Thomas on another, and William the father owned the land on another corner.

Children.

46. Curtis, b. Aug. 20, 1769, d. 1859.
47. Amor, b. 1771, d. Dec. 10, 1820.
48. Harmon, b. April 28, 1775, d. Aug. 24, 1858.
49. Elihu, b. Nov. 24, 1777, d. June 18, 1860.
50. Peter, b. ——— d. in Illinois.
51. Caleb, b. ——— d. in Delaware.
52. Sarah, b. ——— d. in Delaware.
53. John, b. Sept. 25, 1791, d. July 6, 1861.
54. Lewis S., b. June 8, 1794, d. Sept. 3, 1847.
55. Keziah, b. ——— d. in Delaware.
56. Eli, d. in infancy.

ELIHU TALLEY (*14*) married Lydia Forwood, daughter
of Wm. and Sarah (Clark) Forwood.   (See sketch.)

Children.

57.   Amor, b. Jan'y 9, 1780, d. in Ohio.
58.   Sarah, b. Dec. 18, 1781, d. in Delaware.
59.   John Forwood, b. April 1, 1784, d. Dec. 11, 1851.
60.   Mary, b. Nov. 10, 1787, d. Feb'y 16, 1869.
61.   George, b. Jan'y 2, 1793.
62.   Lydia, b. Aug. 14, 1795.
63.   Elihu, b. Aug. 16, 1795, d. in infancy.

The wife Lydia died August 16, 1795, when the
last twin was born.   Elihu married second
Rachel Robinson, daughter of Charles Robinson, who lived on the Robt. Casey farm.

Children of second marriage.

64.   Charles—went to the Mexican War.
65.   Hannah R., b. Aug. 10, 1801, d. April 8, 1879.
66.   Gideon G., b. 1806, d. Nov. 30, 1842.
67.   Hiram, d. unmarried.
68.   Rachel A., b. ——— d. May 20, 1855.

EDWARD TALLEY (*15*) married Elizabeth ——— probably a Talley.   (See his sketch.)

Children.

69.   Cyrus, b. March 7, 1781.
70.   Harlin, b. Sept. 13, 1782—nothing known.
71.   Orpah, b. March 22, 1784—nothing known.
72.   Susanna, b. Nov. 25, 1785.
73.   Enoch, b. May 16, 1787—nothing known.
74.   Samuel, b. March 8, 1790.
75.   Oliver, b. Oct. 23, 1791—nothing known.

These names were found in the Bible of Joseph
Lloyd.   Edward Talley married second, Chris-
tiann Dick, a widow.   No children of this
last marriage.

ESTHER TALLEY, (*16*) married James Council.   They
moved to Ohio.

REBECCA TALLEY (*17*) married Thomas Smith, of Birmingham. He was the son of Wm. Smith, of Elam, Delaware County, Pa.

These last two marriages are proved by a deed made by the heirs-at-law of Wm. Talley, deceased, dated 1790, and Recorded in Book " H," vol. 3, pg. 97, at Wilmington, Del.

SUSANNA TALLEY (*18*) married (tall) Thomas Cartmell, of Quarryville, Del. She was his second wife ; his first wife having been Hannah Foulk (35). All of the children of Thomas Cartmell were in the Talley line of descent.

Children of second marriage.

76.   Jemima, b. Sept. 1, 1793, d. Aug. 31, 1846.
77.   Elizabeth, d. unmarried.
78.   Susanna.
79.   William, m. Jane Pennington.
80.   George, a cooper at Brandywine.

MARTHA TALLEY (*19*) married John Marshall. Nothing is known of them.

PRISCILLA TALLEY (*20*) married Thomas Thompson, an Englishman. Priscilla is buried at St. Martin's Church at Marcus Hook. Thomas is buried at Swedes Church, Wilmington. Priscilla survived her husband a number of years.

Children.

81.   Catharine, b. Sept. 10, 1806, d. 1844.
82.   John, b. July 30, 1809, d. Aug. 19, 1888.
83.   Sallie, b. Nov. 2, 1811.
84.   George, b. Oct. 1, 1814, d. 1898.
85.   Elizabeth, b. 1817, d. ———.
86.   Stephen H., b. Dec. 20, 1823.
87.   Edward T., b. Sept. 17, 1825.
88.   Mary Ann, b. Sept. 17, 1825.

THOMAS TALLEY (*24*), son of Samuel, married Rebecca Lloyd, sister of Jeremiah Lloyd, Feb'y 19, 1784. (See Swedes' Church Record.)

Children.

89.   Amor, m. Lydia Talley.

90. Margaret, m. Aaron Smith.
91. Hannah, m. Samuel Hanby.
92. Rebecca, m. Robinson Beeson.

JOSEPH TALLEY (**25**), son of Samuel, married Susanna Smith June 8, 1798. Susanna died Feb'y 20, 1858.

Children.

93. Jehu (dark hair), b. Sept. 5, 1799, d. July 29, 1882.
94. Susanna, b. Sept. 22, 1801, d. Nov. 17, 1881.
95. Thomas, b. Nov. 30, 1803, d. Nov. 31, 1824.
96. Margaret, b. April 12, 1806, d. young.
97. Margaret, b. June 30, 1809, d. Oct. 29, 1824.

JEHU TALLEY (**26**), son of Samuel, married Jemima Kellam. He lived to the west of, and adjoining, the Ebright farm, near the State line.

Children.

98. Jehu (Blonde), b. June 11, 1802, d. July 22, 1869.
99. Joseph B.
100. Benjamin, d. in Philadelphia, Pa.
101. Jemima.
102. Parthena, m. Robert McClure.
103. Susan.
104. Mary, m. Benjamin Pierce.

SAMUEL TALLEY (**27**), son of Samuel, married Mary Russell Sept. 21, 1796. He resided on the farm now the home of Zach. Ebright. It was sold by Bayard Talley, executor, to Ebright.

Children.

105. Bayard, b. July 25, 1806, d. Aug. 12, 1891.
106. Nelson R., moved to Delaware, Ohio.
107. Alban, d. unmarried.
108. Isabella.
109. Jane, m. John Wilson.
110. Margaret, m. ——— Little.
111. Maria, m. John Cochran.
112. Ann.
113. Martha, b. June 23, 1810, d. April 11, 1861.

SIXTH GENERATION.

JOHN FOULK (*33*) married Jemima Sharpley, Feb'y 27, 1787. He is buried at the Newark Union burying ground. The date of birth on his tombstone agrees with the date in the Foulk Bible. We do not know the names of all his children, but he evidently had a son John, who was John the third. This last John married Ann Grubb, sister of Joseph Grubb. They had a son John, who married Susanna Dutton. The latter had a son John the fifth.

ESTHER FOULK (*34*) married Moses Bullock, Feb'y 7, 1787. They resided near Elam, Pa., and were the ancestors of many of this name in and about Concord Township, Delaware County, Pa.

HANNAH FOULK (*35*) married (tall) Thomas Cartmell. They resided at Quarryville, Del., on the farm of the late Joseph B. Guest.

PRISCILLA FOULK (*36*) married Harmon Talley (48). (See the issue under No. 48.)

SARAH FOULK (*37*) possibly married Powell Clayton, of Delaware County, Pa. It is not certain whether it was Sarah No. 37, or a sister Sarah, born February 7, 1772, that married Mr. Clayton. The old Foulk Bible indicates that Sarah, born 1763, may have died an infant, and that a second child was named Sarah, and was born in 1772. We did not discover this Bible until this genealogy was nearly ready for the printer. John Clayton was the son of Powell and Sarah (Foulk) Clayton. Sarah, then, was the grandmother of Hon. Powell Clayton, Minister to Mexico ; Judge Thomas J. Clayton, of the Delaware County, Pa., Courts ; and Judge.Wm. H. Clayton, of Arkansas.

WILLIAM FOULK (*38*) married ——— Sharpley. They moved to Mill Creek Hundred, Del., and were the ancestors of the Foulks there.

WILLIAM CLOUD (*39*) married Ann Davis, Nov. 2, 1796.

Children.

114. Abner, m. Elizabeth McKay.
115. Ann, m. George Lodge.
116. Charity, did not marry.
117. Maria, did not marry.
118. Lot, m. Rebecca Talley.
119. Joel.

CHARITY CLOUD (*40*) married Valentine Robinson, who lived on the Naaman's Creek Road, Brandywine Hundred. The names of their children are taken from the *Sterne Record*.

Children.

120. Jemima, b. 1790.
121. Lydia, b. 1792.
122. Keziah, b. 1796.
123. Kerenhappuck, b. 1799.
124. Charles, b. 1801.
125. Charity, b. 1807.

WILLIAM TALLEY (*41*) married Ann Day, sister of Benjamin Day, who lived on the Shellpot Creek. Francis Day was the father. William Talley purchased of William McClure's Estate 100 acres of land on the "New Road" to the southeast of Perry's Hotel, and made his home there until his death, in 1839.

Children.

126. Joseph, b. May 15, 1799, d. in Illinois.
127. Thomas, b. June 9, 1801, d. young.
128. Harmon, b. March 31, 1803, d. 1867.
129. Hezekiah, b. Jan'y 12, 1806, d. Nov. 3, 1862.
130. Mary Ann, b. Nov. 8, 1808, d. April 4, 1885.
131. William Grubb, b. May 22, 1813, d. 1898.
132. Samuel M., b. Dec. 27, 1815, d. Aug. 23, 1896.

ADAM TALLEY (*42*) married Rebecca Day, July 15, 1795. She was a sister of Ann and Benjamin Day, and was born March 26, 1774. Adam Talley was an extensive land-owner at Talley's Corner. He devised a farm each to his sons William D., Thomas Miller and Lewis, subject to legacies to his daughters; and a "new house," with a small tract, to Priscilla Hanby (wife of William Hanby) for life, with remainder to her son, Adam Talley Hanby, in fee. His desk and armchair were devised to Lewis. Lewis was appointed executor of the will, and letters were granted to him August 1, 1844. The witnesses to the will were Isaac Grubb and Lewis S. Talley (the preacher). Adam died July 28, 1844. His will bears date May 7, 1842. His wife died April 8, 1838. Adam was a very thrifty and honorable man. Camp-meeting was held in his woods adjoining the Grubb Road for several seasons.

Children.

133. Mary, b. Oct. 10, 1795.
134. Ann, b. June 1, 1797.
135. Hannah, b. Jan'y 16, 1800, d. 1890.
136. Adam G., b. April 3, 1802, d. May 14, 1868.
137. Priscilla, b. Feb'y 20, 1805, d. Jan'y 7, 1869.
138. William D., b. Oct. 6, 1806, d. Nov. 21, 1882.
139. Thomas Miller, b. Aug. 28, 1808, d. March 1, 1873.
140. Lewis, b. Nov. 4, 1810, d. Oct. 9, 1890.
141. Elizabeth, b. Feb. 12, 1812.
142. Rebecca, b. Feb'y 12, 1813, d. July 26, 1893.

THOMAS TALLEY (*43*) was born May 5, 1772, and died at the extreme age of 87 years. He was born on the farm late of Penrose R. Talley, on the Foulk Road. He was a small boy at the date of the Battle of Brandywine, yet he recollected distinctly having seen a part of the American army retreating past his home, going to Chester on the evening of the battle. A portion may have gone by the Foulk Road. Thomas married Mary Weldin, daughter of George and Elizabeth (Allmond) Weldin, who lived on Penny Hill, on the Philadelphia Turnpike. George Weldin was a brother to Jacob Weldin, who married Mary Allmond, sister to Elizabeth. George and Jacob were sons of Isaac, who was a son of the first Jacob. Thomas and Mary, shortly after their marriage, purchased a farm on the lower Shellpot, above

Webster's mill, and moved to it soon after 1800. They spent
the remainder of their life on this farm. Thomas was a very
neat and intelligent man. He was a stone mason by trade,
and helped to erect the immense stone arch which forms the
Naaman's Creek Bridge at Claymont, Del. Thomas was a
patriot and shouldered his musket in the War of 1812.

Children.

143. Eliza A., b. March 8, 1806, d. Nov. 7, 1891.
144. George W., b. Feb'y 8, 1808, d. March 3, 1888.
145. Alban, b. March 15, 1811, d. Oct. 16, 1821.
146. John, b. Nov. 15, 1813.
147. Hannah, b. July 25, 1816, d. Jan'y 5, 1892.

RICHARD TALLEY (**44**) married Sarah Cartmell, daughter of (tall) Thomas Cartmell and Hannah (Foulk) Cartmell.
Richard and his wife lived and died on the Penrose Talley
farm, at Talley's Corner. Richard may have died about the
date of his will, in 1826. He was buried at the Talley–Foulk
burying ground. His wife died about 1833.

Children.

148. Hannah C., b. Oct. 1, 1803.
149. Penrose R., b. May 19, 1805, d. Nov. 27, 1879.
150. Charity, b. 1807.
151. Sarah, b. Jan'y, 27, 1809, d. Aug. 12, 1879.
152. Thomas, b. Nov. 11, 1810, d. Aug. 13, 1899.
153. John R., b. Nov. 7, 1812, d. Feb'y 6, 1890.
154. Peter, b. March 16, 1816, d. Oct. 19, 1884.
155. Nelson L., b. Oct. 15, 1823, d. April 20, 1864.
156. George, d. unmarried.

CHARITY TALLEY (**45**) died unmarried, in 1819, about
one year after her father.

CURTIS TALLEY (**46**) married Mary Baldwin, daughter
of Eli Baldwin. Curtis, after his marriage, resided on the farm
later owned by his son Thomas Lea Talley, adjoining the
Ebright farm in Brandywine Hundred.

Children.

157. Clarissa, b. Sept. 12, 1791, d. April 29, 1843.

158. Elizabeth, b. Feb'y 19, 1793, d. Aug. 6, 1843.
159. Mary, b. Jan'y 26, 1795, d. Feb'y 6, 1840.
160. Keziah, b. June 6, 1797, d. young.
161. William, b. Aug. 12, 1799, d. in the West.
162. Eli Baldwin, b. Nov. 1, 1801, d. Sept. 9, 1875.
163. Samuel, b. March 1803, d. young.
164. Sally Ann, b. June 19, 1805.
165. Curtis, b. Nov. 19, 1807, d. in New Jersey.
166. Margaret, b. April 12, 1810.
167. Thomas Lea, b. June 3, 1812.

These names and dates were taken from an old Bible in the possession of Curtis, son of Thos. Lea Talley, Sr.

AMOR TALLEY (*47*) married Ann Day, daughter of Joseph Day, on January 19, 1797. Amor lived and died close by the "eight-square" school-house, west of the Concord Turnpike. Amor was a man of excellent character and firm integrity. He died at the age of 49 years, and is buried at the Bethel Cemetery, Brandywine Hundred.

Children.

—168. Diana, b. July 3, 1798, d. March 30, 1895.
169. Joseph Day, b. Dec. 4, 1799, d. 1868.
170. Hiram W., b. Dec. 6, 1802, d. 1840.
171. Amor L., b. Sept. 20, 1804.
172. Eliza Ann, b. Oct. 14, 1806, d. 1891.
173. Keziah, b. Oct. 20, 1808, d. Jan'y 5, 1892.
174. Wesley, b. Jan'y 17, 1812, d. 1875.
175. Mary Day, b. Feb'y 22, 1814.

HARMON TALLEY (*48*) married first, Priscilla Foulk, (36.) They were first cousins to each other. He married after the death of Priscilla, Rebecca Grubb, a sister of his son-in-law, Adam Grubb. Priscilla died in 1802, and is buried in the Foulk burying ground. Rebecca, the second wife, died in 1836, and is buried in the Grubb family burying ground on the Grubb Road. Harmon was quite an able man, was a member of the Delaware Legislature in 1828. After the death of his last wife, in 1836, he moved to Ohio, taking almost his entire family with him. He moved from Ohio to Illinois, and died, in 1858, at Piasa, Macoupin County. He was interred in the Mt. Pleasant M. E. Cemetery at that place. He lost his eyesight some years before he died.

Children of first marriage.

176. Julian, b. June 23, 1798, d. Sept. 10, 1877.
177. John Foulk, b. Oct. 26, 1799, d. Nov. 4, 1886.
178. Priscilla—died young.

Children of second marriage.

179. Isaac Grubb, b. Jan'y 10, 1804, d. Feb'y 18, 1888.
180. William Tatnall, b. May 7, 1808, d. May 15, 1885.
181. Margaretta.
182. Charles T.—died in California.
183. Harmon Harrison—died in Kansas.
184. Priscilla, b. Feb'y 14, 1814, d. 1885.

ELIHU TALLEY (*49*) married Ann Twaddell. They are both buried at St. Martin's P. E. Church at Marcus Hook. Elihu was a man of action, and of great influence in his hundred. He held many small offices.

Children.

185. William T., b. May 6, 1817.
186. Charles T., b. Aug. 11, 1819.

PETER TALLEY (*50*) married first, Sarah Carlton. He lived on the Brandywine Creek until some years after his father's death. He moved to Illinois—some say to Ogle County. He married a second time, probably.

Children.

187. Carlton may be same as Lewis, 192.
188. Diana.
189. Hannah.
190. Elvina.
191. Ruth.
192. Lewis.

These were merely reported by Mrs. Lurana Gardner, of Illinois, as Peter's children.

CALEB TALLEY (*51*) married Sarah Brown. He died on the banks of the Brandywine, December 31, 1820. His wife died July 22, 1818, leaving their children quite young,

Hannah being but five months old when her mother died.
Hannah Talley, it appears, was a daughter of Caleb the first.
Her children state it most clearly that their mother was born
towards the Brandywine, and that her father was Caleb Talley ;
that the mother died when Hannah was only a few months
old, and that Hannah was reared partly by Caleb Perkins,
who married Hannah Brown, aunt to Hannah the infant.
Hannah also, in her lifetime, stated that she was entitled to
some land near the Brandywine. Most positive proof has
been found in the family Bible of Hannah ('Talley) Everson,
now in the hands of her daughter at Marcus Hook. It gives
the death of Caleb and his wife, Sarah Talley. If Caleb
married Elizabeth Jones, as has been stated, she was a first
wife, for he surely had a wife Sarah, the mother of Hannah.
Those interested in this matter can follow it up to a definite
conclusion.

Children.

193. Caleb.
194. Hannah, b. Feb'y 14, 1818.

SARAH TALLEY (**52**) married Thomas McKee, of Mc-
Kee's Hill, near Wilmington.

Children.

195. William.
196. Thomas.
197. Mary.
198. Isabella.   } These names were given by
199. Keziah.   J. Henderson Talley, of
200. Diana.   West Chester, Pa.
201. Sarah.

REV. JOHN TALLEY (**53**) married first, Letitia Clark,
daughter of George Clark, who lived at Talley's Corner. He
married second, Ann W. Henderson, of Milford, Del., and
third, Ann Hollingsworth, of Elkton, Md. John Talley was
buried at Mt. Lebanon church-yard, near the Brandywine.
(See sketch.)

Children of first marriage.

202. George C., b. April 21, 1813.

203. James Zebley, b. May 9, 1814.
204. William Wesley.
Children of second marriage.
205. J. Henderson, b. Aug. 2, 1824.
206. Rachel Ann, b, Mch. 12, 1826, d. Mch. 24, 1828.
207. Major, b. 1828, d. March 12, 1828.

There were no issue of third marriage.

REV. LEWIS S. TALLEY (*54*) married Priscilla Clark, a sister of Letitia, the wife of his brother John Talley. He traveled for a time as a Methodist minister, but receiving an injury from a fall, he ceased to travel, and afterwards preached as a local minister, at the same time conducting his farm at Talley's Corner, on the Foulk Road. He is well remembered by the older residents of Brandywine Hundred. He was quite an able man and a forcible preacher. He was above the average in intellect, and a man of influence among his neighbors. He died September 3, 1847, and was interred at the Bethel Cemetery in Brandywine Hundred. He was the father of a large family, among whom was General William Cooper Talley, now of Washington, D. C.

Children.
208. Caleb C., b. April 17, 1816.
209. Eleanor, b. Jan'y 21, 1818, d. June 10, 1842.
210. Letitia H., b. Jan'y 30, 1820.
211. Ann Glover, b. May 20, 1822, d. Aug. 11, 1860.
212. Priscilla, b. March 26, 1824, d. —, 1899.
213. Charlotte, b. Sept. 5, 1826, d. Oct. 13, 1850.
214. Lewis Henry, b. Nov. 5, 1828, d. Nov. 17, 1893.
215. William Cooper, b. Dec. 11, 1831.

This birth is taken from his father's Bible.

KEZIAH TALLEY (*55*) married first, Charles Twaddell. After his death she married Isaac Grubb, uncle to Isaac N. Grubb, of Brandywine Hundred.

No issue of either marriage.

CAPT. AMOR TALLEY (*57*) married Mary Pierce, sister of Adam Pierce. He resided for a time on a farm along the

Foulk Road. He followed his brother John Forwood Talley to Cleremont County, Ohio, where he died at a very full age. (See sketch of his father Elihu.)

Children.

216. Sallie Ann.
217. Timothy.
218. Lydia.   } All supposed to be in Ohio.
219. Elihu.
220. Mary Caroline.

SARAH TALLEY (*58*) married Major Joseph Grubb, who lived at Grubb's Mill, in Brandywine Hundred. He was the owner of many acres of land. Sarah was the " Belle of Delaware." (See sketch of Elihu, her father.)

Children.

221. Amor.
222. Nelson.
223. Matilda B.
224. Lydia Ann.
225. Collingwood Clark.
226. Joseph.

JOHN FORWOOD TALLEY (*59*) married Sarah New-comer, February 26, 1818, in Maryland. He was in the War of 1812. After this he worked at his trade erecting mills. When engaged in erecting a mill in Maryland for Henry New-comer, he became acquainted with the daughter Sarah. This resulted in a marriage. The newly wedded couple resided in Virginia for a time, later they settled in Cleremont County, Ohio, where they spent the remainder of their very successful life. Cleremont County was, when John moved there, well on the frontier. He has told, that in the early day he was offered the best lot in Cincinnati for a load of lumber. Thus show-ing how new Cincinnati was at that day. John Forwood Talley, by his push and energy, acquired a vast amount of lands in Ohio ; and when he died he was the wealthiest man in Cleremont County. His wife died July 8, 1851. He turned from her death-bed saying, " I have nothing to live for now." From that time he declined, and passed away December 11, 1851. He was particular in his dress, kept good horses, and enjoyed a dashing drive. He was tall and muscular, and was possessed of an iron will. He, though a very silent man, would not stand an insult, and would resent the same even if it led to a personal encounter. He left to survive him five children, who became men and women of great ability and of influence in the State of Ohio.

Children.

227. Henry N., b. June 12, 1819, d. Nov. 13, 1888.
228. Lydia, b. Oct. 3, 1820, d. Sept. 17, 1840.
229. Elizabeth, b. Oct. 19, 1823, d. Nov. 10, 1896.
230. Elihu, b. Sept. 4, 1825, d. Jan'y 17, 1896.
231. John William, b. Aug. 5, 1830, d. Mch. 22, 1895.
232. Sarah L., b. Dec. 25, 1833.

MARY TALLEY (**60**) married first, Harmon Talley, second, Thos. Smith. Harmon was a carpenter, and resided along the Foulk Road, on a farm afterward owned by Samuel Forwood. He was in the army of 1812, and was encamped near Marcus Hook. He was born July 31, 1781, and died February 10, 1821.

Children.

233. Lydia, b. April 20, 1807, d. young.
234. Rebecca, b. Oct. 2, 1808, d. young.
235. Washington, b. Dec. 20, 1810, d. young.
236. Lurana A., b. Jan'y 25, 1812, d. April 6, 1893.
237. Isaac Jones, b. Feb'y 8, 1814, d. Sept. 17, 1873.
238. Leah, b. April 19, 1815, d. young.
239. Mary Jane, b. Sept. 4, 1818.
240. Elizabeth M., b. April 21, 1821.

Children of second marriage.

241. George W., m. Anna M. Grubb.
242. Ann, m. Thomas J. Pierce, (Concord.)

LYDIA TALLEY (**62**) married Amor Talley, son of Thomas, son of Samuel first. (See No. 89 for issue of this marriage.)

CHARLES TALLEY (**64**) married ———— , moved to Harrisburg, Pa., went to the Mexican War, and was never heard of again.

HANNAH R. TALLEY (*65*) married, January 31, 1822, Jehu Talley, (dark-haired) No. 93. They resided on the Concord Turnpike, above Perry's Hotel. They are buried at Siloam M. E. burying ground, Delaware County, Pa.

Children.

243. Lewis Smith, b. April 8, 1824, d. Mch. 13, 1855.
244. Thomas C., b. July 29, 1826, d. Dec. 26, 1886.
245. Julia Ann, b. Feb'y 1, 1829, d. Nov. 21, 1850.
246. Charles Parker, b. March 3, 1831, d. young.
247. Hiram G., b. Sept. 12, 1833, d. Nov. 29, 1875.
248. Elizabeth M., b. June 2, 1836, d. Jan'y 22, 1898.
249. Susan Jane, b. Dec. 12, 1838, d. Jan'y 4, 1897.
250. Walter Marsh, b. March 28, 1841, d. young.
251. Joseph E., b. May 31, 1843, d. young.
252. Mary Emma, b. Feb'y 17, 1845, d. Nov. 23, 1892.

GIDEON GILPIN TALLEY (*66*) married first, Elizabeth Lloyd (271), sister of Joseph Lloyd. After her death he married a widow named Paiste, of Delaware County, Pa.

Child of first marriage.

253. Edgar L., b. Nov. 26, 1834, d. July 14, 1854.

Children of second marriage.

254. Martha H., b. Jan'y 28, 1838, d. young.
255. Hiram H., b. Feb'y 3, 1840. In California.

Elizabeth, the first wife, was visiting in the West. She was out of doors, and heard the cry of " mad dog." She suddenly turned to run in the house, and in some way ruptured a blood vessel, from the effects of which she shortly died.

RACHEL A. TALLEY (*68*) married John Thompson, (82) January 10, 1833. He was a carpenter, and resided in Chester, Pa. He is buried at the Newark Union Cemetery, Brandywine Hundred.

Children.

256. George, b. Feb'y 2, 1834, d. young.
257. Thomas, b. April 4, 1835, d. young.
258. Elizabeth J., b. Jan'y 19, 1837.
259. Gideon Gilpin, b. Feb'y 2, 1840.
260. John L., b. Jan'y 23, 1842, d. young.

261. William T., b. Nov. 3, 1843.
262. Charles A., b. June 4, 1846.
263. Lydia A., b. Dec. 10, 1848, d. young.
264. Stephen E., b. Dec. 29, 1849, d. young.
265. Thomas Rawson, b. April 13, 1851, d. young.

Cyrus Talley (**69**) married Mary ———. He may have resided near Philadelphia.

Children.

266. James Smith, b. June 15, 1811, d. Sept. 20, 1873.
267. Alexander. (Perhaps.)
268. Henry, b. April 22, 1819, d. 1884.

Susanna Talley (**72**) married Jeremiah Lloyd, May 2, 1805. He resided near the Delaware River. Susanna has been described, by those who knew her, as a lady of refinement and great kindness.

Children.

269. Samuel, b. Nov. 30, 1806. Resided in Indiana.
270. Joseph, b. Aug. 6, 1808, d. March 1, 1855.
271. Elizabeth, b. April 6, 1811, d. April 12, 1835.
272. Orpah, b. Nov. 3, 1813. Resided in Indiana.
273. Susan, b. Sept. 25, 1817.
274. Isaac, b. July 4, 1825.

Samuel Talley (**74**) married Jemima Talley (101). This is not definitely known, but it is supposed to be right, from the fact that a grave is found in the Foulk Cemetery marked, "Margaret, the daughter of Samuel and Jemima Talley, died April 24, 1839, at the age of 18 years." We know of no other Samuel or Jemima who were of the age to have a child born about 1821. Then, again, Mary Talley, the mother of Willard Galbreath, was the daughter of Jemima Talley, and Willard states that his grandfather was buried in the Foulk Cemetery.

Children.

275. Margaret, b. 1821, d. April 24, 1839.
276. Mary, b. Aug. 27, 1826, d. April 17, 1861.
There may have been other children.

JEMIMA CARTMELL. (*76*) married Warren Rawson about 1810. (See sketch of Thomas G. Rawson.)

Children.

277. Elizabeth.
278. Susanna.
279. Regina, b. Aug. 26, 1815.
280. A daughter died in infancy.
281. A daughter died in infancy.
282. Thomas George, b. Jan'y 9, 1823.
283. William Warren, b. April 1, 1825.

CATHERINE THOMPSON (*81*) married John McDade. They are both interred at St. Martin's, Marcus Hook, Pa.

Child.

284. Rachel, m. Thomas Hansell.

JOHN THOMPSON (*82*) married Rachel A. Talley. (See No. 68 for the issue.)

SALLIE THOMPSON (*83*) married Robert Bird, Feb'y 28, 1833. He was a shoemaker. He died at his home at Penny Hill, Brandywine Hundred.

Children.

285. Mary Ann.
286. Rebecca.
287. Priscilla.
288. George.

GEORGE THOMPSON (*84*) married Sarah Ann Prince, daughter of Isaiah Prince, brother of ~~John~~ Adam Prince.

Child.

289. Mary Eliza—died a young woman.

ELIZABETH THOMPSON (*85*) married Nehemiah Broomall.

Children.

290. Thomas Thompson, unmarried.
291. Mary, m. James Rusk.
292. Martha S.
293. Jesse, d. young.

294. Nehemiah, d. young.
295. Ella L., m. Samuel Mullen.
296. John Talbot, unmarried.
297. Sarah T., married James Bullock.
298. Lydia Jane, m. Isaac Venn.
299. Victor I. Du Pont, m. May Mower.

STEPHEN II. THOMPSON (*86*) married Henrietta M. Guest, Dec. 6, 1861.

Child.
300. Mary F., b. Dec. 6, 1865, m. Wm. J. Quigley.

EDWARD T. THOMPSON (*87*) married Mary Schuster.

Children.
301. Eliza.
302. Edward.
303. Florence.
304. Priscilla.
305. Thomas J. Y.

MARY ANN THOMPSON (*88*) married John G. Burke, May 23, 1849. She is a widow, and has, of late years, resided at Chester, Pa. She and her daughters get along very snugly at their home. Her memory is good, and she has given much information for the book.

Children.
306. Mary A., b. Feb'y 25, 1850.
307. Ellen H., b. Jan'y 7, 1853.
308. Lizzie E., b. Sept. 5, 1864.

AMOR TALLEY (*89*) married Lydia Talley (62).

Child.
309. Samuel, b. 1820, d. 1887.

MARGARET TALLEY (*90*) married Aaron Smith, of Delaware County, Pa. They lived close by the circular line.

Children.
310. John.
311. Rebecca.
312. Susan, d. at nine years of age.

HANNAH TALLEY (*91*) married Samuel Hauby, who lived near Siloam M. E. Church. They and all of their children are deceased, and are buried in the Siloam Cemetery.

REBECCA TALLEY (*92*) married Robinson Beeson, May 25, 1826. They resided, after their marriage, on the land of Thomas Talley, now the William Weer farm, on the Naaman's Creek Road.

—— Robinson Beeson, b. Oct. 17, 1797, d. Spt. 18, 1877.
—— Rebecca Talley, b. Sept. 23, 1800, d. Jan. 11, 1867.

Children.

313. Thomas Talley, b. April 23, 1827.
314. Amor, b. March 1, 1828.
315. Wesley C., b. Dec. 14, 1830.
316. Hannah A., b. Dec. 14, 1830.
317. Margaret, b. May 1, 1834.
318. Charles, b. Nov. 7, 1836.
319. Charlotte, b. March 27, 1840.
320. Emily, b. March 27, 1840
—— Rebecca.

JEHU TALLEY, dark hair (*93*), married Hannah R. Talley. (See No. 65 for issue of this marriage.)

SUSANNA TALLEY (*94*) married John McKeever. They are both buried in the Bethel Cemetery. Susanna died at the age of 81 years and her husband at the age of 82 years.

Children.

321. Thomas T., b. April 26, 1830, d. July 19, 1868.
322. Margaret, married Jacob R. Pennell.
323. Isabella, d. seven years old.

JEHU TALLEY (*98*), blonde, married Hannah Smith, daughter of James and Jane Smith, of Elam, Delaware Co., Pa. He owned considerable land at Elam.

Children.

324. James Smith, b. Aug. 11, 1834, d. 1864.
325. Jehu, b. April 18, 1836.
326. Jane, b. July 15, 1838.
327. Hannah A., b. June 25, 1840.

JOSEPH B. TALLEY (*99*), son of John, married Maria —.

Children.

328. Aaron Dickinson—went West.
329. Thomas — killed by explosion of Du Pont's powder wagons in Wilmington.
330. Mary—went West.
331. Joseph, d. unmarried.

BENJAMIN TALLEY (*100*) married ———, had children, and died in Philadelphia, Pa.

JEMIMA TALLEY (*101*) may have married first, Samuel Talley, (74) son of Edward. Children, (See No. 74.) Jemima, after the death of Samuel, married, about 1844, Robert Galbreath.

Child of second marriage.

332. Robert Clay, b. Feb'y 14, 1856.

PARTHENA TALLEY (*102*) married Robert McClure. He lived along the Foulk Road, and had something to do with the log house known as the "Booth house." It is said that he moved to Wilmington, and his descendants may be living there to-day.

SUSAN TALLEY (*103*) married Benjamin Brown.

Children.

333. Thomas—went to Ohio.
334. Frank—went to Ohio.
335. Sarah Jane—nothing further known.
—— John.

MARY TALLEY (*104*) married Benjamin Pierce. Know nothing further of this family.

BAYARD TALLEY (*105*), son of Samuel, the son of Samuel the first, married, February 5, 1835, Elizabeth Smith, daughter of James and Jane Smith, of Elam, Delaware County, Pa. Bayard, later in life, moved to Oak Hill, Lancaster County, Pa. He and his wife are buried at St. John's P. E. Church Cemetery, Concord, Pa.

Children.

336. Anna Maria, d. an infant, in 1836.
337. Nelson Smith, d. Sept. 17, 1890, in his 53d year.
338. Mary Jane, b. Aug. 1, 1840.

NELSON R. TALLEY (*106*) married ———, moved to Delaware, Ohio.

Children.

339. A. J. Talley, Belle Point, Ohio. (Others, but not found.)

ISABELLA TALLEY (*108*) married ———. Nothing further known of her.

JANE TALLEY (*109*) married John Wilson. They resided near Centreville, Christiana Hundred.

Children.

340. Sabilla, d. unmarried.
341. Lydia A., single.
342. Hannah, single.
343. Adaline, m. ——— Baird.
344. Mary Jane, m. James Ewing.
345. Priscilla, married Eli Seal.
346. Alban J., m., and lives in Montgomery Co., Pa.

MARGARET TALLEY (*110*) married ——— Little.

MARIA TALLEY (*111*) married John Cochran.

MARTHA TALLEY (*113*) married Daniel Himes, of Chester County, Pa., about 1833. He was born August 11, 1811, and died February 2, 1895. She was born June 23, 1810, died April 11, 1861.

Children.

347. John S., b. Nov. 22, 1835.
348. Samuel, b. Dec. 31, 1836, d. young.
349. Mary Elmira, b. June 12, 1839.
350. Nelson T., b. Oct. 15, 1840, d. Sept. 21, 1861.
351. William S., b. March 16, 1842.
352. George B., b. May 18, 1844.

353. Anna Maria, b. Aug. 8, 1847, d. 1849.
354. Louis D., b. July 9, 1850, d. 1858.
355. Victorene, b. April 16, 1852, d. February, 1892.

SEVENTH GENERATION.

The Foulk line for lack of information cannot be shown farther. The Foulk numbers are 33 to 38, inclusive.

ABNER CLOUD (*114*) married Elizabeth McKay.
Children.
356. William, m. Sarah Derrickson.
—— Sarah Jane, m. John J. Krider, Philadelphia, Pa.

ANN CLOUD (*115*) married George Lodge, who resided at Lodge's Hill, on the Philadelphia Turnpike, Brandywine Hundred. She died a few years after her marriage, leaving only one child.
Child.
357. William C. He died in 1899.

LOT CLOUD (*118*) married Rebecca Talley (142), daughter of Adam Talley.
Children.
358. Elmira, unmarried.
359. Joel, unmarried.
360. George Lodge.
361. Ann M.
362. Charity, d. unmarried.
363. William, m. Mary Clemson.
364. Elizabeth, m. Joseph Husbands.

JOSEPH TALLEY (*126*) married Anna Maria Denny, sister of Randolph Denny. They moved to Piasa, Macoupin County, Ill., at a very early day. They died at Piasa. Several children survived them; but no word has been received from them.

HARMON TALLEY (*128*) married Harriet Johnson, daughter of Robert Johnson. No issue.

HEZEKIAH TALLEY (*129*) married Julian Bird, March 7, 1831. He owned a farm southeast of Perry's Hotel, in Brandywine Hundred. He raised fine peaches at an early date, and in large quantities. They were sold at remunerative prices. He was a man of fine attainments, and was most upright in all his dealings.

Children.

365. William Henry, b. Oct. 30, 1833, d. Oct. 30, 1869.
366. Sarah Anne, b. Oct. 30, 1833, d. July 20, 1899.
367. Anne Mary, b. Feb'y 25, 1836, d. Sept. 28, 1896.
368. Harriet Jane, b. Feb'y 25, 1836, d. Aug. 22, 1836.
369. Edwin, b. May 31, 1838.
370. Harmon Harrison, b. Nov. 1, 1840, d. Sept. 24, 1864.
371. John Day, b. Nov. 10, 1843.

MARY ANN TALLEY (*130*) died unmarried, at Wilmington, Del., and is buried at Bethel Cemetery.

WILLIAM GRUBB TALLEY (*131*) married Margaret Ann Bell. They resided at Brandywine Village for a number of years. He was well known as the village wheelwright. He died at Wilmington, and is buried at Bethel.

Children.

372. Harmon, b. Aug. 20, 1837, d. Feb'y 27, 1897.
373. Ann Elizabeth, b. 1841, d. 1848.
374. William Elwood, b. 1842, d. 1856.
375. Charles L., b. 1844.
376. Mary Emma, b. Aug. 25, 1848.
377. Wilhelmina, b. 1852.
378. Alfred G., b. 1857, unmarried.

SAMUEL M. TALLEY (*132*) married Sarah Aldred Day, December 30, 1840. (See sketch.)

Children.

379. Ellen Aldred, b. June 29, 1842.
380. Harriet Jane, b. May 2, 1844.
381. Winfield Scott, b. Aug. 31, 1847.
382. Francis D., b. June 11, 1854.

383. Joseph Harley, b. Feb'y 5, 1858.
384. Samuel M., b. Nov. 11, 1859.

MARY TALLEY (*133*), daughter of Adam Talley, married John Aldred. They moved to Ohio. So far as we have ascertained their children are as follow :

    385. Wm. Massey.
    386. John A.
    387. Adam.
    388. Thomas.
    389. Sarah A.
    390. Mary.
    391. Ellen.
    392. Rebecca or Eliza, (?)
    393. Catharine.

ANN TALLEY (*134*), daughter of Adam Talley, married Joseph Quigley, as his second wife.

Child.

    394. Rebecca Ann.

HANNAH TALLEY (*135*) married Joseph Grubb, son of Richard. In after life they removed to their farm near Newport, Del. Hannah died at Wilmington and is buried at Bethel Cemetery.

Children.

    395. Lydia Ann, m. William Babb.
    396. Rebecca, b. 1829, d. Aug. 18, 1890.
    397. George, m. Rebecca Lynam.
    398. Joseph Lybrand, m. Priscilla Rowland.
    399. Hannah Elizabeth, m. J. Fesmire.
    400. Alfred—went away and was not heard of.
    401. Mary, m. John Lynam.
    402. Beulah C., b. Oct. 10, 1842, d. Nov. 29, 1882.

ADAM G. TALLEY (*136*) married Sarah Aldred, March 28, 1825. They went to Ohio, and later to Iowa, where nearly all of the descendants now reside. The children, grandchildren and great-grandchildren number more than one hundred. Adam was major in the Pennsylvania militia before he emigrated to the West. He was a remarkably large man.

Children.

403. Thomas Aldred, b. May 18, 1828, d. Aug. 3, 1842.
404. Catharine R., b. Nov. 13, 1829, d. Aug. 24, 1899.
405. Albert, b. Dec. 31, 1832, d. July 9, 1840.
406. Mary, b. Oct. 3, 1834, d. Aug. 20, 1894.
407. Helen, b. Oct. 23, 1836, d. Nov. 22, 1836.
408. Isaac A., b. Aug. 17, 1838.
409. Benjamin F., b. Jan'y 25, 1841.
410. Sarah E., b. July 28, 1843.

PRISCILLA TALLEY (*137*) married William C. Hanby. He was born October 17, 1804; died August 1, 1885.

Children.

411. John, b. March 12, 1828.
412. Rebecca, b. Nov. 4, 1830.
413. Adam Talley, b. Dec. 29, 1832, d. 1864.
414. Louisa, d. young.
415. Charity, d. young.
416. William H., b. Aug. 29, 1835, d. 1885.
417. Rachel A., b. Oct. 27, 1839.
418. Charlotte, b. May 10, 1842.
419. Priscilla, b. Jan'y 10, 1846, d. 1899.
420. Mary Elizabeth, b. Dec. 1, 1847.

WILLIAM D. TALLEY (*138*) married Elizabeth H. Bullock. She is sister of Jacob Bullock, who married Elizabeth Talley (141). By these two marriages Elizabeth Bullock became Talley, and Elizabeth Talley became Bullock.

Children.

421. Adam Clark, b. May 12, 1839, d. Jan'y 28, 1863.
422. John D., b. April 22, 1841, d. Oct. 20, 1864.
423. William B., b. Feb'y 26, 1843.
424. Sarah M., b. Aug. 7, 1845, d. Nov. 10, 1884.
425. Isabella G., b. March 12, 1847, d. 1860.
426. Martha A., b. May 7, 1849.
427. Mary E., b. Aug. 31, 1853.
428. Emma L., b. Aug. 31, 1855.

429. Clara R., b. March 6, 1857.
430. Joseph G., b. May 6, 1860, d. young.
431. Lewis C., b. Sept. 16, 1863, d. young.
432. Wesley H., b. April 6, 1865.
433. Jessie S., b. May 6, 1868.

THOMAS MILLER TALLEY (*139*) married first, Elizabeth Goudy; second, Hannah Foulk; and third, Susan Rambo, January 29, 1857. Susan now lives in the old, well preserved house which belonged to the Rambo family. It is more than one hundred years old.

Children of first marriage.
434. Mary G., b. March 19, 1835.
435. Rebecca, b. April 12, 1837.
436. John A., b. March 6, 1840.

Children of second marriage.
437. Sarah Jane, b. Nov. 7, 1842, d. young.
438. Elwood M., b. March 11, 1844, deceased.
439. Esther Foulk, b. Aug. 1, 1845.
440. Hannah G., b. Oct. 31, 1846. Went to Califor'a.
441. Eli Sinex, b. Sept. 4, 1848, d. young.
442. Caroline S., b. May 5, 1850, d. young.
443. William Foulk, b. Dec. 9, 1851.
444. Lewis C., b. April 16, 1855.

Children of third marriage.
445. Thomas R., b. Nov. 23, 1857, d. young.
446. Rachel E., b. Nov. 22, 1859, d. young.
447. Elizabeth, b. Jan'y 22, 1861.
448. Charles H., b. Feb'y 4, 1865.
449. Jesse P., b. Aug. 4, 1867.

LEWIS TALLEY (*140*) married Elizabeth Zebley, Feb'y 27, 1834. She was born February 12, 1814, and is now in her 86th year. (See sketch.)

Children.
450. Thomas Miller, b. Dec. 27, 1834.
451. William A., b. April 2, 1836.
452. Robert, b. Aug. 29, 1837.
453. Mary, b. July 23, 1839.

454. Hannah, b. March 12, 1841.
455. Lewis F., b. March 26, 1843.
456. Elizabeth J., b. April 9, 1847.
457. Beulah Z., b. Nov. 9, 1849.
458. Albert, b. Feb'y 22, 1852, d. young.
459. Clara V., b. Feb'y 12, 1858, d. Aug. 3, 1895.

ELIZABETH TALLEY (*141*) married Jacob Bullock.
They resided at Wilmington, Del.

Children.

460. John, b. June 9, 1841.
461. Sharpley,
462. Anna Mary.
463. Margery.
464. Emma.
465. Elizabeth,
466. Jacob.

These names are quoted
from vol. 1, page 320, of
the Biog. and Genealogi-
cal History of Del.

REBECCA TALLEY (*142*) married Lot Cloud (118).
For the issue see No. 118.

ELIZA A. TALLEY (*143*) never married. (See sketch.)

GEORGE W. TALLEY (*144*) married, April 12, 1838,
Lavinia Beeson, daughter of Joseph and Susanna Smith Beeson.
(See sketch.)

Children.

467. Mary Anna, b. Jan'y 20, 1839, d. Feb'y 24, 1860.
468. John Smith, b. May 23, 1840.
469. Charles W., b. Sept. 25, 1842.
470. George A., b. Sept. 27, 1844.
471. Thomas J., b. March 13, 1846.
472. Phebe Jane, b. Oct. 10, 1847.
473. Ella, b. July 22, 1850.
474. Beulah Emma, b. Aug. 29, 1852.
475. Joseph Beeson, b. Jan'y 11, 1855.
476. Anna Lavinia, b. Jan'y 10, 1861.

JOHN TALLEY (*146*) married, in the early part of
1853, Sarah A. Stidham. (See sketch.)

Children.

477. Eliza Jane, b. Sept. 25, 1853.
478. Isaac S., b. Dec. 29, 1855.
479. John R., b. Sept. 15, 1857, d. young.
480. Anna Mary, b. Dec. 6, 1859.
481. John Thomas, b. Jan'y 10, 1862.
482. Sarah Louisa, b. Oct. 18, 1863.

HANNAH TALLEY (*147*) married Jacob R. Weldin.
(See sketch.)

Children.

483. Eliza, b. March 7, 1846.
484. Isaac, b. Jan'y 30, 1849, d. young.
485. Lewis, b. Oct. 6, 1851, d. young.
486. Jacob Atwood, b. Jan'y 31, 1855.
487. Thomas Talley, b. Aug. 18, 1857.

HANNAH C. TALLEY (*148*), daughter of Richard
Talley, married Curtis Bullock, November 19, 1822.

Children.

488. Curtis Talley, b. Oct. 3, 1823, d. Aug. 23, 1867.
489. Priscilla, b. July 26, 1825.
490. Esther, b. Aug. 14, 1827.

Curtis having died in 1829, Hannah C. married second,
Jesse M. Lane, January 12, 1837.

Children.

491. Louis, b. Feb'y 8, 1838.
492. Margaret G., b. July 15, 1839.
493. Hannah M., b. Oct. 11, 1842.

PENROSE R. TALLEY (*149*) married Edith G. Smith,
December 8, 1831. She was daughter of Thomas and Margery
(Bullock) Smith. Penrose lived at Talley's Corner, and was
a very prosperous farmer, and owned considerable land.

Children.

494. Ezra, b. Nov. 6, 1832, d. young.
495. Thomas S., b. Nov. 13, 1833, d. April 2, 1890.
496. Charles, b. March 4, 1835, d. Oct. 1, 1898.
497. Louisa, b. Feb'y 28, 1837, d. young.
498. Brinton L., b. June 29, 1839, d. Jan'y 29, 1889.

499. Sarah M., b. June 14, 1841, d. Feb'y 7, 1872.
500. Eliza J., b. Oct. 20, 1842.
501. Edith G., b. April 24, 1845.
502. Penrose R., b. Aug. 16, 1847.
503. Abner C., b. Oct. 1, 1849, d. May 13, 1876.

CHARITY TALLEY (*150*) married Nathaniel Booth, December 7, 1826.

Children.

504. Elizabeth Ann, b. Nov. 28, 1827.
505. Isaac, b. April 19, 1829.
506. Eber W., b. March, 1835.
507. Enoch, b. July 5, 1831, d. Sept. 14, 1855.
508. Sarah, b. Nov., 1833.
509. Nathaniel, b. Dec. 9, 1838.
510. Jemima, b. March 6, 1841, d. young.
511. John, b. July 15, 1843.

SARAH TALLEY (*151*) married Joseph Pierce, March 2, 1829. He died April 23, 1878, aged 81 years.

Children.

512. Alfred D., b. Nov. 18, 1829.
513. Joseph M., b. Jan'y 27, 1836.
514. William H., b. Nov. 25, 1838.

THOMAS TALLEY (*152*) married Elizabeth Bird, about 1849. She died April 9, 1887, aged 71 years.

Children.

515. Daughter, d. in infancy.
516. Leah, b. June 2, 1852.

JOHN R. TALLEY (*153*) married Eliza Ann Kizer. They resided on the farm now owned by Nelson L. Talley. John R. and Eliza Ann are interred at Mt. Pleasant M. E. Cemetery, Delaware.

Children.

517. Jesse Lane, b. Oct. 14, 1838, d. March 7, 1896.
518. Edward, b. 1841, d. July 21, 1864.
519. Henry C., b. Feb'y 1, 1844.
520. John L., b. Jan'y 19, 1846.

521.   Isaac, b. Feb'y, 1849, d. Aug. 14, 1869.
522.   Nelson L., b. April 7, 1852.
——   Albin, b. July 5, 1855.

PETER TALLEY (*154*) married Mary (Mousley) Bullock, a widow, December 29, 1841. She was born August 3, 1813; died May 5, 1889.

Children.

523.   Curtis M., born Feb'y 17, 1843.
524.   Norris W., b. Sept. 28, 1845, d. May 14, 1889.
525.   Almira, b. April 1, 1848, d. young.
526.   Sarah Jane, b. Feb'y 7, 1850, d. May 14, 1869.

NELSON L. TALLEY (*155*) married Rachel Ann Wilson, September 3, 1846. She was born October 19, 1826. He was a carpenter, but later became a farmer in Brandywine Hundred, Del.

Children.

527.   James Wilson, b. Sept. 6, 1847.
528.   John C., b. March 13, 1850, d. April 29, 1882.
529.   William T., b. March 17, 1853, d. young.
530.   Sarah Emma, b. June 17, 1855, d. young.
531.   Rachel Anna, b. May 31, 1857.
532.   Mary Ella, b. July 26, 1862, d. young.

CLARISSA TALLEY (*157*) married William Wilson.

Children.

533.   Hannah, b. April 6, 1814.
534.   Mary, b. May 5, 1816.
535.   Norris, b. Feb'y 12, 1818.
536.   Martha, b. Aug. 12, 1820.
537.   Louis, b. Aug. 22, 1823.
538.   William, b. July 2, 1826.
539.   Sarah A., b. Aug. 9, 1829.
540.   Ellen, b. Oct. 15, 1831.

ELIZABETH TALLEY (*158*) married James McKay, of Concord Township, Delaware County, Pa.

Children.

541.   Mary, m. Isaac Booth.
542.   Rachel, m. Isaac Smith.

543. Curtis Talley, never married.
544. William T., m. Evelyn Bullock.
545. James.

MARY TALLEY (*159*) married William Smith, who lived in Chandler's Hollow, on the present Ramsey farm.

Children.

546. Diana, m. John Saville.
547. Mary, m. Thomas Wilson.
548. Eli Baldwin.
549. William Penn.
550. Ann Jane, m. Jonathan Mechem.
551. Emma, m. John Tucker.

WILLIAM TALLEY (*161*) married ——, went to Columbus, Ohio, and reared a family.

Children.

552. Eli Baldwin. It is said he died from wounds received in the Civil War.
553. William. It is said he died from wounds received in the Civil War. It is said that there were daughters, but nothing further is known.

ELI BALDWIN TALLEY (*162*) married Mary Jane Mancill, March 3, 1828. (See sketch.)

Children.

554. Curtis, b. Nov. 20, 1828, d. Sept. 18, 1851.
555. William, b. May 6, 1830, d. Jan'y 24, 1896.
556. John W., b. May 3, 1832, d. April 12, 1864.
557. Eli Baldwin, b. March 27, 1834, d. young.
558. Mary Jane, b. April 27, 1836, d. young.
559. Elihu, b. May 29, 1838.
560. James A. Bayard, b. Oct. 21, 1840, d. young.
561. Lydia Ann, b. April 4, 1843, d. March 8, 1867.
562. Caroline E., b. May 11, 1845, d. June 17, 1881.
563. Harriet Ellen, b. May 29, 1848.

SALLY ANN TALLEY (*164*) married Amos W. Wickersham. She was born February 25, 1806.

Children.

564. Theodore Lea, b. June 22, 1831.
565. Curtis T., b. Sept. 7, 1832.
566. Mary E., b. May 7, 1835.
567. Amanda M., b. Sept. 1, 1836.
568. Josephine L., b. Aug. 28, 1838.
569. Victoria Veturia, b. Aug. 28, 1838.
570. Orlando Linneus, b. Feb'y 28, 1840.
571. William Francis, b. Dec. 10, 1842.

These names were taken from an old Bible in possession of Curtis Talley, son of Thomas Lea Talley.

REV. CURTIS TALLEY (*165*) married Miss Crane, of Pennington, N. J. He joined the Philadelphia M. E. Conference, and preached in New Jersey. Upon the division of the Conference he remained with the New Jersey Conference. He preached at Bethel when making visits to his old home in Delaware. He taught school at the Talley school house when a young man. Curtis died in New Jersey.

Child.

572. A daughter—name not known.

MARGARET TALLEY (*166*) married first, William Day, son of John Day. John was possibly uncle to John W. Day.

Child.

573. Mary Ellen.

Margaret married second, Isaac Thompson. No issue.

THOMAS LEA TALLEY (*167*) married first, Mary Ann Hanby, daughter of John and Charity Hanby ; second, Elizabeth M. Talley, (248).

Children.

574. Abner P., b. April 2, 1836.
575. Curtis B., b. Oct. 14, 1839.
576. William W., b. Oct. 5, 1845.
577. Margaret, b. Aug. 10, 1847. Deceased.
578. John Hanby, b. March 5, 1849.
579. Sallie Ann, b. Feb'y 26, 1851.
580. Eli Baldwin, b. Feb'y 22, 1853.

581. Thomas Lea, b. —— 1834.
582. Mary.
583. Agnes.
584. Elizabeth.
No issue of second marriage.

DIANA TALLEY (*168*) married Charles Forwood, May 15, 1823. They lived at first near the Forwood School House. Diana lived to the remarkable age of 96 years.

Children.
585. Ann, b. Dec. 26, 1825, d. 1848.
586. Jehu, b. Jan'y 5, 1827, d. young.
587. Mary, b. Aug. 26, 1828, d. 1846.
588. Amer Talley, b. Feb'y 22, 1831, d. 1887.
589. Charles Wesley, b. July 19, 1833, d. 1894.
590. William Robinson, b. Sept. 28, 1836.

JOSEPH DAY TALLEY (*169*) married Margaret Shades. He lived and died near the "Eight Square" School House.

Children.
591. Joanna D.
592. Mary E., unmarried.
593. Margaret H., unmarried.
594. Amor S.
595. Emeline P.
596. Ellen D., d. unmarried.
597. Elizabeth, d. unmarried.
598. Armanella W., unmarried.
599. Joseph D., d. young.
600. Elihu, d. young.
601. Anne E.

HIRAM W. TALLEY (*170*) married Elizabeth Dutton, January 31, 1831. He resided in Wilmington, Del., and probably died there.

Children.
602. Willamina, d., one year old.
603. Joseph G., b. Aug., 1834, d. 1847.
604. Mary Elizabeth.

AMOR L. TALLEY (*171*) married Mary Rutter, sister of Blythe Rutter.

Children.

605. James Blythe.
606. Amor L.
607. Annie.
608. Elwood, died in infancy.
609. John, died in infancy.
610. Jacob Hailman.

ELIZA ANN TALLEY (*172*) married William Johnson. They resided at Johnson's Corner. (See sketch of Thomas W. Johnson.)

Children.

611. Margaret W., b. Dec. 9, 1826.
612. Anna D., b. Sept. 9, 1829.
613. Thomas Webster, b. Jan'y 7, 1833.
614. Mary Jane, b. Feb'y 3, 1835.
615. Harriet J., b. Sept. 22, 1838.

KEZIAH TALLEY (*173*) married James Hannum. She died at the age of 84 years.

Children.

616. Elizabeth, b. 1827.
617. Amor T., b. 1829.
618. James N.
619. Ann Eliza.
620. Hiram W.
621. Thomas, b. March 7, 1837.

WESLEY TALLEY (*174*) married Charlotte Mulford. He taught school, and afterwards resided in Wilmington, Del., where he died.

Child.

622. Frank W., practicing physician at Philad'a, Pa.

MARY DAY TALLEY (*175*) married Robert Johnson, March 7, 1833. They resided first near the "Eight Square" School House, in Brandywine Hundred. They later resided on their farm in Bethel Township, Delaware County, Pa.

Children.

623. David, b. July 4, 1834, d. young.
624. William Wesley, b. Feb'y 22, 1837.
625. Lizzie Day, b. April 26, 1839.
626. Robert S., b. Oct. 28, 1841.
627. Mary Emma, b. April 16, 1845, d. 1866.
628. Andrew Carey, b. Oct. 1, 1848, d. young.
629. Anna Amanda, b. Sept. 29, 1853, d. Aug. 15, 1896.
630. Margaret Ella, b. Oct. 8, 1856.

JULIAN TALLEY (*176*) married Adam Grubb, August 3, 1815. He was a farmer, and a local preacher in the M. E. Church.

Children.

631. Louis Henry, b. Feb'y 6, 1817, m. Mary Ford.
632. Harman Wesley, b. Sept. 26, 1818, m. Sidney Smith, of Ohio.
633. Priscilla, b. Jan'y 16, 1821.
634. Isaac N., b. March 25, 1823.
635. John T., b. Feb'y 21, 1825, m. Elizabeth Love.
636. Margaretta C., b. June 21, 1827.
637. Anna Maria, b. Sept. 5, 1829, m. Geo. W. Smith. ✓
638. Francis H., b. Oct. 17, 1832, d. in Illinois.
639. Rebecca T., b. March 14, 1835.
640. Charles E., b. July 18, 1837, m. Phebe Smith.

JOHN FOULK TALLEY (*177*) married Hannah Poulson, September 11, 1819. They moved to Ohio. John F. Talley lived to be 87 years old. He was County Surveyor of Morgan County for about twenty-two years. He surveyed and laid out nearly all towns in the county. He was also Justice of the Peace for many years. He was a very liberal man, rarely charging anything for writing wills or acknowledging deeds. He was a fine mathematician, and a decidedly useful man in his county.

Children.

641. Anna, b. June 17, 1820.
642. Rebecca, b. Nov. 7, 1822.
643. Priscilla, b. Feb'y 5, 1824.
644. Jane, b. Feb'y 6, 1825.

645.   Julian, b. Nov. 17, 1826.
646.   Harman, b. Nov. 16, 1828.
647.   John P., b. Oct. 26, 1830.
648.   Hannah P., b. Sept. 14, 1834.
649.   Margaretta, b. May 29, 1836.
650.   Priscilla.

ISAAC GRUBB TALLEY (*179*) married first, Mary Simmons, April 5, 1827 ; married second, Rachel J. Grubb, December 19, 1833.

Children of first marriage.

651.   Harmon G., b. Jan'y 20, 1828.
652.   John Simmons, b. Feb'y 28, 1830.
653.   Lydia S., b. 1832, d. young.

Children of second marriage.

654.   William H., b. May 26, 1837, d. young.
655.   Rebecca J., b. June 6, 1840, d. Feb'y, 1889.
656.   Isaac Elwood, b. May 11, 1844, d. young.
657.   Valentine J., b. March 18, 1846, d. young.

WILLIAM TATNALL TALLEY (*180*) married Anna Mary Elliott, December 23, 1835. (See sketch.)

Children.

658.   Isaac Elliott, — d. an infant.
659.   Harman H., — d. an infant.
660.   William Cloud, — d. aged 18 years.
661.   E. Hillis, — d. April 4, 1861.
662.   E. Jennie E.

MARGARET TALLEY (*181*) married first, John Simmons, and second, Frank Shades of Ohio.

Child of first marriage.

663.   John T., b. Jan'y 11, 1829.

Child of second marriage.

664.   William Talley, b. Jan'y 11, 1844.

CHARLES T. TALLEY (*182*) married Evaline Kellam. He died in California.

HARMAN H. TALLEY (*183*) married in Ohio, later moved to Kansas. No information has been obtained.

PRISCILLA TALLEY (*184*) married Moses Bullock, of Ohio.

WILLIAM T. TALLEY (*185*) married Elizabeth Heyburn, of Birmingham, Penna., November 16, 1843. They reside in Beaver Valley. William T. Talley is a man of means, and of fine character. He is quite active, although more than 80 years old.

Children.
665. Elihu Dallas, b. Dec. 25, 1844.
666. Sarah Ann, b. Oct. 1, 1848.
667. John Heyburn, b. Dec. 3, 1852.
668. Letitia B., b. Nov. 12, 1856.

CALEB TALLEY (*193*), son of Caleb, may have gone to Illinois and died there, for there is probate of an estate at West Chester, Pa., of Caleb Talley, of Illinois, died about 1857.

HANNAH TALLEY (*194*) married Albert Everson, of Marcus Hook, Pa., January 10, 1839.

Children.
669. Sarah Jane, b. Oct. 3, 1839.
670. Rachel W., b. Dec. 27, 1840.
671. Mary Ann, b. March 9, 1844.
672. William B., b. Aug. 31, 1846.
673. George A. H., b. Feb'y 24, 1849.
674. Virginia, b. July 13, 1851.
675. Orpha E., b. Nov. 27, 1854.
676. Adeline C., b. June 29, 1856.
677. Laura C., b. Feb'y 10, 1858.
678. Newlin, b. July 15, 1860.

GEORGE C. TALLEY (*202*) married Eliza Crawford, 1848.

Children.
679. John C., b. May 14, 1849.
680. James, b. Sept. 2, 1852.
681. Matilda, b. Jan'y 28, 1855.
682. Mary, b. June 3, 1860.
683. Charles, b. Aug. 20, 1865.

684. Mary Ann.
685. Henry Lewis.
686. Sarah Jane.
687. George.

JAMES ZEBLEY TALLEY (*203*) married Elizabeth T.
Lyons. He carried on the plastering business in Chester, Pa.,
and resided and died within a few feet of the Penn Landing
Stone on the Delaware River, at Chester.

Children.

688. Letitia, b. ———, d. young.
689. Arabella, b. Oct. 12, 1841.
690. Zelina, b. April 29, 1844, d. young.
691. Emma, b. Jan'y 11, 1846, d. young.
692. Clara, b. May 3, 1848, d. young.
693. Henry, b. Aug. 25, 1850, d. young.
694. Melissa, b. March 9, 1852.
695. James Edgar, b. Jan'y 15, 1857.

WILLIAM WESLEY TALLEY (*204*) married Charity
Hanby. No issue.

J. HENDERSON TALLEY (*205*) married Elizabeth R.
Fisher (niece of Jesse Ford), on December 30, 1846. She was
born December 24, 1824. (See sketch.)

Children.

696. Sarah Ann, b. July 8, 1848, d. 1849.
697. Willie Ann, b. Jan'y 6, 1850.
698. Arabella, b. Oct. 15, 1851.
699. Mary E., b. Sept. 11, 1853, d. 1857.
700. Charles Wesley, b. March 6, 1857.
701. Sallie Fisher, b. March 2, 1859.
702. Edward Cooper, b. Nov. 18, 1861.
703. Samuel Henderson, b. Sept. 30, 1863.
704. Eugene Franklin, b. Sept. 23, 1869.

LETITIA H. TALLEY (*210*) married Humphrey Pyle,
September 1, 1842.

Child.

705. H. Alban Louis, b. Sept. 1, 1847. He was an attorney-at-law, Phila., Pa. Now deceased.

ANN GLOVER TALLEY (*211*) married Dr. Reuben J. Allmond, of Brandywine Hundred, November 10, 1841. They moved to Ohio first, and afterward located at Palmyra, Macoupin County, Ill Doctor Allmond was a remarkably active man, and of very large stature, and of almost unfailing endurance. It has been asserted that in his practice in Illinois he exceeded all others in the number of hours spent in travel among his patients. All calls were answered, if within his power, whether in the daytime or at night. He was, as a family physician, most faithful, interested and skillful. He, at one time, had gathered much historical and genealogical data of the Talleys, with a view of printing the same. His work has all been lost or mislaid. He was interested in all good works, and was an active member of the Methodist Church.

Children.

706. Lurana Cooper, b. Nov. 23, 1842.
707. Mary Ellen, b. 1843, d. 1848.
708. Lewis S. T., b. 1844, d. 1848.
709. Letitia Ann, b. Jan'y 22, 1846, d. 1878.
710. Priscilla T., b. March 1, 1848.
711. Phebe Ellen, b. May 5, 1851.
712. Julia E., b. March 25, 1853.
713. Florence V., b. Oct. 2, 1856.
714. Ida M., b. Oct. 2, 1858.
715. Tenth child buried with its mother, 1860.

PRISCILLA TALLEY (*212*) married Wm. McCracken, who lived near Media, Pa.

Children.

716. Letitia, m. Samuel A. Field.
717. Mary, m. John Bodley.
718. Sydney, m. George Adams.
719. Hannah, m. Joseph Rogers.
720. James, unmarried.

LEWIS HENRY TALLEY (*214*) married first, Sarah J. Boise. They lived in Wilmington, Del., for a few years. In later life, Lewis Henry resided at Bridgeton, N. J., and died there.

Children.

721.   A boy, d. in infancy.
722.   A boy, d. in infancy.
723.   Laura V., b. 1852, d. Aug. 3, 1877.
724.   Harriet L., b. Oct. 27, 1856.

The first wife having died, he married second, Margaret K. Garton, October 6, 1858.

Children of second marriage.

725.   Priscilla Clark, b. Jan'y 16, 1860.
726.   Lewis Henry, b. July 16, 1862.
727.   Charles G., b. Feb'y 5, 1865.
728.   Mary Elizabeth, b. May 15, 1867.
729.   Samuel Harlan, b. Oct. 3, 1869.
730.   Albin Pyle, b. Feb'y 10, 1872.

GEN'L WILLIAM COOPER TALLEY (*215*), son of Lewis S. Talley, a minister, married Mary J. Webb. They resided in Delaware County, Pa. In recent years they have lived in Washington, D. C. (See sketch.)

Children.

731.   Priscilla, b. 1861.
732.   Mary F., b. March 2, 1864, d. 1865.
733.   Stella, b. March 30, 1866, d. young.
734.   Eleanor, b. May 11, 1867.
735.   William C., b. April 18, 1869.
736.   Frank G., b. Nov. 8, 1871.
737.   Horace W., b. Nov. 16, 1873.
738.   Georgia, b. Jan'y 15, 1876.
739.   Ethel, b. Jan'y 11, 1880.
740.   Katherine, b. March 4, 1884.

SALLIE ANN TALLEY (*216*) married Enos Shades, of Ohio.

Children.

741.   Amor.
742.   Francis.

TIMOTHY TALLEY (*217*) married Ann Harvey, of Ohio.

Children.

746. Amor.

747. Sarah.

748. Lydia.

749. Mary.

LYDIA TALLEY (*218*) married George Smith, of Ohio.

MARY CAROLINE TALLEY (*220*) married Newton Carter, of Ohio.

Children.

750. William.

751. Charles.

AMOR GRUBB (*221*) and NELSON GRUBB (*222*) went on the ocean as masters of ships, owned by Stephen Girard, of Philadelphia, Pa. They were lost in a storm at sea, or by mutiny of the crews.

MATILDA B. GRUBB (*223*) married George Cummins, of Delaware County, Pa.

Children.

752. James R.

753. Lydia Ann, m. Edward Baker.

754. John R. Lives in Minnesota.

755. Joseph G., m. Sarah Otley.

756. Jesse, m. Matilda Cofman.

757. Richard R. Lives at Yellowstone Park.

LYDIA ANN GRUBB (*224*) married George Walter, January 7, 1832.

Children.

758. Ann Marshall, b. April 6, 1833, unmarried.

759. Sarah Grubb, b. Dec. 31, 1834.

760. Lewis P., b. July 2, 1838, m. Sarah Trainor.

761. Matilda B., b. Mch. 2, 1841, m. Wm. S. Goodley.

762. Harriet Mansell, b. June 19, 1843, m. Moses
         Bullock.
763. George Cummins, b. Sept. 7, 1846, m. Emma
         Bower.
764. Amor Grubb, b. Oct. 26, 1850, m. Mary Pyle.

COLLINGWOOD C. GRUBB (*225*) married first, Rachel
Bailey. They moved to Kansas.
Children of first marriage.
765. Eli B.
766. Alfred.
Children of second wife (Charlotte Webb).
767. Matilda.
768. Lydia.
—   Rachel.
769. Walter.
770. Nancy.
771. Mary.
772. Martha.
773. James.

JOSEPH GRUBB (*226*) married Ann Cricks, of Trenton, N. J.
Children.
774. Amor.
775. George.
776. Joseph.
777. Henry.
778. Matilda.
779. Sarah.
780. John.
781. Edward.
782. Jess.
783. Sherman.

HENRY N. TALLEY (*227*) married Martha P. Fish-
back, January 30, 1850. Henry N. Talley was a lawyer of
prominence in Southern Ohio.

Children.

784. Sarah A., b. Feb'y 3, 1853, d. Aug. 11, 1890.
785. Frank F., b. May 4, 1855.

LYDIA TALLEY (*228*) married Lindsey Moore, April 22, 1838. He had quite a reputation in Ohio as a geologist.

Child.

786. Elizabeth T., b. July 24, 1840.

ELIZABETH TALLEY (*229*) married Rev. James F. Chalfant, July 17, 1845. He was a Methodist minister, and at one time Presiding Elder of a district in the Cincinnati Conference. No children.

ELIHU TALLEY (*230*) married Amanda E. Hitch, January 16, 1860. He was a chemist.

Children.

787. Rowena, b. Jan'y 13, 1861.
788. Kate, b. Jan'y 28, 1864.

JOHN WILLIAM TALLEY (*231*) married Amanda J. Kyle, Aug. 4, 1853. He was a farmer in Indiana.

Children.

789. Mary L., b. Sept. 8, 1854.
790. Orville B., b. Sept. 24, 1860.

SARAH L. TALLEY (*232*) married Benjamin F. Dye, January 8, 1856. He was an extensive farmer and stock-raiser of Paxton, Ill. No issue.

LURANA A. TALLEY (*236*), daughter of Harman and Mary Talley, married George Anderson, who lived near Media, Pa.

Children.

791. Elizabeth, b. Dec. 18, 1834.
792. Isaac J., b. Feb'y 13, 1836.
793. John H., b. July 22, 1840.
794. Lydia J., b. Feb'y 9, 1844.
795. George W., b. Oct. 12, 1846.
796. David P., b. Sept. 11, 1849.

ISAAC JONES TALLEY (*237*) married Eliza Grubb. He resided at Madison, Indiana.

Children.

797. Emma.
798. George L.
799. Elby.

MARY JANE TALLEY (*239*) married first, Brinton L. Smith, April 16, 1835 ; and second, Daniel Pyle, June 15, 1856.

Children of first marriage.

800. Elizabeth Ann, b. June 23, 1839.
801. Thomas T., b. April 12, 1842.
802. Isaac W., b. Sept. 5, 1846.
803. Brinton P., b. Sept. 17, 1849.

Child of second marriage.

804. Ella.

ELIZABETH M. TALLEY (*240*) married Philip Pierce, son of Amos and Mary Pierce. They lived on their farm near the Blue Ball Hotel, in Brandywine Hundred.

Children.

805. Joseph Jackson, b. Oct. 2, 1844.
806. Isabella, b. July 5, 1849.
807. Emma L., b. Feb'y 17, 1855.
808. James Bayard, b. Jan'y 21, 1858.
809. Ella K., b. Oct. 31, 1860.
810. Mary E.
811. Anna M.

GEORGE W. SMITH (*241*) married Anna M. Grubb, (637) sister of Isaac N. Grubb. Children's names not known.

ANN SMITH (*242*) married Thomas J. Pierce, of Concord, Delaware County, Pa. Have no information about children.

LEWIS SMITH TALLEY (*243*) married Lydia Jane Perkins, daughter of Moses Perkins, of Concord, Delaware County, Pa. He resided in Philadelphia.

Children.

812. Hannah P.
813. Elizabeth.

THOMAS C. TALLEY (**244**) married Sarah Ann Ervin, October 13, 1853. She was born December 27, 1829. They resided in Delaware County, Pa., and later in Philadelphia.

Children.

814. Henry Irving, b. Aug. 11, 1854.
815. Thomas C., b. Sept. 11, 1856.
816. Hannah Ellen, b. Jan'y 31, 1859, d. young.
817. Annie Dutton, b. July 4, 1862, d. in 1894.
818. Bessie Gertrude, b. Sept. 19, 1866.

JULIA ANN TALLEY (**245**) married William Johnston, of Wilmington, Del.

Child.

819. Harry.

HIRAM G. TALLEY (**247**) married Hannah A. Beeson, (316).

Children.

820. Mary Eva, b. Nov., 1861, d. unmarried.
821. Hannah Rebecca, b. Aug. 28, 1867.

ELIZABETH M. TALLEY (**248**) married Thomas Lea Talley, Sr., as his second wife. No issue.

SUSAN JANE TALLEY (**249**) married Thos. E. Lukens, a wheelwright, of Wilmington, Del. No issue.

MARY EMMA TALLEY (**252**) married James Blythe Rutter, October 19, 1869. They have resided in Philadelphia, Pa., for several years.

Children.

822. Florence May, b. Aug. 5, 1870.
823. Laura Irene, b. 1873.
824. Blanche, b. 1876.
825. Mabel Lillian, b. May 14, 1879.
826. Marion Emma, b. May 14, 1882.
827. Walter Fleetwood, b. Aug. 17, 1885.

ELIZABETH J. THOMPSON (*258*) married George Crawford, of Chester, Pa.

Children.

828. Robert.
829. Rachel A.

CHARLES A. THOMPSON (*262*) married ―――― Smith.

JAMES SMITH TALLEY (*266*), son of Cyrus Talley, son of Edward, married Catharine ――――.

Children.

830. Mary.
831. James.
832. Elizabeth.

HENRY B. TALLEY (*268*) married Ann Eliza Bispham, March 27, 1845. She was born January 18, 1821. They resided in Philadelphia, Pa.

Children.

833. Henry Bispham, b. Jan'y 6, 1846.
834. George Washington, b. Oct. 16, 1847.
835. Elizabeth G., b. Oct. 24, 1849.
836. Daniel Bispham, b. Feb'y 24, 1852.
837. Kate, b. Feb'y 6, 1854.
838. Charles M. Y., b. Aug. 16, 1856.
839. Frank Albert, b. July 28, 1859.

SAMUEL LLOYD (*269*) married Margaret Rambo. They moved to and resided in Putnam County, Indiana.

Children.

840. Elizabeth.
841. Jane.
842. Susanna.
843. Maggie.
844. Orpah.
845. Isaac.
846. Richard.
847. Eber.
848. Joseph.
849. Samuel.
850. Edward.

JOSEPH LLOYD (*270*) married Beulah Pennell, January 16, 1834. They resided at Lodge's Hill, on the Philadelphia Turnpike, near the Delaware River.

Children.

851. Margaretta P., b. Sept. 8, 1834, d. 1855.
852. Susanna, b. July 31, 1836, d. 1837.
853. Wellington G., b. Aug. 1, 1838, d. July 29, 1863.
854. George L., b. June 26, 1840, d. Nov. 19, 1886.
855. William Henry, b. Feb'y 17, 1842.
856. Mary B., b. Jan'y 19, 1844.
857. John B., b. Oct. 16, 1846.
858. Sarah, b. July 18, 1849, d. 1849.
859. Orpah, b. July 12, 1850.
860. Joseph, b. Dec. 1, 1852.
861. James P., b. Feb'y 14, 1855, d. young.

ORPAH LLOYD (*272*) married Caleb Perkins, January 8, 1835. Moved to Putnam County, Ind.

Children.

862. Joseph.
863. Edward.
864. Emeline.
865. Susan.
866. Harriet.
867. Orpah.

SUSAN LLOYD (*273*) married William Phillips. They lived along the River Shore at Holly Oak, Del., and later purchased the Cartmell farm at Quarryville, Del. They both died on this farm.

Child.

868. George W., b. Oct. 31, 1843.

ISAAC LLOYD (*274*) married Elizabeth Bradley. They lived in the West.

Children.

869. Caroline.
870. Sarah.
871. Frank.

872. Harry.
873. Lewis.
874. Virginia.

Mary Talley (**270**) married —— Martin, first, and after his death she married Wallace Wardell Galbreath. He died October 20, 1892.

Children.

875. Willard Talley, b. Feb'y 14, 1856.
876. Thomas A.

Thomas George Rawson (**282**) married first, Mary A. Kimber, January 1, 1845. She died July 18, 1873. He married second, Emma McAffee, Aug. 20, 1879. (See sketch.)

Children of first marriage.

877. Mary Kimber, b. July 29. 1846, d. young.
878. Sarah Ellen, b. Feb'y 16, 1850, d. young.
879. Laura Celinda, b. June 20, 1856, d. young.
880. Emma Jane, b. April 25, 1859, d. March 1, 1877.
881. Warren T., b. March 18, 1873.

Child of second marriage.

882. George Cartmell, b. June 30, 1880.

Martha S. Broomall (**292**) married William H. Priest, January 12, 1870. They have resided in the vicinity of Linwood, Pa., since their marriage. He has been Assistant Station Agent at the Linwood Station on the P., W. and B. R. R. for twenty-five years.

Samuel Talley (**309**) married Elizabeth A. Bullock, daughter of Lewis Bullock, of Elam, Pa., on June 15, 1848.

Children.

883. Lydia.
884. Charles B., b. April 14, 1852.
885. Leslie C., b. Nov. 8, 1855.
886. Amor, b. Jan'y 24, 1859.
887. Ida Lottie, b. Dec. 15, 1861.
888. Mary E., b. July 12, 1867, d. young.

John Smith (**310**) married ——.

Children.
889. Thomas Talley.
890. Isaac.
891. William H. Harrison.
892. Theodore.
893. Susan.
894. Mary Eliza.

REBECCA SMITH (*311*) married William Bishop.
Children.
895. Samuel.
896. Rebecca.

THOMAS TALLEY BEESON (*313*) married Susan Price, daughter of Dr. Phineas Price.
Children.
897. Wilmer.
898. Horace.

AMOR BEESON (*314*) married Louisa Cloud.
Children.
899. Henry.
900. Edwin R.
901. Martha.

WESLEY G. BEESON (*315*) married Sarah Larkin.
Children.
902. Edward L., m. Bertha Witsil.
903. W. Calmer, m. Florence Pierce.
904. Mary, m. Alfred Mousley.
905. Ola.

CHARLES BEESON (*318*) married Maggie Minshall.
Children.
906. Thomas.
907. John.
908. Chandler.

EMILY BEESON (*320*) married Robert Talley (452).

JAMES SMITH TALLEY (*324*) married Sarah Hannum.
They both died at an early age, leaving only one child, whose
name is—

    909. James Ely, b. July 22, 1864. A physician at
        Philadelphia, Pa.

JEHU TALLEY, of Elam (*325*), married Phebe Carter,
November 14, 1861. He resides adjoining the M. E. Church,
at Elam, Pa.

Children.
    910. Mary Elizabeth, b. Sept. 26, 1862.
    911. Hannah Emma.
    912. Ruthanna, b. Sept. 17, 1866.
    913. Ida L.
    914. Harry M., b. Feb'y 14, 1869.
    915. Jesse.

JANE TALLEY (*326*) married Samuel M. Lenderman.
She is a widow and resides at Johnson's Corner, Delaware
County, Pa.

Children.
    916. Anna Jane, b. Oct. 5, 1863, d. young.
    917. Abraham L., b. Jan'y 29, 1865.
    918. Hanna R., b. July 6, 1866.
    919. Joseph, b. Oct. 20, 1868, d. 1898.

HANNAH A. TALLEY (*327*) married Ellis Hendrickson. She resides at Elam, Pa.

Children.
    920. Harry.
    921. Mary.

MARY JANE TALLEY (*338*), daughter of Bayard
Talley, married S. Harvey Scott, February 25, 1869. They
reside at Oak Hill, Lancaster County, Pa.

Children.
    922. Laura E.
    923. Alice A.
    924. Mary Jane.

925. Ella May.
926. Nelson A.
927. Bertha V.

EIGHTH GENERATION.

GEORGE LODGE CLOUD (*360*) married Sallie A. Prince, daughter of Adam and Charlotte Prince.

Children.
928. Eva May, b. May 27, 1871.
929. William Lot, b. July 16, 1873.
930. Cassandra Prince, b. Feb'y 24, 1876.
931. Ann Krider, b. May 6, 1880.

ANN M. CLOUD (*361*) married Robert Casey. They reside at Claymont, Del.

Children.
932. Lot C.
933. Robert P.

WILLIAM HENRY TALLEY (*365*) married Hannah Elizabeth Bright, daughter of Wm. Bright, of Wilmington, Del., Nov. 18, 1857. William Henry died in early manhood. He held a responsible position in the Farmers' Bank, at Wilmington, Del., and was also a member of the St. Paul's M. E. Church, Wilmington. He was a man of fine character, and of the strongest integrity.

Children.
934. Sarah Bright, b. Aug. 15, 1858, d. Oct. 31, 1872.
935. May Anne, b. May 9, 1861, d. Feb'y 15, 1892.
936. William Paul, b. May 9, 1861, d. Jan'y 16, 1864.
937. Virginia Bird, b. Nov. 6, 1863, d. Nov. 25, 1868.
938. Elizabeth Henry, b. Oct. 17, 1868.

SARAH ANNE TALLEY (*366*) married James A. Bayard Perkins, April 12, 1860, son of Joseph Perkins, of Holly Oak, Del.

Children.
939. Joseph Leslie, b. Nov. 15, 1861.
940. Julia May, b. March 28, 1866, m. Geo. T. Barlow,
      Sept. 29, 1887.

EDWIN TALLEY (*369*) married Sara B. Davis.

Children.

941. Lelia Ada.
942. Edwin Howard.
943. Anna Sophia.
944. Edna Emilie.

JOHN DAY TALLEY (*371*) married Mary De Vou,
March 23, 1871.

Children.

945. Preston Lea, b. Feb'y 8, 1872.
946. Fannie Bird, b. March 19, 1874.
947. Sadie Iola, b. May 8, 1875.
948. Anne Mary, b. June 27, 1878.
949. John Day, b. Oct. 11, 1880.
950. Elizabeth Francis, b. March 20, 1884.

HARMON TALLEY (*372*) married Eliza Long, born April
10, 1838. He was born in New Castle County, Del. He learned
the wheelwright trade with his father, in Brandywine Village.
He later in life resided in Philadelphia, Pa., and served faithfully on the Police force of the last named city for twenty-three
years. He was a member of the Masonic Order. His death
was caused by pneumonia, in 1897.

Children.

951. William Elwood, b. Sept. 13, 1863.
952. Mary Emma, b. Jan'y 13, 1866.
953. Lizzie, b. Aug. 6, 1868, d. 1870.
954. Harry W., b. Oct. 29, 1870.
955. John B., b. March 2, 1873.
956. Ella, b. Jan'y 5, 1875.
957. Harmon, b. May 2, 1877.
958. Margaret Ann, b. Jan'y 8, 1882, d. 1883.

CHARLES L. TALLEY (*375*) married Rebecca McBride.

Children.

959. Leonard K., b. 1868.
960. Ann McBride, b. 1876.

MARY EMMA TALLEY (*376*) married Dr. Aquilla Nebeker. He was born April 22, 1843. They reside in Philadelphia, Pa.

Children.

961. Mary Boys, b. May 6, 1867.
962. Aquilina Allen, b. May 17, 1871.
963. Emma Talley, b. June 4, 1873.
964. Myrtle L., b. March 29, 1878.

WILHELMINA TALLEY (*377*) married John Moore, September 14, 1874. They reside in Wilmington, Del.

Children.

965. Mary Isabelle, b. July 31, 1875.
966. Margaret Talley, b. Oct. 17, 1878.
967. Alfred Garfield, b. Sept. 9, 1881.
968. James, b. June 28, 1884, d. 1886.
969. William H., b. Feb'y 3, 1888.
970. John, b. Dec. 18, 1893.

HARRIET J. TALLEY (*380*) married Wm. F. Green, of Delaware County, Pa., March 13, 1866. They now reside in Wilmington, Del. Mr. Green was born Nov. 2, 1837.

Children.

971. Ida, b. Dec. 24, 1866.
972. William Arthur, b. June 14, 1875.
973. Samuel Talley, b. Jan'y 9, 1877.

WINFIELD SCOTT TALLEY (*381*) married Mary Forwood, in 1872. They reside near Centreville, Del.

FRANCIS D. TALLEY (*382*) married, in 1875, Clemma Lane.

Children.

974. Francis D., b. May 23, 1876.
975. Walter White, b. Dec. 7, 1879.
976. Elsie May, b. Oct. 4, 1881.
977. Lena, b. Oct. 28, 1884.
978. Ella Aldred, b. April 9, 1886.
979. Ada Harrison, b. Nov. 23, 1888.

JOSEPH HARLEY TALLEY (*383*) married Ellathera Campbell. No children.

SAMUEL M. TALLEY, JR. (*384*) married Alice Way, November 10, 1897.

REBECCA ANN QUIGLEY (*394*) married Wm. Mayne. They reside in Wilmington, Del.

Children.

980. Lillie O., b. Aug. 8, 1864, m. John T. Talley.
981. Naomi, m. Thomas Hendrickson.
982. Harry.
983. William, m. Ella Baynard.
984. Edgar, m. Florence Thompson.
985. Mary.
986. Leonard.
987. James.

REBECCA GRUBB (*396*) married Stephen Blackwell.

Children.

988. Hannah Mary, b. Dec. 8, 1858, d. Jan. 28, 1882.
989. John.
990. Stephen.

BEULAH C. GRUBB (*402*) married Wm. B. Talley (423). See children's names under No. 423.

CATHARINE R. TALLEY (*404*) married Benjamin W. Ford, February 14, 1850.   Reside in the West.

Children.

991. Mary V., b. Nov. 20, 1850.
992. Josephine, b. March 13, 1853.
993. Irenous W., b. Nov. 26, 1854.
994. Alice J., b. Oct. 23, 1855.
995. Sarah E., b. June 8, 1857.
996. Emily Vic., b. Dec. 1, 1859.
997. George A., b. Jan'y 31, 1862.
998. William L., b. May 10, 1866.
999. Benjamin F., b. April 27, 1868.
1000. John B., b. June 20, 1871.

MARY TALLEY (*406*) married Michael Stahl, November 10, 1854.

Children.

1001. Melissa E., b. Jan'y 11, 1856.
1002. Sarah E., b. Aug. 25, 1858.
1003. Catharine J., b. Dec. 2, 1860.
1004. Martha A., b. Aug. 11, 1862.
1005. Mary J., b. April 14, 1864.
1006. Ulysses Grant, b. Feb'y 9, 1866.
1007. William Sherman, b. Jan'y 16, 1868.
1008. Luella T., b. April, 1870.
1009. Eva F., b. Feb'y 14, 1876.
1010. Edgar.

ISAAC A. TALLEY (*408*) married Nancy Keller, Feb'y 9, 1860. They reside in Iowa.

Children.

1011. Mary E., b. March 12, 1861.
1012. John W., b. June 13, 1862.
1013. Ella I, b. Oct. 25, 1863.
1014. Anna M., b. May 14, 1867.
1015. Cora B., b. May 14, 1867.
1016. Henry E., b. Oct. 2, 1869.
1017. Sarah C., b. Aug. 27, 1871.
1018. William W., b. March 25, 1873.
1019. Melvin R., b. May 3, 1875.
1020. Jessie N., b. Feb'y 4, 1880.
1021. Louis F., b. Dec. 3, 1883.

BENJAMIN F. TALLEY (*409*) married Sarah C. Kellar, December 25, 1860. Reside at Mt. Ayr, Iowa.

Children.

1022. Adam C., b. April 29, 1863.
1023. Ambrose E., b. May 31, 1866.
1024. Lloyd, b. Jan'y 14, 1870.
1025. Mary M., b. Sept. 14, 1873.
1026. Gilbert H., b. July 8, 1876.
1027. Nora May, b. Dec. 2, 1881.
1028. Charles D., d. in infancy.

1029. Cleo, d. in infancy.
1030. Ellis B., died in infancy.

SARAH E. TALLEY (*410*) married Benjamin Kellar, February 9, 1860.

Children.

1031. Clarinda E., b. Nov. 24, 1860.
1032. Mary V., b. Nov. 3, 1862.
1033. Rosa B., b. Nov. 1, 1864.
1034. George E., b. Sept. 29, 1866.
1035. Ensign K., b. Dec. 21, 1868.
1036. John N., b. April 10, 1871.
1037. Sarah E., b. April 18, 1873.
1038. Catharine J., b. Oct. 24, 1875.
1039. Jesse Franklin, b. Jan'y 21, 1880.
1040. C. Eunice, b. March 18, 1882.
1041. Benjamin Adam, b. March 9, 1885.
——   Eva J., b. Feb'y 28, 1877.

WILLIAM B. TALLEY (*423*) married Beulah C. Grubb (402).

Children.

1042. Stephen B., b. May 25, 1865.
1043. Hannah, m. Samuel Stott.
1044. Howard F.

SARAH M. TALLEY (*424*) married Henry Roberts, February 14, 1866. He was born May 8, 1840. Resides at Linwood, Pa.

Children.

1045. Margaret M., b. Jan'y 29, 1867.
1046. Mary E., b. Nov. 13, 1868.
1047. Martha A., b. April 29, 1870.
1048. Emma L., b. June 7, 1872.
1049. Clara R., b. March 22, 1875.
1050. Bertha M., b. July 13, 1879.

MARTHA A. TALLEY (*426*) married first, Mark H. West, of Upland, Pa., December 16, 1879.

Child.

1051. Ethel Bullock, b. Jan'y 23, 1881.

Mr. West died Jan'y 12, 1883, and she married second, Walter Lye, March 9, 1890.

MARY E. TALLEY (*427*) married William T. Foster, of Cecil County, Md.

Children.

1052. William.
1053. Jesse.
1054. Theodore.
1055. Carrie.
1056. Raymond.
1057. Ernest.
1058. Ethel.
1059. Ellis.
1060. Edna.

EMMA L. TALLEY (*428*) married Charles Slawter. They live at Phillipsburg, N. J.

Children.

1061. Bertha E., b. Dec. 14, 1877.
1062. Charles B., b. Aug. 26, 1880.
1063. Anna M., b. June 10, 1883.
1064. Paul B., b. Dec. 19, 1890.

CLARA R. TALLEY (*429*) married Pennell Larkin, April 15, 1878. They reside in Chichester Township, Delaware County, Pa.

Children.

1065. Hannah S., b. April 25, 1881.
1066. Ida J., b. Oct. 9, 1884.

WESLEY H. TALLEY (*432*) married Hannah M. Renner, September 10, 1891. She was born May 7, 1873.

Children.

1067. William D., b. Feb'y 7, 1892.
1068. Wesley H., b. Sept. 1, 1893.
1069. Kate R., b. Sept. 1, 1895.
1070. Annie R., b. Oct. 27, 1897.

JESSIE S. TALLEY (*433*) married John F. Cramp, of Chester, Pa.

Children.

1071. Blanche L.
1072. Mabel E.
1073. John F.
1074. Mary F.
1075. Alfred C.
1076. Edmund O.

WILLIAM A. TALLEY (*451*) married first, Emily Forwood, February 22, 1866. She was born July 8, 1834 ; died April 20, 1892. (See sketch.)

Children.

1077. Ida I., b. Nov. 28, 1866, d. July 18, 1867.
1078. Hannah A., b. March 2, 1868, d. Feb'y 19, 1877.
1079. Lydia A., b. Feb'y 11, 1870.
1080. Samuel Alfred, b. Jan'y 12, 1872.
1081. Carrie Lizzie, b. Dec. 29, 1874.
1082. Lewis Corliss, b. Dec. 21, 1876.
1083. William Dalgren, b. Feb. 4, 1879, d. June 3, 1880.
        He m. second, Katherine (Twaddell) Sharpley, Feb'y 22, 1894. She was born Aug. 5, 1845.

ROBERT TALLEY (*452*) married Emily Beeson, March 8, 1866. (See sketch.)

Children.

1084. Robinson Beeson, b. May 12, 1867.
1085. Lewis, b. May 9, 1868, d. young.

MARY TALLEY (*453*) married Charles Wesley Poole, December 29, 1863. She is a widow, and resides at Chelsea, Delaware County, Pa.

Children.

1086. Mary Elizabeth, b. Nov. 24, 1864, d. Feb. 16, 1893.
1087. Hattie B., b. Feb'y 22, 1868.
1088. Sarah A., b. March 20, 1875.

HANNAH TALLEY (*454*) married John M. C. Prince, October 9, 1862. (See sketch.)

Child.

1089. William E., b. June 28, 1863, d. young.

LEWIS F. TALLEY (455) married Mary Miller, Feb'y 10, 1870. (See sketch.)

Children.

1090. Leonard C., b. Dec. 24, 1871.
1091. Lewis Prince, b. Nov. 19, 1873.
1092. Clyde E., b. Feb'y 1, 1876, d. young.
1093. Jennie E., b. April 12, 1878.
1094. Howard B., b. Oct. 4, 1880, d. young.
1095. Watson, b. Jan'y 9, 1883.

ELIZABETH J. TALLEY (456) married Henry C. Bird, January 7, 1875.

Child.

1096. Mary W., b. Nov. 8, 1875.

BEULAH Z. TALLEY (457) married Clark W. Baldwin, December 23, 1869. They reside at Booth's Corner, Delaware County, Pa.

Children.

1097. Lillie M., b. Jan'y 25, 1871.
1098. Reese H., b. Aug. 16, 1874, d. young.
1099. Sarah W., b. Aug. 25, 1878.
1100. Hannah P., b. June 25, 1880.
1101. Rebecca E., b. Dec. 23, 1882.
1102. John, b. Aug. 4, 1885.

CLARA V. TALLEY (459) married J. Atwood Weldin, (486). See names of children under No. 486.

MARY ANNA TALLEY (467) was the oldest child of George W. and Lavinia (Beeson) Talley. She was born January 20, 1839, and died February 24, 1860, at the age of 21 years. She was not of a robust constitution, but rather of the delicate and refined type, fitted more for the spiritual and devotional side of life than for its rougher activities. She joined the Methodist Church early in life, and continued to worship within its doors until her young life faded away with consumption. She was greatly esteemed for her piety and purity of character by all who knew her.

JOHN SMITH TALLEY (*468*) married Mary Ellen Beeson, January 17, 1867. (See sketch.)

Children.

1103. George Edward, b. Nov. 20, 1867.
1104. Howard Cookman, b. Aug. 20, 1870, d. 1876.
1105. Homer Beeson, b. Sept. 4, 1877.
1106. Nellie May, b. Nov. 20, 1879.
1107. Walter Weldin, b. March 9, 1885.

CHARLES W. TALLEY (*469*) married Sarah Jane Perkins, 1866. (See sketch.)

Children.

1108. Ella May, b. June 26, 1867.
1109. Charles P., b. Dec. 28, 1868.
1110. Stillman J., b. Dec. 27, 1871, d. July 19, 1892.
1111. Julia L., b. Dec. 17, 1873, d. June 14, 1899.
1112. Paul, b. Jan'y 6, 1876, d. June 2, 1899.
1113. Herbert, b. June 1, 1879.

GEORGE A. TALLEY (*470*) married Julia Emma Perkins, August 18, 1868.

Children.

1114. Everett H., b. July 24, 1869, d. July 18, 1870.
1115. Alta Perkins, b. Dec. 30, 1875, d. Mch. 12, 1876.
1116. Mabel, b. June 20, 1879.

THOMAS J. TALLEY (*471*) married Maria E. Clearwater, daughter of Dr. Jacob Clearwater, of Litchfield, Ill. They resided, when first married, at Litchfield, where he was engaged in the drug business with his brother, John Smith Talley. They sold out the store there, about 1874, and Thomas returned to Wilmington, Del., and engaged in the saw-mill business with his brother, Charles W. Talley. He, after a few years, accepted the position of fuel agent on the Philadelphia, Wilmington and Baltimore Railroad. Later he engaged in the lumber and timber trade in Wilmington and Philadelphia, and has succeeded in building up an extensive business.

Children.

1117. Clayton C., b. Oct. 2, 1873, d. young.
1118. Thomas J., b. July 7, 1875.
1119. Perle C., b. Feb'y 13, 1878.
1120. Claude D., b. July 4, 1881.

PHEBE JANE TALLEY (*472*) married Thomas S. Robinson, October 26, 1871. They reside on the Philadelphia Turnpike, near the Wilmington City line.

Children.

1121. Mary L., b. June 27, 1879.
1122. Elsie T., b. June 5, 1881.
1123. William J., b. Aug. 17, 1889.

BEULAH EMMA TALLEY (*474*) married Francis E. Gallagher, November, 1872. They reside in Wilmington, Del. He is engaged in the drug business in the Ninth Ward, and has been quite successful in this line, as well as dealing in real estate.

Children.

1124. Florence E., b. Dec., 28, 1874, d. Jan'y 20, 1879.
1125. Alice Maude, b. Oct. 6, 1879.
1126. Francis E., b. June 20, 1891.

JOSEPH BEESON TALLEY (*475*) married first, Hannah Mary Blackwell (988), January 28, 1877 ; and second, married Sarah J. Lodge, April 4, 1889.

Child of first marriage.

1127. George S., b. Oct. 7, 1878.

Children of second marriage.

1128. Florence A., b. Oct. 23, 1890.
1129. Howard J., b. Aug. 2, 1893.
1130. Ella J., b. July 22, 1894, d. June 10, 1897.
1131. Elsie L., b. March 13, 1898.

ANNA L. TALLEY (*476*) married Harrie M. Perkins, March 23, 1892. They reside at Holly Oak, Del. He is a contractor and builder.

Child.

1132: Mildred Chase, b. Feb'y 19, 1893.

ELIZA JANE TALLEY (*477*) married Isaac R. Staats. They reside at Townsend, Del. He is a land-owner and is prominent in his neighborhood.

ISAAC S. TALLEY (*478*) married Eliza Beeson. They reside near Carrcroft, Brandywine Hundred, Del. He owns a valuable farm, purchased at the settlement of his father-in-law's estate. Isaac is an active business man, is a director in the Cherry Island Marsh Company, and a trustee in the Mt. Pleasant M. E. Church.

Children.

1133. Ira S., b. July 31, 1879.
1134. Etna, b. Nov. 25, 1880.
1135. Sara A., b. Aug. 6, 1882.
1136. L. Emma, b. Dec. 28, 1883.
1137. Edward B., b. Sept. 5, 1885.
1138. Leah M., b. Jan'y 7, 1887.

ANNA MARY TALLEY (*480*) married Lewis McCrea. They reside on their farm on McKee's Hill, near Wilmington, Delaware.

Children.

1139. Elsie, b. Oct. 21, 1894.
1140. Edith, b. Jan'y 20, 1896.
1141. Sarah T., b. Aug. 11, 1897.

JOHN THOMAS TALLEY (*481*) married Lillie O. Mayne (980), November 24, 1891. (See sketch.)

Children.

1142. Henry S., b. July 14, 1893.
1143. Helen R., b. Feb'y 19, 1896.
1144. Marguerite E., b. May 20, 1897.

SARAH LOUISA TALLEY (*482*) married J. C. Fremont Carver. They reside in their very neat home in East Lake Park, Wilmington, Del. He is a machinist by trade.

JACOB ATWOOD WELDIN (*486*) married Clara V. Talley (459), Jan'y 28, 1879. (See sketch.)

Children.

1145. Jacob R., b. May 26, 1881.
1146. Howard L., b. Dec. 20, 1883.
1147. Hannah Elizabeth, b. Feb'y 9, 1885.
1148. Freddie L., b. Jan'y 20, 1887, d. young.
1149. Mabel, b. Feb'y 10, 1890, d. young.
1150. Ethel M., b. May 6, 1894, d. young.
1151. Paul, b. July 23, 1895.

THOMAS TALLEY WELDIN (*487*) married Emma M. Naylor. (See sketch.)

Children.

1152. Eva P., b. Oct. 16, 1883.
1153. Thomas T., b. Sept. 16, 1886.
1154. Meta N., b. Dec. 2, 1888, d. young.
1155. Hannah P., b. Jan'y 3, 1892, d. young.
1156. Herbert F., b. Dec. 8, 1895.

THOMAS SMITH TALLEY (*495*) married Sarah Elizabeth Hanby, March 13, 1862. (See sketch.)

Children.

1157. Ella J., b. Feb'y 25, 1863, d. Oct. 29, 1895.
1158. William H., b. May 23, 1865.
1159. Penrose R., b. Nov. 2, 1869.

CHARLES TALLEY (*496*) married Mary Zebley, daughter of Thomas Zebley, March, 1858.

Children.

1160. Wilmer, b. Nov. 20, 1858.
1161. Penrose R., b. July 25, 1861.
1162. Sarah Anna, b. Feb'y 21, 1865, d. 1885.
1163. Mary Ellen, b. June 28, 1868.
1164. Charles, b. July 22, 1872.
1165. Thomas Zebley, b. Dec. 12, 1874.

BRINTON L. TALLEY (*498*) married Rebecca T. Weldin. They resided on their farm north of Booth's Corner, Delaware County, Pa.

Children.

1166. Francis E., b. Oct. 6, 1867.
1167. Addie B., b. July 22, 1870, d. young.

1168. Atmore S., b. July 22, 1870, d. young.
1169. Harry C., b. May 12, 1875, d. young.

SARAH M. TALLEY (*499*) married Lewis Hickman, February 18, 1862.

Children.

1170. Laura, b. July 10, 1863, d. Jan'y 26, 1885.
1171. Edith G., m. William Hance.
1172. Alfred B., b. Sept. 5, 1868.

ELIZA J. TALLEY (*500*) married George W. Weldin. (See sketch.)

Children.

1173. Harry M., b. Nov. 4, 1866.
1174. Estella J., b. Oct. 8, 1867.
1175. Beulah M., b. May 8, 1869.
1176. L. Emma, b. Feb'y 28, 1871.
1177. Lewis, b. May 21, 1872, d. young.
1178. Sallie H., b. Oct. 21, 1873, d. young.
1179. Charles P., b. April 11, 1875.
1180. George H., b. Feb'y 18, 1877.
1181. Winifred, b. Feb'y 5, 1879. .
1182. Bertha V., b. July 26, 1881.
1183. Florence H., b. July 31, 1884.

NATHANIEL BOOTH (*509*) married Elizabeth Booth, March 7, 1865. (See sketch.)

Children.

1184. Thomas Wheeler, b. June 23, 1866.
1185. Joseph Elmer, b. 1870 ; deceased.
1186. Henry Wilson, b. 1872 ; deceased.
1187. Cora Jane, b. 1880.

JOHN BOOTH (*511*) married Margaret A. Phillips, December 20, 1866. (See sketch.)

Children.

1188. Thomas P., b. Nov. 30, 1867.
1189. Charity Eva, b. Oct, 7, 1869.
1190. Julia Emma, b. April 25, 1872.
1191. John, b. Feb'y 1, 1874.

1192. Oliver H. P., b. Aug. 1, 1877.
1193. George, b. Dec. 9, 1879.
1194. Frank, b. June 23, 1882, d. young.
1195. Frederick, b. June 23, 1882, d. young,
1196. Irwin P., b. April 21, 1891.

ALFRED D. PIERCE (*512*) married Louisa Pierce.
Children.
—— Ida E. ; deceased.
—— Joseph E.
—— Thomas Jefferson.
—— Charles Alfred.
1197. Mary Ole.

WILLIAM H. PIERCE (*514*) married Susanna Forwood.
No issue.

LEAH TALLEY (*516*) married Thomas Booth, January
12, 1871.
Children.
1198. Laura E., b. Dec. 9, 1871.
1199. Thomas A., b. March 5, 1874.

JESSE LANE TALLEY (*517*) married Eliza J. Frame,
October 17, 1866. They resided in Wilmington, Del., where
he died in 1896.
Children.
1200. Eleanor, b. July 17, 1868.
1201. Leonard G., b. Jan'y 23, 1870, d. 1870.
1202. Etta Jane, b. Feb'y 23, 1871.
1203. Reba May, b. Nov. 18, 1872.
1204. Cena A., b. April 15, 1874.
1205. Ebert Lincoln, b. Feb'y 5, 1876.
1206. Hycen Grant, b. Dec. 23, 1879.
1207. Owen Garfield, b. Oct. 19, 1881.
1208. Walter Blaine, b. Nov. 4, 1887.
1209. Nellie G., b. May 2, 1889, d. 1890.
1210. Emma L., b. Dec. 1, 1892, d. 1892.

HENRY C. TALLEY (*519*) married Anna Mary Mousley,
November 7, 1867. (See sketch.)

Children.

1211. Edward H., b. Oct. 4, 1868, d. young.
1212. Ella Lavenia, b. Feb'y 7, 1871.
1213. Elwood M., b. Nov. 26, 1873.
1214. Clara Arcelia, b. July 24, 1876.
1215. Ada, b. Nov. 5, 1880.
1216. Henry C., b. Feb'y 2, 1884.
1217. Mary Viola, b. April 5, 1887.

JOHN L. TALLEY (*520*) married Margaret Lenderman, daughter of Isaac Lenderman, of Brandywine Hundred, Del. They resided for a few years in this hundred, but later purchased a farm in Mill Creek Hundred, where they now reside.

Children.

1218. Calver Grant, b. April 2, 1873.
1219. J. Leslie, b. July 21, 1875.
1220. Conrow, b. Jan'y 6, 1879.

NELSON L. TALLEY (*522*) married Lavania Simons, November 13, 1873. (See sketch.)

Children.

1221. Eliza Ann, b. Jan'y 30, 1875.
1222. Clara N., b. Jan'y 17, 1877.
1223. Nelson L., b. Jan'y 12, 1881.
1224. Howard, b. May 1, 1884.
1225. Wilmer J., b. Feb'y 21, 1886.
1226. Jos. Chandler, b. Aug. 14, 1888.
1227. Herbert L., b. May 2, 1893.

CURTIS M. TALLEY (*523*) married Anna Mary Miller, March 7, 1867. (See sketch.)

Children.

1228. Laura Virginia, b. Aug. 14, 1868.
1229. Mary Anna, b. Feb'y 9, 1873.
1230. Linda B., b. Oct. 31, 1883.

NORRIS W. TALLEY (*524*) married Sarah Jane Kirk, February 17, 1870. He resided on his farm at Talley's Corner, Brandywine Hundred, until his decease. He was thrifty, and a very much respected citizen.

Children.

1231. Sallie J., b. Jan'y 7, 1871.
1232. Robert P., b. Aug. 27, 1872.
1233. Blanche A., b. June 17, 1874.
1234. Kate E., b. Dec. 21, 1878.
1235. Mary, b. March 4, 1882.

JAMES WILSON TALLEY (*527*) married Margaret E. Cartmell. (See sketch.)

Children.

1236. James Walter, b. Aug. 21, 1871.
1237. Mary Ida, b. Oct. 23, 1873.
1238. Laura May, b. March 27, 1876.

JOHN C. TALLEY (*528*) married Anna Mary Langley, widow of J. Langley, January 1, 1878.

Children.

1239. John Nelson, b. Nov. 26, 1878.
1240. Mary Lena, b. Jan'y 10, 1882.

RACHEL ANNA TALLEY (*531*) married Pliney Likens, July 27, 1876. They reside at Baltimore, Md.

Children.

1241. Lewis Edward, b. Nov. 8, 1876.
1242. John Talley, b. Sept. 1, 1883.
1243. Bertha May, b. May 23, 1890.
1244. Arthur Earl, b. Dec. 21, 1898.

SARAH A. WILSON (*539*) married Thomas R. Day, February 24, 1858.

Children.

1245. William W.
1246. Lewis H.
1247. Helen G.

WILLIAM TALLEY (*555*) married Sarah Elizabeth Langley, daughter of Joseph and Mary Langley, February 9, 1869.

Children.

1248. John W., b. Dec. 7, 1871.
1249. Mary E., b. Nov. 6, 1873.

ELIHU TALLEY (**559**) married Anna E. Hanby, November 19, 1868. They reside near Talleyville, Brandywine Hundred, Del.

Children.

1250. Eli Baldwin, b. April 22, 1869, d. young.
1251. Gertrude L., b. Dec. 6, 1870.
1252. Samuel H., b. Dec. 5, 1872, d. young.
1253. Francis Bayard, b. Jan'y 1, 1874.
1254. Sadie H., b. Aug. 18, 1876.
1255. Lewis S., b. Oct. 27, 1879.

LYDIA ANN TALLEY (**561**) married Martin V. Palmer, March 22, 1864. Mr. Palmer died November 19, 1869.

Child.

1256. Mary T., d. in infancy.

CAROLINE ELIZABETH TALLEY (**562**) married Lewis Reese Springer, December 21, 1868. He is an architect at Wilmington, Del.

Children.

1257. Ellen T., b. Nov. 4, 1869, d. 1875.
1258. Baldwin, b. Dec. 14, 1870. An attorney-at-law at Wilmington, Del.
1259. Wilber L., b. Jan'y 27, 1873, d. young.
1260. Lucile, b. July 10, 1875.
1261. Lewis Reese, b. Aug. 6, 1877. A civil engineer with the Maryland Steel Co., at Sparrow's Point, Md.
1262. Thomas Bayard, b. Sept. 19, 1879, d. young.

HARRIET ELLEN (**563**) is unmarried, and resides at Wilmington, Del.

ABNER P. TALLEY (**574**) married first, Sarah J. Graves ; and second, Hannah Mary Harkins. (See sketch.)

Children of first marriage.

1263. Eber Y., b. May 30, 1858.
1264. Thomas Lea, b. Nov. 22, 1859.
1265. Mary E., b. Oct. 29, 1860.
1266. Elizabeth M., b. Oct. 31, 1861, d. Nov. 29, 1893.

1267. Caroline S., b. Feb'y 17, 1863.
1268. John G., b. April 18, 1864.
1269. Josephine, b. Sept. 16, 1865.
1270. Susanna A., b. Feb'y 12, 1867.
1271. William Harry, b. Feb'y 16, 1868.
1272. Frank H., b. March 10, 1869, d. young.
1273. James H., b. Sept. 7, 1870, d. young.

Children of second marriage.

1274. Abner P., b. Dec. 19, 1872.
1275. Eli Baldwin, b. June 17, 1874, d. young.
1276. Samuel T., b. Oct. 22, 1876.
1277. Hannah B., b. Dec. 19, 1878.
1278. Clarence, b. Oct. 19, 1880.
1279. Lawrence, b. Oct. 19, 1880, d. young.
1280. Fanny, b., June 19, 1882.
1281. Elsie May, b. Dec. 22, 1884.
1282. Emma L., b. May 5, 1886.
1283. Matilda.
1284. Lidie May, b. Feb'y 22, 1890.
1285. Reba, b. Oct. 8, 1893.
1286. Anna D., b. Dec. 13, 1895.
1287. Arthur, b. April 10, 1897.

CURTIS B. TALLEY (**575**) married Rachel E. Harvey.
She was born December 3, 1843.

Children.

1288. Lewis H., b. Feb'y 5, 1864.
1289. Mary A., b. Jany'y 19, 1870.
1290. Curtis B., b. May 18, 1880.

WILLIAM W. TALLEY (**576**) married R. Emma Baker,
April 26, 1870. She was born November 5, 1850, and was
daughter of Dilworth and Hannah Baker, of ·Chester Co., Pa.

Children.

1291. James Lea, b. Feb'y 12, 1871, d. young.
1292. Mary Caroline, b. March 16, 1872, d. young.
1293. Anna Galena, b. July 26, 1873.
1294. Mabel Garfield, b. June 1, 1880.

MARGARET TALLEY (**577**) married Miller Forwood. He was born January 27, 1845.

Children.

1295. Lottie May, b. July 14, 1869.
1296. William Marshall, b. Dec. 26, 1872.
1297. Joseph Bayard, b. Sept. 16, 1875.
1298. Lydia Bertha, b. Oct. 12, 1878.
1299. Thomas Clayton, b. May 28, 1883.

JOHN HANBY TALLEY (**578**) married Lydia H. Street. She was born August 9, 1854.

Children.

1300. Florence, b. Jan'y 15, 1874.
1301. Curtis Lea, b. Feb'y 8, 1876.
1302. Amos Street, b. Aug. 18, 1878.
1303. Margaret, b. Feb'y 3, 1881.
1304. Ernest Cleveland, b. Oct. 17, 1883.
1305. John Morrison, b. March 7, 1886.
1306. Walter, b. Nov. 12, 1889.
1307. Blanche, b. March 12, 1892.

SALLIE ANN TALLEY (**579**) married first, Benjamin R. Teat, June 19, 1870; and second, Thomas A. Galbreath, July 5, 1891.

Children of first marriage.

1308. Thomas Lea, b. March 28, 1871.
1309. Oliver Perry, b. Feb'y 16, 1873.
1310. William, b. July 11, 1875.
1311. Mary A., b. May 19, 1878.
1312. Rachel Emma, b. March 28, 1885.

Children of second marriage.

1313. Eva G., b. Feb'y 18, 1894.
1314. Hattie T., b. Nov. 12, 1895.
1315. Willard G., b. May 7, 1898.

ELI BALDWIN TALLEY (**580**) married Emma Lurana Pierce (807), February 24, 1876.

Children.

1316. Howard D., b. April 19, 1877.

1317.   Ella Belle, b. Oct. 14, 1889, d. young.
1318.   Bessie, b. Dec. 28, 1892, d. young.

THOMAS LEA TALLEY (*581*) married Isabella Pierce, (806). He was born January 9, 1844. She was born 1849.
Children.
1319.   William Lea, b. Dec. 6, 1867.
1320.   Mary Ella, b. Aug. 6, 1869.
1321.   John Howard, b. Sept. 21, 1871.
1322.   James Bayard, b. Sept. 28, 1873.
1323.   Emma Lurana, b. Oct. 22, 1875.
1324.   Elizabeth Pierce, b. Aug. 27, 1883.
1325.   Elbie Thomas, b. Aug. 26, 1890.

WILLIAM ROBINSON FORWOOD (*590*) married Rachel Ann Smith, daughter of Isaac and Rachel Smith, of Elam, Pa., March 26, 1872.
Children.
1326.   Charles, b. Sept. 29, 1873.
1327.   Martha, b. Aug. 26, 1880.
1328.   Howard, b. Sept. 9, 1882.

JOANNA D. TALLEY (*591*) married Edward Griswold.
Children.
1329.   Ellen D.
1330.   Rachel.
1331.   Mary P.
1332.   Taylor.
1333.   Lydia.
1334.   Amor.
1335.   Josephine.
1336.   Edward.

AMOR S. TALLEY (*594*) married Edith S. Campbell.
Children.
1337.   Morton L., b. Dec. 3, 1873.
1338.   Martha C., b. Aug. —, 1874.
1339.   Emmor S., b. Nov. 1, 1875.

EMELINE P. TALLEY (*595*) married John Larkin.

Children.

1340. Belle D.
1341. Frank L.
1342. John L.

ANNE E. TALLEY (*601*) married George W. Springer.

Children.

1343. Armanella P., b. Aug. 4, 1874.
1344. Leonard H., b. March 27, 1875.
1345. Margaret T., b. Aug. 2, 1878.
1346. Sarah A., b. July 28, 1881.
1347. Frank L.
1348. Isabel H., b. Oct. 31, 1886.
1349. Harriet.

MARY ELIZABETH TALLEY (*604*) married Charles H. Heald.

Children.

1350. William H.
1351. Josephine.

JAMES BLYTHE TALLEY (*605*) married Belle ———.

Children.

1352. Samuel.
1353. Mary.
1354. Emma.
1355. Gus.

AMOR L. TALLEY (*606*) married Kate Williams.

Children.

1356. Howard W.
1357. Frederick.

JACOB HAILMAN TALLEY (*610*) married Susan Samples.

Children.

1358. Annie M.
1359. Florence V.
1360. Percy E.
1361. Archie J.

1362. Norman H.
1363. Elwood.
1364. R. Clifford.
1365. Bessie.
1366. Walter.
1367. Leon.
1368. Edgar T.

MARGARET W. JOHNSON (*611*) married John Wesley Hance, January 31, 1856.
Children.
1369. Mary Eliza, b. July 14, 1858.
1370. Andrew Johnson, b. Sept. 2, 1860.
1371. William J. Wesley, b. July 12, 1866.

ANNA D. JOHNSON (*612*) married Daniel Husbands.
Children.
1372. William J.
1373. T. Lawrence.
1374. Eliza B.

THOMAS WEBSTER JOHNSON (*613*) married Sallie Poole. (See sketch.)
Children.
1375. Mary Eva, b. Dec. 3, 1857, m. L. Cass Weldin.
1376. Harriet Eliza, b. Nov. 2, 1859, m. John K. Hipple.
1377. Lottie Talley, b. Feb. 28, 1862, m. Geo. Drayton.
1378. Maggie Anna, b. July 19, 1863, m. Geo. J. Palmer.
1379. William Wesley, b. June 29, 1865, m. Cornelia Watkins.
1380. Sallie Emma, b. Sept 7, 1867, d. aged 22.
1381. Laura Edna, b. Oct. 6, 1869.
1382. Mattie Walter, b. March 16, 1873, m. Howard Ely.
1383. Thomas Webster, b. June 28, 1876.

MARY JANE JOHNSON (*614*) married Minshall Hinkson, February 16, 1858.
Children.
1384. Anna Elizabeth, b. May 9, 1860.
1385. Harriet Laura, b. Jan'y 7, 1865.
1386. William Henry, b. Dec. 1, 1866.

HARRIET J. JOHNSON (*615*) married George W. Todd. For a number of years he was President of the Diamond State Iron Company, Wilmington, Del.

Children.

1387. Eleanor A., b. Nov. 29, 1873, m. Howard De Haven Ross.
1388. James C., b. March 6, 1877, d. in infancy.
1389. Hattie G., b. April 22, 1880, d. Dec. 12, 1886.

THOMAS HANNUM (*621*) married Hannah Dunn.

Children.

1390. Anna Elizabeth.
1391. T. Leslie.
1392. Maggie K.
1393. William H.

DR. WILLIAM WESLEY JOHNSON (*624*) married first, Bettie A. Ford, March 12, 1866. No issue. Married second, Mariana Burns, December 18, 1869.

Child.

1394. Maggie B., b. April 3, 1870, m. Wm. Grey Clyde.

He married third, Lizzie Morgan.

Dr. W. W. Johnson has been in active practice in Chester, Pa., for a number of years.

LIZZIE DAY JOHNSON (*625*) married James K. Foulk, July 4, 1871.

Child.

1395. Mary B., b. July 29, 1879.

ROBERT S. JOHNSON (*626*) married Annie Cullingworth.

ANNA AMANDA JOHNSON (*629*) married Geo. H. Hance, December 20, 1877.

Children.

1396. Walter E., b. May 25, 1879.
1397. William Johnson, b. July 5, 1883.

ISAAC N. GRUBB (*634*) married Julia E. Smith, March 20, 1859. (See sketch.)

Children.

1398. Jennette S., b. Oct. 1, 1862, d. Jan'y 24, 1899.
1399. Newton L., b. Sept. 19, 1864.

JOHN FOULK TALLEY's children married as follows :
Ann Talley (*641*) m. Thomas Farra.
Rebecca Talley (*642*) m. Bonam Reed.
Priscilla Talley (*643*) m. Joseph Reed.
Jane Talley (*644*) m. A. J. Mondew.
Julian Talley (*645*) m. Anderson Evans.
Hannah P. Talley (*648*) m. John W. Waller.
Margaretta Talley (*649*) m. William Hall.

JOHN P. TALLEY (*647*) married Rebecca M. Ford, of
Philadelphia, May 20, 1858.

Children.

1400. Lillian, b. April 4, 1859.
1401. Anna, b. June 22, 1861.
1402. E. Hilles, b. May 15, 1863.
1403. Frank L., b. Jan'y 28, 1865.
1404. William T., b. Nov. 15, 1867.
1405. Laura, b. Aug. 30, 1869.
1406. Jessie May, b. May 30, 1871.
1407. John F., b. May 4, 1874.

HARMON G. TALLEY (*651*) married Louisa Ann
Hodges, January 13, 1853. She was born April 21, 1833. He
resides at Piasa, Macoupin County, Ill.

Children.

1408. Isaac Lillian, b. Oct. 24, 1853.
1409. William E., b. Aug. 3, 1856.
1410. Mary Simmons, b. April 4, 1859.
1411. Hattie E., b. Feb'y 7, 1862.
1412. Dora A., b. Sept. 21, 1866.
1413. Lula Hodges, b. Sept. 26, 1869.
1414. Harmon Grubb, b. Feb'y 20, 1872.

John Simmons, grandfather of Harmon Gregg Talley,
died October 15, 1824, aged 60 years.

Lydia Simmons, grandmother of Harmon G. Talley,
died October 11, 1824, aged 57 years.

Mary Talley, wife of Isaac G. Talley, daughter of John and Lydia Simmons, died March 15, 1833, aged 35 years.

Harmon Talley, grandfather of Harmon G. Talley, died at Piasa, Ill., August 24, 1858, aged 83 years.

JOHN SIMMONS TALLEY (*652*) married first, Elizabeth F. Hill, Jan. 16, 1855. He married second, Sarah W. Taggart, March 4, 1885, and third, Sarah A. Pierson, May 2, 1888.

Children of first marriage.

1415.   William Gregg.
1416.   Hannah M.
1417.   John W.

REBECCA J. TALLEY (*655*) married first, Hugh E. Mearns, November 27, 1862. He died March 12, 1870. She married second, Leonzo E. Baylis, June 6, 1871.

Children of second marriage.

1418.   Isaac L., b. Aug. 11, 1872.
1419.   Harry E., b. Sept. 24, 1875.
1420.   Clarissa N., b. July 3, 1878.
1421.   Leonard K., b. May 24, 1881.

E. JENNIE E. TALLEY (*662*) married Samuel M. Rutledge, October 11, 1876. They reside on the Muskingum River, nine miles south of Zanesville, Ohio.

Children.

1422.   William Cloud, b. Feb'y 23, 1879.
1423.   George Armstrong, b. May 20, 1885.

JOHN T. SIMMONS (*663*) married first, Martha Arganbright, in 1852. He married second, Jennie S. Bryant, of Birmingham, Iowa, in 1894. (See sketch.)

Children of first marriage.

1424.   Lydia Jane.
1425.   Francis William.
1426.   George B.
1427.   J. W.
1428.   Kittie Luella.
1429.   Edmund.

WILLIAM TALLEY SHADES (*664*) m. ——.

JOHN HEYBURN TALLEY (*667*) married Josephine Mac-Donald. He is grocer and postmaster near Perry's Hotel, Brandywine Hundred.

Children.

1430. Florence Heyburn, b. Dec. 31, 1879.
1431. Howard W., b. July 15, 1881.
1432. Elizabeth, b. April 18, 1884.

JOHN C. TALLEY (*679*) married Margaret Frame.

Children.

1433. Sarah Emma, b. June 13, 1881.
1434. Mary, b. June 18, 1884.
1435. Sidney R., b. April 13, 1887.
1436. Margaret, b. May 24, 1890.

ARABELLA TALLEY (*689*) married William D. Pullen, of Chester Pa., April 7, 1864.

Children.

1437. Kate, b. Dec. 7, 1866.
1438. William D., b. Feb'y 7, 1868.

MELISSA TALLEY (*694*) married first, David Corson ; married second, —— Paulsworth.

Child of first marriage.

1439. Lizzie.

JAMES EDGAR TALLEY (*695*), of Bay Mills, Michigan, married Kate Lamade, February 21, 1881.

Children.

1440. Frederick William, b. July 19, 1882.
1441. Caroline Elizabeth, b. July 11, 1884.
1442. James Andrew, b. Oct. 18, 1886.
1443. John Truman, b. Sept. 2, 1892.

WILLIE ANN TALLEY (*697*) married James Rea, May 5, 1881.

Child.

1444. Emma Davis, b. Jan'y 9, 1882.

ARABELLA TALLEY (*698*) married Francis M. Dowlin, of Chester County, Pa., January 24, 1872.

Children.

1445. Albert Scott, b. Jan'y 11, 1873.
1446. Henderson Talley, b. Aug. 7, 1874.
1447. Sallie Edna, b. Nov. 18, 1875.
1448. Francis M., b. Nov. 12, 1877.

CHARLES WESLEY TALLEY (*700*) married Mary E. Hoffman, February 15, 1888.

Children.

1449. Ruth F., b. Oct. 24, 1888.
1450. John Henderson, b. May 30, 1890.

EDWARD COOPER TALLEY (*702*) married Alice Standring, May 25, 1887.

Children.

1451. Maud A., b. March 3, 1888.
1452. Mary E., b. Dec. 14, 1889.
1453. Clarence E., b. Aug. 16, 1891.
1454. Ralph S., b. Feb'y 1, 1895.
1455. George Marion, b. Oct. 17, 1897.

SAMUEL H. TALLEY (*703*) married Clara Freeman, March 15, 1888.

Children.

1456. Florence May, b. Jan'y 13, 1891.
1457. Arthur M. F., b. March 12, 1897.

H. ALBIN LOUIS PYLE (*705*) married Anna Hare, of Wilmington, Del.

LURANA COOPER ALLMOND (*706*) married Joseph L. Gardner, December 24, 1863. They reside at Hettick, Macoupin County, Illinois.

Children.

1458. Leslie A., b. Aug. 8, 1865.
1459. Lewis H., b. March 24, 1867.
1460. Harmon W., b. Sept. 7, 1870.
1461. Letitia May, b. June 4, 1873.

1462. Ida B., b. Jan'y 10, 1876.
1463. Leonora B., b. June 17, 1878.
1464. William W., b. April 10, 1880.

LETITIA A. ALLMOND (*709*) married Dr. Wm. C. Day, February 20. 1866.

Children.

1465. Lewis Roach, b. Dec. 6, 1867. A practicing physician.
1466. James Allmond, b. Oct. 29, 1869. A practicing physician.
1467. Anne Agnes, b. Feb'y 12, 1872.
1468. Gertrude Lois, b. June 4, 1874.

PRISCILLA T. ALLMOND (*710*) married Thomas H. Padget.

Children.

1469. Anna G. A., b. March 4, 1868.
1470. Reuben J., b. Nov. 23, 1869.
1471. Ella E., b. Aug. 16, 1873.
1472. Eddie C., b. Dec. 3, 1875.
1473. Thomas C., b. Sept. 29, 1878.
1474. Francis R., b. April 19, 1880.
1475. Earl R., b. Sept. 1, 1883.
1476. Geneva P., b. Jan'y 8, 1885.
1477. Gacey E., b. Sept. 4, 1889.
1478. Powell Clayton, b. Dec. 29, 1890.

PHEBE ELLEN ALLMOND (*711*) married Andrew J. Crum, September 9, 1873.

Children.

1479. Nellie May, b. June 12, 1874.
1480. Edwin Wallace, b. March 21, 1876. A physician.
1481. Lee Burnett, b. Sept. 16, 1878.
1482. Joseph Reuben, b. Sept. 26, 1880.
1483. Robert Roy, b. Aug. 14, 1882.
1484. Golda T., b. Nov. 3, 1884.
1485. Ola Bertram, b. Dec. 17, 1886.
1486. Carroll Clayton, b. Dec. 25, 1888.

1487. Glenn Palmer, b. March 3, 1891.

1488. Ferris Bertrand, b. July 27, 1893.

JULIA E. ALLMOND (*712*) married J. Huston Grimmet, 1875.

Children.

1489. Clarence C., b. Nov. 15, 1876.

1490. Ethel M., b. Nov. 2, 1878.

1491. Ora B., b. Aug. 21, 1880.

1492. Dennis E., b. March 11, 1883.

1493. Sartoris R., b. Jan'y 28, 1884.

1494. Stella T., b. Jan'y 2, 1886.

1495. Theresa M., b. Dec. 21, 1888.

1496. Charles O., b. Nov. 15, 1891.

1497. Lella M., b. April 6, 1895.

1498. Leitta F., b. April 6, 1895.

FLORENCE V. ALLMOND (*713*) married Chas. W. Rice, 1875.

Children.

1499. Charles W., b. May 27, 1876.

1500. Minnie M., b. Aug. 26, 1879.

1501. Freddie A., b. Dec. 12, 1880.

1502. Anna I., b. Jan'y 7, 1882.

1503. Pearl Hattie Valentine, b. Feb'y 14, 1884.

1504. Chester O., b. Oct. 19, 1886.

1505. Opal Farmer, b. Sept. 4, 1888.

1506. Carrie Bell, b. Aug. 8, 1890.

1507. Grace, b. 1897.

IDA M. ALLMOND (*714*) married Dr. W. B. Sprinkel, 1880.

Children.

1508. Clyde, b. July 4, 1886.

1509. Marie, b. Feb'y 3, 1892.

LETITIA McCRACKEN (*716*) married Samuel A. Field.

Child.

1510. Elizabeth.

MARY McCRACKEN (*717*) married John Bodley, W. Va.

SIDNEY McCRACKEN (*718*) married George Adams.

Children.

1511. George.

1512. Harry.

HANNAH MCCRACKEN (*719*) married Joseph Rogers, of Media, Pa.

Children.

1513. William.

1514. Mary.

HARRIET L. TALLEY (*724*) married Thomas Blest, of Wilmington, Del., January 3, 1883. She is engaged in the millinery business.

Children.

1515. May Forest, b. May 4, 1884.

1516. Henry Lewis Flinn, b. March 15, 1890.

1517. Mabel Talley, b. Nov. 22, 1895.

PRISCILLA CLARK TALLEY (*725*) married John E. Lach, Kansas City, Mo., January 21, 1890.

MARY ELIZABETH TALLEY (*728*) married —— Alexander, of West Philadelphia, Pa.

SAMUEL HARLAN TALLEY (*729*) married Emma Webb, January 11, 1890. She died September 25, 1897.

PRISCILLA TALLEY (*731*) married Charles W. Scudder, November, 1884, at Washington, D. C.

Children.

1518. Margaret, b. March, 1886.

1519. Edith, b. March, 1891.

1520. Catharine, b. Dec., 1896.

ELEANOR TALLEY (*734*) married Daniel Cronin, at Washington, D. C., September 17, 1887.

Children.

1521. Evelyn, b. July 8, 1888.

1522. Eleanor, b. April 2, 1890, d. young.

SARAH A. TALLEY (*784*) married Zachary T. Hook, February 3, 1883. They reside in Ohio.

Child.

1523. Richard, b. Dec. 8, 1883.

FRANK F. TALLEY (*785*) married Esther F. McMurchy, October 28, 1880. He is a prominent business man

of New Richmond, Ohio.   He is editor of the *New Richmond
Independent* and postmaster of that town.

Children.

1524.   Martha, b. Aug. 28, 1882.
1525.   Harriet, b. Nov. 9, 1893.

ELIZABETH T. MOORE (*786*) married Robert A. Johnston, October 21, 1858.   He was for many years a Judge of
the Common Pleas Court in Cincinnati.   She was a beautiful
woman and an artist.

Children.

1526.   Campbell M., b. Oct. 31, 1859.
1527.   Lindsey C., b. Nov. 25, 1861.
1528.   Elizabeth C., b. Dec. 11, 1863.
1529.   Thomas S., b. Oct. 7, 1866.
1530.   Roberta A., b. Oct. 3, 1872.
1531.   Robert A., b. April 15, 1874.

ROWENA TALLEY (*787*) married Harrie L. Moore,
October 2, 1879.   In Ohio.

Children.

1532.   Olive H., b. June 10, 1882.
1533.   Harriette L., b. March 28, 1885.

KATE TALLEY (*788*) married Charles A. Elliott.

MARY L. TALLEY (*789*) married Charles C. Sedgwick,
May 24, 1876.

Children.

1534.   Shirley, b. Nov. 27, 1879, d. 1891.
1535.   Charles C., b. May 1, 1892.

ORVILLE B. TALLEY (*790*) married Helen E. Lighty,
June 15, 1892.   They reside at Sioux City, Iowa.   He is engaged in preparing Abstracts of Title and Searches of all
matters connected with land titles in his county.   He was
Clerk to the Committee on Printing of the National House of
Representatives for three years.   He is active and persistent
in everything he undertakes.   He has labored faithfully to
make our book a success, and is delighted that success is in

sight. What others consider labor in searching out our family history he treats as mere pleasure. He is loyal to our family standard and glories in whatever tends to its advancement.

Child.

1536. Eleanor Frances, b. Sept. 2, 1899.

JOHN H. ANDERSON (*793*) married Harriet Ahn, December 21, 1865.

Children.

1537. Joseph, b. 1866.
1538. George, b. 1868.
1539. Charles, b. 1870.
1540. Estella, b. 1872.
1541. Calver, b. 1874.
1542. Henry, b. 1877.
1543. Emma, b. 1880.

JOSEPH JACKSON PEIRCE (*805*) married Mary A. Patterson, of West Chester, Pa., Nov. 7, 1867. He is engaged in the Real Estate and Conveyancing business at Wilm., Del.

Children.

1544. Charles M., b. Oct. 10, 1868, d. 1868.
1545. John Bail, b. Oct. 20, 1869.
1546. James Frank, b. Oct. 15, 1871.
1547. George M., b. June 12, 1876.
1548. Edward P., b. Jan'y 30, 1885.

JAMES BAVARD PEIRCE (*808*) married Harriet B. Seymour, of Toronto, Canada, August 17, 1893. They reside in Wilmington, Del.

ELLA K. PEIRCE (*809*) married John C. Husbands, March 21, 1894.

Children.

1549. Philip P., b. Feb'y 22, 1895.
1550. Hannah Louisa, b. Aug. 4, 1897.

HANNAH P. TALLEY (*812*) married George Mervine.

Children.

1551. Mamie.
1552. Clara.
1553. George.

HENRY IRVING TALLEY (*814*) married Caroline Louisa Clarke, October 17, 1895. No issue. (See sketch.)

THOMAS C. TALLEY (*815*) married Henrietta Smith. No issue.

ANNIE DUTTON TALLEY (*817*) married George Hamilton Anderson, January 18, 1893.

Child.
1554.   Thomas Henry, b. Jan'y, 1894.

BESSIE GERTRUDE TALLEY (*818*) married William Egan, October 9, 1890. He was born June 24, 1862.

Children.
1555.   Willie, b. Sept. 11, 1891.
1556.   Annie May, b. Oct. 23, 1893.
1557.   Bessie Gertrude, b. July 17, 1898.

HANNAH R. TALLEY (*821*) married William Barnett, October 23, 1889. They reside at Clifton Heights, Delaware County, Pa.

Children.
1558.   Walter Morris, b. Dec. 11, 1892.
1559.   William Horace, b. Jan'y 20, 1895.
1560.   Percy Franklin, b. Oct. 5, 1898.

CHARLES M. Y. TALLEY (*838*) married Mary Tomlin. He is a shoe merchant at Philadelphia, Pa.

Children.
1561.   Mary T., b. May 7, 1880.
1562.   Charles M., b. Aug. 12, 1894.

GEORGE W. PHILLIPS (*868*) never married. He was the only child of his parents. He resides on the Quarryville Farm, which he inherited from his father. He favored the Trolley line which passes through his farm, and was liberal in granting the right of way for the same. George is up to date in his views of public improvement. He is a great sufferer from rheumatism, but is very cheerful in the midst of it all, and is filled with good feeling for humanity.

WILLARD TALLEY GALBREATH (*875*) married Eliza E. Morrow.

Children.

1563. Amy E., b. Dec. 19, 1879.
1564. John P., b. June 4, 1883.
1565. Jennie C., b. Dec. 3, 1888.
1566. Ella May, b. April 19, 1893.

WARREN T. RAWSON (*881*) married Maggie Lefferts.

Children.

1567. Bessie.
1568. Grant Kimber.

CHARLES B. TALLEY (*884*) married first, Harriet Risdon Bishop, February 3, 1874. She died October 28, 1894. He married second, Ida A. Williamson.

Children of first marriage.

1569. Lawrence E., b. Dec. 6, 1874.
1570. J. Wilmer, b. Aug. 16, 1877.
1571. Anna S., b. Aug. 16, 1877.
1572. Harlan H., b. April 13, 1883.
1573. Edgar S., b. May 27, 1887.

AMOR TALLEY (*886*) married Ella J. Petitdemange.

Children.

1574. Hattie Florence, b. Jan'y 28, 1886.
1575. Myrtie J., b. Sept. 4, 1887.
1576. L. Blanche, b. Aug. 1, 1889.
1577. Mamie E., b. June 30, 1891.
1578. Evelyn, b. Nov. 12, 1893.
1579. Clarence H., b. May 30, 1896.
1580. Albert Dewey, b. Feb'y 7, 1898.

IDA LOTTIE TALLEY (*887*) married William S. Hanby, son of William and Sarah Hanby, June 14, 1889.

Children.

1581. Harry Clayton, b. Feb'y 16, 1891.
1582. Frank Herbert, b. Feb'y 27, 1894.

DR. JAMES ELY TALLEY (*909*) married Isabella M. Andrews, of Canandaigua, N. Y., 1894. (See sketch.)

MARY ELIZABETH TALLEY (*910*) married Richard M. Mathues, Jan. 9, 1881. They reside at Nicetown, Phila., Pa.

Children.

1583.   Ida May, b. Oct. 3, 1881, m. Wm. G. Steck.
1584.   John Richie, b. Oct. 8, 1883.
1585.   Elizabeth Rust, b. Feb'y 28, 1886.
1586.   William, b. March 29, 1888.

HANNAH EMMA TALLEY (*911*) married Howard McAllister, September 16, 1886.

RUTHANNA TALLEY (*912*) married Howard J. Cheyney, April 9, 1885.

Children.

1587.   Alice, b. June 6, 1886, d. young.
1588.   Gertrude, b. Feb'y 8, 1889, d. young.
1589.   Warren, b. Oct. 29, 1892.
1590.   Margaret R., b. Dec. 14, 1896.
1591.   Emily, b. Dec. 6, 1898, d. young.

ABRAHAM L. LENDERMAN (*917*) married Abbie Sharpless, October 20, 1892.

Children.

1592.   Anna J., b. Aug. 27, 1893.
1593.   Emily R., b. July 31, 1895.
1594.   Elsie L., b. June 17, 1897.

NINTH GENERATION.

MAY ANNE TALLEY (*935*) married Garrett Jefferson Hart, Feb'y 12, 1885. She died 1892 without issue.

PRESTON LEA TALLEY (*945*) married Mary Edith McNeil, Oct. 12, 1898.

SADIE IOLA TALLEY (*947*) married Milton Blackwood, June 16, 1896.

Child.

1595.   Milton, b. March 23, 1897.

WILLIAM ELWOOD TALLEY (*951*) married Blanche Horner.

Children.

1596. Elwood Harmon, b. Jan'y 18, 1887, d. 1887.
1597. Laura, b. March 11, 1888.
1598. William, b. Oct. 20, 1889.
1599. Harmon, b. Nov. 6, 1891.
1600. Robert W., b. Dec. 4, 1898.

MARY EMMA TALLEY (*952*) married Harry Haddock, born April 9, 1862.

Children.

1601. Harry, b. Nov. 16, 1885.
1602. Lizzie, b. June 22, 1890.
1603. Florence, b. July 29, 1893.
1604. Harmon, b. Nov. 15, 1896.

HARRY W. TALLEY (*954*) married Emma Dean, born December 25, 1871.

Children.

1605. Harmon, b. May 30, 1890.
1606. William, b. Nov. 16, 1891.
1607. Henry W., b. Nov. 25, 1892.
1608. John B., b. Jan'y 16, 1896.
1609. Lizzie, b. Oct. 20, 1898.

MARY BOYS NEBEKER (*961*) married William Volk-hardt, born June 5, 1867.

Children.

1610. Aquilla Nebeker, b. Nov. 25, 1897.
1611. Myrtle Nebeker, b. Oct. 9, 1898.

AQUILINA ALLEN NEBEKER (*962*) married Paul Euo.

EMMA TALLEY NEBEKER (*963*) married William Preston Craig.

MARY V. FORD (*991*) married William Stanford.

Child.

1612. Eva, b. April 26, 1874.

IRENOUS W. FORD (*993*) married Ida E. Taylor, November 11, 1880.

Children.

1613. James A., b. Sept. 8, 1881.
1614. Carl B., b. June 1, 1885.
1615. Lalah I., b. Dec. 7, 1890.

ALICE J. FORD (*994*) married William Stanford, March 2, 1879.

Children.

1616.   Mary E., b. Oct. 17, 1879.
1617.   Ernest E., b. Feb'y 4, 1881.
1618.   Josephine G., b. Nov. 13, 1883.
1619.   Clifton B., b. Jan'y 21, 1885.
1620.   Edmund Ames, b. March 12, 1887.
1621.   William C., b. May 29, 1889.
1622.   Jennie R., b. May 10, 1890.
1623.   Catharine V., b. Sept. 15, 1894.

EMILY VIC. FORD (*996*) married Wm. W. Schwinn, November 25, 1884.

Children.

1624.   John N., b. Aug. 30, 1885.
1625.   Mary K., b. April 15, 1887.
1626.   William H., b. Oct. 21, 1888.
1627.   Bernice E., b. July 11, 1891.
1628.   Thomas G., b. July 9, 1893.
1629.   Mildred A., b. June 6, 1895.

JOHN B. FORD (*1000*) married Elizabeth E. Stern, May 26, 1894.

MELISSA E. STAHL (*1001*) married George E. Shafer, August, 1869.

Children.

1630.   Ida.
1631.   Charles W.
1632.   Alonzo, b. Feb'y 2, 1873.
1633.   Mary E., b. May 28, 1875.
1634.   Inez C., b. March 25, 1877.
1635.   Annabell.
1636.   Nora L., b. April 11, 1879.
1637.   Grace M., b. May 29, 1883.
1638.   Laura E.
1639.   Chester A., b. June 16, 1887.
1640.   Sarah R., b. Nov. 14, 1890.
1641.   Mabel L., b. April 4, 1893.

MARY J. STAHL (*1005*) married Charles King, January 1, 1886.

Children.
1642. Mary E., b. 1886.
1643. Helen M., b. 1890.
1644. Merrill Stahl, b. 1893.
1645. Florence, b. 1896.
1646. Bridice, b. 1898.

ULYSSES GRANT STAHL (*1006*) married Nannie McCahan, August, 1891.

Child.
1647. Bessie M., b. June 30, 1892.

JOHN W. TALLEY (*1012*) married Celia S. Bentley, May 17, 1885.

Children.
1648. G. Ross, b. May 31, 1886.
1649. Fred. G., b. Jan'y 2, 1890.
1650. J. Warren, b. Oct. 11, 1891.
1651. J. Earl, b. Dec. 11, 1895.

ELLA I. TALLEY (*1013*) married H. E. Myers, August 20, 1889.

Children.
1652. Evangeline Belle, b. Aug. 22, 1890.
1653. Joy Uberto, b. April 3, 1892.
1654. Paul Spurgeon, b. Dec. 11, 1893.
1655. Vivian Armanilla, b. Dec. 1, 1896.

CORA B. TALLEY (*1015*) married Edgar Price, August 17, 1891.

Child.
1656. Vesper, b. June 30, 1897.

HENRY E. TALLEY (*1016*) married Mabel Houdysheldt, December 13, 1893.

Children.
1657. Joyce.
1658. Helen Marie, b. Jan'y 23, 1897.

SARAH C. TALLEY (*1017*) married George W. Worrell, November 8, 1898.

Child.

1659. Daughter, b. Aug. 20, 1899.

WILLIAM W. TALLEY (*1018*) married Melissa Coddington, March 4, 1896.

ADAM C. TALLEY (*1022*) married Olive Hughes, July, 1889. He is a practical newspaper man.
Children.
1660. True H., b. March 18, 1891.
1661. Merrill K., b. May 16, 1892.
1662. Victor W., b. April 2, 1894.
1663. Bonham B., b. Oct. 28, 1896.

AMBROSE E. TALLEY (*1023*) married Blanche Dana, September, 1895. He is a minister of the Methodist Church in Des Moines Conference.
Children.
1664. Russell D., b. Aug. 22, 1896.
1665. Herald H., b. Oct., 1897.

MARY M. TALLEY (*1025*) married Walter H. Beall, June 30, 1897.

MARY V. KELLER (*1032*) married John M. Bentley, September 20, 1882.
Children.
1666. Viola M., b. July 2, 1883.
1667. Jennie P., b. April 6, 1885.
1668. Charles E., b. Jan'y 21, 1887.
1669. B. Harrison, b. April 8, 1889.
1670. Mabel, b. May 14, 1891.
1671. Ray, b. Sept. 14, 1893.
1672. Jessie, b. Dec. 5, 1895.

ENSIGN K. KELLER (*1035*) married Eva Lulu Eckard, September 24, 1892.
Children.
1673. Vera Fern, b. Aug. 21, 1893.
1674. Cecil Earl, b. Nov. 14, 1898.
1675. Mildred Pearl, b. Nov. 14, 1898.

JOHN N. KELLER (*1036*) married Harriet Reynolds, November 12, 1894.

Child.

1676.   Chester Arthur, b. Feb'y 19, 1896.

SARAH E. KELLER (*1037*) married Harry Reynolds, March 1, 1894.

Children.

1677.   Ora, b. Jan'y 16, 1895.
1678.   Laura Arminta, b. Sept. 17, 1896.

STEPHEN B. TALLEY (*1042*) married Lillie Turner, December 16, 1886. She was born July 28, 1864. He is a Car Inspector at South Chester, Pa.

Children.

1679.   Beulah C., b. July 14, 1889.
1680.   Myrtle B., b. July 26, 1899.

HANNAH TALLEY (*1043*) married Samuel Stott, of Philadelphia, Pa.

HOWARD F. TALLEY (*1044*) married Mary Boyler. They reside in Brooklyn, East, N. Y. He is a printer.

(Children—Howard ; Mary.)

MARGARET M. ROBERTS (*1045*) married William James Jacquette, April 24, 1887.

Children.

1681.   Maud I., b. July 12, 1892.
1682.   William Carl, b. Sept. 21, 1895.

MARY E. ROBERTS (*1046*) married George W. Barber.

Children.

1683.   Edith E., b. June 24, 1891.
1684.   Ethel, b. Oct. 14, 1896.

MARTHA A. ROBERTS (*1047*) married Eugene M. Plummer.

Child.

1685.   Adolphus, b. March 2, 1889.

EMMA L. ROBERTS (*1048*) married Jas. Blanchard Gill.

Children.
1686. Ida May, b. March 10, 1893.
1687. Harry F., b. Dec. 7, 1894.
1688. Mary E., b. Feb'y 16, 1898.

CLARA R. ROBERTS (*1049*) married Benjamin F. Klee.
Child.
1689. Benjamin F., b. Jan'y 11, 1898.

ETHEL BULLOCK WEST (*1051*) married Clarence Stewart, of Eddystone, Pa., January 20, 1899.

LYDIA A. TALLEY (*1079*) married G. Albert Hinkson, October 8, 1890.
Children.
1690. Emily T., b. Nov. 15, 1891.
1691. William Thomas, b. Feb'y 12, 1894.

SAMUEL ALFRED TALLEY (*1080*) married L. Anna Cheyney, April 28, 1897.
Child.
1692. Alfred Edwin, b. March 16, 1899.

CARRIE LIZZIE TALLEY (*1081*) married John W. Talley (1248), September 6, 1893. He was born December 7, 1871.
Children.
1692. William C., b. Aug. 14, 1894.
1693. Mary E., b. Feb'y 12, 1896.
1694. Alfred H., b. June 5, 1897.
1695. Lillian E., b. Dec. 29, 1898.

MARY ELIZABETH POOLE (*1086*) married Thomas B. Hibberd.
Child.
1696. Laura May, b. Feb'y 27, 1892.

HATTIE B. POOLE (*1087*) married Walter T. Hibberd.

LEONARD C. TALLEY (*1090*) married Anna J. Clark, November 3, 1897. He is engaged with the Edgemoor Iron Co., and resides at Wilmington, Del.

LEWIS PRINCE TALLEY (*1091*) married Cassandra Prince Cloud (930), October 13, 1897. He resides near Carpenter's Station, Brandywine Hundred, Del.

Child.

1697. Jennie Elizabeth, b. Jan'y 23, 1899.

MARY W. BIRD (*1096*) married Joseph Petitedemange.

Child.

1698. Irene H., b. March 26, 1895.

LILLIE M. BALDWIN (*1097*) married Dr. ——— Matthews, of Concord, Delaware County, Pa.

GEORGE EDWARD TALLEY (*1103*) married Cora Koopman, April, 1898. They reside at Terre Haute, Ind.

ELLA MAY TALLEY (*1108*) married Alfred G. Cummings, January 16, 1889. They reside at Terre Haute, Ind.

CHARLES PERKINS TALLEY (*1109*) married Belle Henry, Sept. 7, 1895. They reside at Terre Haute, Ind.

THOMAS J. TALLEY, JR. (*1118*) married Florence Richards Primrose, April 6, 1899. They reside at Wilmington, Del.

ELLA J. TALLEY (*1157*) married Lewis Henry Day, son of Thomas R. Day.

Child.

1699. Sadie, b. about Oct. 2, 1887.

WILLIAM H. TALLEY (*1158*) married Carrie May Poole, daughter of George W. and Emma Poole.

PENROSE R. TALLEY (*1159*), son of Thos. S. Talley, married Mary Pyle, daughter of Owen Z. and Anna M. Pyle.

Child.

1700. Lawrence, b. Nov. 12, 1896.

WILMER TALLEY (*1160*) married Mary Barlow, April 11, 1882. They reside near Harvey's Station, Brandywine Hundred, Del.

Children.

1701. Charles Wesley, b. Jan'y 27, 1883.
1702. Edna I., b. April 3, 1885.
1703. Wilmer, b. Oct. 8, 1886.
1704. Horace H., b. July 30, 1892.
1705. George B., b. Sept. 23, 1896.

PENROSE R. TALLEY (*1161*), son of Charles Talley, married Hannah L. Foulk, daughter of Lewis Foulk, of Wilmington, Del., April 2, 1890. They also reside near Harvey's Station, on B. and O. R. R.

Children.

1706.   Leroy F., b. June 5, 1891.
1707.   J. Wallace, b. Nov. 5, 1892.
1708.   Mary Z., b. June 9, 1896.

ALFRED B. HICKMAN (*1172*) married Mary E. Talley (1249), June 5, 1895. She is daughter of Wm. and Sarah E. Talley.

Child.

1709.   Sarah Elizabeth, b. March 4, 1899.

ESTELLA J. WELDIN (*1174*) married William F. Robinson.

Child.

1710.   Elsie W., b. Oct. 11, 1892.

BEULAH M. WELDIN (*1175*) married Warren Missimer.

Children.

1711.   Naomi T., b. March 11, 1895.
1712.   Ruth W., b. March 11, 1895.
1713.   Bertha E., b. Aug. 30, 1897.

THOMAS WHEELER BOOTH (*1184*) married Emma Phillips, February 26, 1896.

THOMAS P. BOOTH (*1188*) married Stella Stevenson, January 1, 1889. They reside at Boothwyn, Delaware County, Pa. He is a contracting plasterer, and is progressive and energetic.

CHARITY EVA BOOTH (*1189*) married Frank D. Pyle, October 31, 1891. He keeps a general store at Boothwyn, Pa.

Children.

1714.   Julia Phillips, b. Sept. 24, 1893.
1715.   Margaret E., b. Aug. 30, 1895.

ELEANOR TALLEY (*1200*) married Thos. W. Eynon, June 20, 1898.

ETTA JANE TALLEY (*1202*) married Thos. D. Holmes, October 3, 1889.

Children.

1716. Thomas, aged 9 years.

1717. Jesse, aged 6 years.

REBA MAY TALLEY (*1203*) married William L. Morrow, April 22, 1891.

Children.

1718. Reuel L., b. April 20, 1892.

1719. Eleanor May, b. Sept. 4, 1895.

1720. Ruth, b. Oct. 28, 1897.

CENA A. TALLEY (*1204*) married Preston M. Baird.

Children.

1721. Charles Taylor, b. Oct. 2, 1893.

1722. Preston Walter, b. July 7, 1895.

1723. Leroy Marshall, b. Jan'y 13, 1899.

EBERT LINCOLN TALLEY (*1205*) married Delia Brennan. They reside in Philadelphia, Pa.

Children.

1724. Edith Theresa, b. 1895.

1725. Mabel May, b. Dec. 21, 1897.

ELLA LAVENIA TALLEY (*1212*) married Abel Hanna, May 28, 1891.

CLARA ARCELIA TALLEY (*1214*) married William L. Wilson, Jr., son of William L. and Hetty Wilson, April 27, 1897.

CALVER GRANT TALLEY (*1218*) married Mamie Hicks. She was born January 2, 1878. They reside in Mill Creek Hundred, Del.

ELIZA ANN TALLEY (*1221*) married William Vanaman, April 3, 1895.

Children.

1726. Nelson T., b. Sept. 9, 1896.

1727. William R., b. Dec. 7, 1898.

LAURA VIRGINIA TALLEY (*1228*) married George Webster, son of Clark Webster. George was born February 18, 1862.

Children.

1728. Howard C., b. Aug. 14, 1890.

1729. Albert, b. Jan'y 19, 1892.

1730. Elsie Martha, b. May 30, 1893.

1731. Rebecca A., b. Nov. 15, 1894.

1732. Infant, not named, d. 1897.

MARY ANNA TALLEY (*1229*) married J. Wesley Davenport. Married by Rev. Chas. H. Williams.

Child.

1733. J. Clarence, b. June 26, 1898.

SALLIE J. TALLEY (*1231*) married Charles E. Webster, April 13, 1893. He is son of Clark Webster, of Brandywine Hundred, Del.

Child.

1734. Herman, b. June 30, 1897.

BLANCHE A. TALLEY (*1233*) married Andrew H. Hinkson, April 1, 1896. They reside at Chester, Pa. He is in the harness business.

Child.

1735. Irene B., b. Feb. 1, 1897.

REV. JAMES WALTER TALLEY (*1236*) married Elva Palmatary. They were married Sept. 8, 1892. (See sketch.)

Children.

1736. Wilson M., b. June 10, 1893.

1737. Ethel, b. Jan'y 7, 1896.

GERTRUDE L. TALLEY (*1251*) married Clifton A. Perkins, of Holly Oak, Del. He is a Contractor and Builder.

Children.

1738. Sarah Anna, b. Sept. 8, 1893, d. in infancy.

1739. Clifton Talley, b. Oct. 2, 1895, d. in infancy.

1740. Gladys Le Van, b. Nov. 10, 1896.

1741. Herbert Amor, b. June 3, 1898.

SADIE H. TALLEY (*1254*) married Anthony McGarvey. They reside in Brandywine Hundred.

EBER Y. TALLEY (*1263*) married Barbara A. Nicholson, December 4, 1877. She was born September 11, 1855. He is engaged in the ice-cream business on the Concord Turnpike, above Perry's Hotel.

Children.

1742. George T., b. Feb'y 4, 1880.

1743. Joseph E., b. June 16, 1883.

THOMAS LEA TALLEY (*1264*) married Harriet Laura Hinkson, February 26, 1890. He is a farmer.

Child.

1744. Mary Elizabeth, b. Sept. 2, 1894.

MARY E. TALLEY (*1265*) married Joseph W. Nicholson. He was born December 14, 1857, and is a farmer.

Children.

1745. Lewis E., b. Sept. 24, 1885.

1746. Carrie S., b. Nov. 15, 1890.

1747. Harry J., b. Feb'y 23, 1894.

ELIZABETH M. TALLEY (*1266*) married John R. Mousley. She died November 29, 1893.

Child.

1748. Corene, b. Nov. 15, 1893.

CAROLINE S. TALLEY (*1267*) married Joel C. Pierce, son of Walter Pierce, of Brandywine Hundred.

Child.

1749. Thomas Leroy, b. Aug. 4, 1891.

JOHN G. TALLEY (*1268*) married Ida L. Pyle, Feb'y 13, 1888. They reside at Elam, Pa. He is a farmer.

Children.

1750. Frank D., b. June 4, 1889.

1751. Norman R., b. Aug. 22, 1890.

1752. Ethel E., b. April 29, 1894.

1753. J. Earl, b. May 17, 1897.

JOSEPHINE TALLEY (*1269*) married John W. Davis, June 26, 1884. He is a farmer of Bethel Township, Delaware County, Pa.

Children.

1754. William L., b. March 26, 1885.

1755. Thomas Walter, b. March 16, 1888.

1756. Addie Graves, b. Jan'y 1, 1894.
1757. John Warren, b. Nov. 27, 1896.
1758. Charles A., b. April 11, 1899.

SUSANNA A. TALLEY (*1270*) married Willard S. Hanby.
He is a farmer at Hanby's Corner, Brandywine Hundred.

Children.
1759. Jacob Carroll, b. Aug. 4, 1892.
1760. Paul W., b. Feb'y 25, 1896.

WILLIAM HARRY TALLEY (*1271*) married Fannie C.
Henvis, March 30, 1898. He is a farmer in the "old Hundred" of Brandywine.

Child.
1761. Harry Darlington, b. June 22, 1899.

ABNER P. TALLEY (*1274*) married Ida Furey.

Children.
1762. William, b. March 18, 1896.
1763. Melba, b. Feb'y 28, 1898

HANNAH B. TALLEY (*1277*) married Alphonso
Oliphant.

Child.
1764. Mabel, b. May 15, 1899.

MARY A. TALLEY (*1289*) married George W. Anderson, August 11, 1892. He was born September 2, 1868. He
resides at Wilmington, Del.

Children.
1765. Myrtle A., b. Feb. 3, 1896. Deceased.
1766. Harvey E., b. April 28, 1898. Deceased.

WILLIAM LEA TALLEY (*1319*) married Clara Lysinger.
Live at Wilmington, Del.

MARY ELLA TALLEY (*1320*) married Pemberton D.
Sheldon.

Children.
1767. Paul, b. July 19, 1891.
1768. Mark W., b. Jan'y 17, 1893.
1769. Thomas Lea, b. Feb'y 6, 1895.

JOHN HOWARD TALLEY (*1321*) married Caroline French.
Child.
1770. Ethel, b. April 19, 1898.

ANNA GALENA TALLEY (*1293*) married Joseph Edwards, June 29, 1898.

HOWARD D. TALLEY (*1316*) married Jennie Hinkson, March 29, 1899.

CHARLES FORWOOD (*1326*) married Lidie Colehower. He resides at Elam, Delaware County, Pa.
Child.
1771. Howard D., b. May 27, 1895.

ELLEN D. GRISWOLD (*1329*) married John L. Price.
Children.
1772. William.
1773. Clarence A.
1774. Mabel A.
1775. Elsie.
1776. Helen.
1777. Mary.
1778. Josephine.

MARY P. GRISWOLD (*1331*) married Charles W. Walton.
Children.
1779. Elsie.
1780. Mildred.
1781. Albert.
1782. Emma.
1783. Mary Francis.
1784. Charles.
1785. Joanna.

BELLE D. LARKIN (*1340*) married Edward S. Hickman.
Children.
1786. Jessie J.
1787. Edward S.
1788. Helen.
1789. Margaret.

MARGARET T. SPRINGER (*1345*) married J. Leedom Palmer.

MARY ELIZA HANCE (*1369*) married Thomas B. Cartmell, April 25, 1895.

Child.

1790. George Edwin.

ANDREW J. HANCE (*1370*) married Annabel Downs, May 6, 1887.

Children.

1791. Wallace Eugene.
1792. Andrew Johnson.

WILLIAM J. WESLEY HANCE (*1371*) married Edith G. Hickman (1171), December 25, 1891.

Children.

1793. Mary Alfreda.
1794. William Wesley.

✓ JENNETTE S. GRUBB (*1398*) married William L. Jefferis, October 6, 1885.

Children.

1795. Julia P., b. June 10, 1888, d. 1894.
1796. Jennette G., b. June 1, 1891.
1797. William G., b. Dec. 16, 1894.

JOHN W. TALLEY (*1417*) married Emma Worth, March 25, 1885.

Child.

1798. Ralph W., b. June 15, 1886.

WILLIAM D. PULLEN (*1438*) married Lelia M. Valentine, June 18, 1891. They reside at Chester, Pa.

Children.

1799. Margaret V., b. Dec. 7, 1892.
1800. Mildred J., b. Feb'y 2, 1896.

HENDERSON TALLEY DOWLIN (*1446*) married Annie E. Hill, August 12, 1899.

SALLIE EDNA DOWLIN (*1447*) married Rev. Joseph E. Gurnsey, of Bridgeport, Conn., June 21, 1899.

LETITIA MAY GARDNER (*1461*) married Clinton L. Reynolds, August, 1894.

Children.

1801. Lois Marion, b. April, 1896.
1802. James Lewis Dale, b. May, 1897.
1803. Leroy Wade, b. Aug., 1898.

ANNA G. A. PADGET (*1469*) married —— Granthom. They have three children ; names not known.

DR. LEWIS ROACH DAY (*1465*) married Lottie Gordon, August 15, 1895. Live in Illinois.

ANNE AGNES DAY (*1467*) married David Grant Mayes, January 1, 1891.

Child.

1804. William C. D., b. Feb'y 13, 1892.

NELLIE MAY CRUM (*1479*) married Henry White, June 15, 1892.

Children.

1805. Neoto May, b. May 5, 1893.
1806. Mildred G., b. April 20, 1895.
1807. Edith A., b. July 11, 1896.
1808. Opal L., b. Nov. 30, 1897.

ETHEL M. GRIMMET (*1490*) married George W. Edwards, January, 1898.

Child.

1809. Harry Otho, b. Jan'y 6, 1899.

CAMPBELL M. JOHNSTON (*1526*) married Elizabeth F. Swing, April 27, 1887.

Child.

1810. Campbell S., b. Sept. 3, 1888.

ELIZABETH C. JOHNSTON (*1528*) married Harries C. Hulbert, November 12, 1884. They reside at Clifton, Cincinnati. She has artistic talent ; has produced some fine pieces of painting and sculpture, and has studied in Europe and Japan.

Children.

1811. William P., b. Sept. 2, 1885.
1812. Lea M., b. Dec. 22, 1888.
1813. Caroline, b. Oct. 3, 1892.

ROBERTA A. JOHNSTON (*1530*) married Harley J. Morrison, November 16, 1893.

Children.

1814. John, b. April 28, 1896.
1815. Robert Johnston, b. Dec. 12, 1898.

JOHN BAIL PEIRCE (*1545*) married Frances A. Clark, of Philadelphia, Pa., October 2, 1894.

J. FRANK PEIRCE (*1546*) married Ella M. Mull, of Wilmington, Del., October 20, 1897.

GEO. M. PEIRCE (*1547*) married Eva Nickerson, of Wilmington, Del., June 6, 1897.

Child.

1816. Mary C., b. April 18, 1898.

TENTH GENERATION.

EVA STANFORD (*1612*) married William E. Lawson, September 5, 1894.

Child.

1817. Son, d. in infancy, April 29, 1896.

MARY E. SHAFER, (*1633*) married Alonzo Beymer, March 30, 1898.

Child.

1818. George, b. April 24, 1899.

UNCLASSIFIED NAMES.

List of those whose names came in too late to be classified in their regular order :

PRISCILLA TALLEY (*184*), the youngest daughter of Harman and Rebecca (Grubb) Talley, married Moses Bullock, in 1835. They removed from Delaware to Ohio, in 1837. They, in 1872, moved to Charlotte County, Va. Priscilla was born February 15, 1814, died January 15, 1885. She was a member of the M. E. Church.

Children.

1819. Elizabeth G., b. 1836.
1820. Marshall H., b. 1838.

1821. Rebecca T., b. 1840.
1822. James K. Polk, b. 1844.
1823. Julia Ann, b. 1851.
1824. William T., b. 1855.
1825. John Wesley, b. 1858.

JOSEPH LYBRAND GRUBB (*398*) was born January 6, 1828. Married Priscilla Rowland.

Children.
1826. George R., b. Nov. 6, 1865.
1827. Clara M., b. May 29, 1867.
1828. Harry Judd, b. Jan'y 1, 1869.
1829. Helen B., b. June 19, 1871.
1830. Joseph J., b. May 18, 1877.
1831. Frank W., b. May 18, 1877.

GEORGE W. GRUBB (*397*), born January 21, 1824; died February 5, 1898. Married Rebecca Lynam.

Children.
1832. Hannah C., b. April 17, 1855.
1833. Springer Lynam, b. Aug. 26, 1857.
1834. Joseph Rush, b. Jan'y 20, 1860.
1835. George Newlin, b. June 20, 1861.
1836. Christiana C., b. July 12, 1863.
1837. Robert Flinn, b. Aug. 6, 1865.
1838. Lewis Weldin, b. July 24, 1867.
1839. Bettie R., b. March 6, 1869.
1840. Ratia Lukens, b. Sept. 17, 1871.

HANNAH ELIZABETH GRUBB (*399*), born March 4, 1836; died June 7, 1898. Married Josiah K. Fesmier.

Children.
1841. Howard F., b. July 12, 1857.
1842. Lucy E.. b. Oct. 24, 1829.
1843. Addie L., b. Sept. 5, 1861.
1844. Simon P., b. May 6, 1863.
1845. William C., b. Oct. 4, 1864.

CHARLES T. TALLEY (*182*), son of Harmon. Married Evaline Kellam. He died in California. We have received the following about the family :

Children.

1846. David K.   Resides at St. Louis, Mo.
1847. Edmund.   Resides in California.
1848. Eva.   Resides in Oklahoma.

PRISCILLA BULLOCK (*489*) married Willis T. Sedgwick.

ESTHER BULLOCK (*490*) married Wm. T. Reese.

JOSEPH M. PIERCE (*513*) married Susanna T. Barlow.
(See sketch.)

Children.

1849. Frank C.
1850. Mary Louie.
1851. Nellie V.
1852. Sarah Emma.
1853. Jennie R.
1854. Florence E.

FRANK C. PIERCE (*1849*) married Pauline A. Rothouse.

Children.

1855. Joseph M.
1856. Bertha L.
1857. William R.
1858. F. Pauline.
1859. Frank C.
1860. Ruth M.

MARY LOUIE PIERCE (*1850*) married William W. Day.

Children.

1861. J. Herbert.
1862. F. Irene.

NELLIE V. PIERCE (*1851*) married S. Larkin Hanby.

Children.

1863. Alma V.
1864. E. Emma.

SARAH EMMA PIERCE (*1852*) married Frank J. Merion.

Children.

1865. Frances J.
1866. Helen E.

JENNIE R. PIERCE (*1853*) married William I. Harvey.

Children.
1867.   Frank J.
1868.   Albert B.

FLORENCE E. PIERCE (*1854*) married W. Calmer
Beeson (903).
Child.
1869.   M. Louie.

JOHN TALLEY (   ) married Mary ——. Said to
have lived at Wilmington, Del. Have not been able to place
this family, as it came in late.
Children.
1870.   George. Deceased.
1871.   Charles A., b. at Wilmington ; d. Jan. 20, 1873.

CHARLES A. TALLEY (*1871*) married Margaret Broome.
She died September 4, 1877.
Children.
1872.   George W., b. July 1, 1863.
1873.   Mary Emma, b. June 30, 1865.
1874.   Charles A., b. April 4, 1867.
1875.   William Henry, b. Nov. 3, 1870.

GEORGE W. TALLEY (*1872*) married Mary A. Nei-
meyer, December 17, 1887. They reside at Trenton, N. J.
Children.
1876.   William Henry, b. Dec. 12, 1889.
1877.   George W., b. Aug. 18, 1891.
1878.   Margaret May, b. Sept. 8, 1894.

HENRY B. TALLEY (*833*) married, December 28, 1873,
Sarah E. Brennen. She was born June 26, 1852. They reside
at Philadelphia.
Children.
1879.   Richard S. J., b. Oct. 10, 1874, married Winifred
        McDevitt, b. July 25, 1876. One child,
        Henry, b. March 2, 1897.
1880.   Joseph Harley, b. March 31, 1877, d. 1877.
1881.   Oscar R., b. Oct. 31, 1878.
1882.   George B. B., b. Dec. 2, 1880.

1883.   Henry A., b. Jan'y 7, 1883, d. 1884.
1884.   Delilah N., b. March 1, 1885.
1885.   Ann B. K., b. March 11, 1887.
1886.   Edmund B., b. April 25, 1889, d. 1889.
1887.   Essie W., b. July 18, 1890.
1888.   Isabella M., b. May 11, 1892.
1889.   May, b. May 11, 1894, d. 1894.
1890.   Matthias Seddinger, b. March 9, 1897.

GEORGE W. TALLEY (*834*), of Atlantic City, born October 16, 1847, married and has two children.

DANIEL BISPHAM TALLEY (*836*) married Lydia N. Hutton, January 22, 1882. They reside at Tacony, Philadelphia. No issue.

KATE TALLEY (*837*) married Theo. Street. They reside at Philadelphia. No issue.

ELIZABETH G. TALLEY (*835*) married Leonard Hasher, of Philadelphia, Pa.

Children.

1891.   Florence Ida, b. Oct. 2, 1872.
1892.   Louise Mary, b. July 8, 1879.
1893.   Frank, b. July 2, 1881.
1894.   Leonard, b. April 26, 1883.
1895.   Harry, b. Dec. 26, 1885.
1896.   George Washington, b. July 4, 1887.
1897.   Charles Walter, b. Sept. 20, 1889.

MARY TALLEY (*582*), daughter of Thos. Lea Talley, Sr., married Oliver H. Parry, of Brandywine Hundred. Their children are as follows : Cordelia, Thomas Lea, William, Oliver H., Mamie and Oda. Mrs. Parry now resides in Wilmington, Del.

WM. HENRY LLOYD (*855*) married Maggie Sayers.

MARY V. LLOYD (*856*) married Wm. H. Edwards.

JOHN B. LLOYD (*857*) married Alice Sparks.

ORPAH PERKINS LLOYD (*859*) married Irwin W. Pierce.

JOSEPH LLOYD (*860*) married Matilda Sparks.

GEO. L. LLOYD (*854*) married —— at Cleveland, Ohio.
Children.
1898. Wellington.
1899. Guy.

JOHN S. HIMES (*344*) married Mary E. Pugh.

MARY E. HIMES (*349*) married John Prizer.

WILLIAM S. HIMES (*351*) married Margaret Hartman.

GEORGE B. HIMES (*352*) married Sarah S. Farmer.

NELSON T. HIMES (*350*). Enlisted in Co. K, 4th Reg.
Pa. Reserves, and died near Washington, D. C., Sept. 21,
1861, in his 21st year.

VICTORENE HIMES (*355*) married Wm. H. Snyder.

HARRY M. TALLEY (*914*) married Nellie J. Wolf, in
1891. They reside at Nicetown, Philadelphia, Pa. She was
born January 9, 1873.
Children.
1900. Edith N., b. July 10, 1893.
1901. Mabel W., b. Jan'y 12, 1896.

FRANK A. TALLEY (*839*) married ——. He resides
at Hendricks, Montgomery County, Pa.

BIOGRAPHY.

In this department is given a short sketch of the Grubb Ancestry, as well as a few sketches of persons now living and of some who have, in recent years, passed away. This field was not intended for a selected class, but was open to all. Many cared not for mention in this way. Modern thought would indicate that in this course they erred, and thereby detracted much from the value of the book. Matter of this kind must be invaluable after the lapse of a few years. If every one decided not to permit his biography to appear, how could a satisfactory book be issued? Individual wishes must oftentimes yield to that which may result in good to others.

The sketches following were mostly prepared by the author, voluntarily, as a small tribute to those who took active part in working for the book, and to those who donated funds to aid in the printing when it was clearly discernible, that unless aid were given the undertaking must result in failure. This movement added many pages to the book, and many more could have been added had the funds been donated for the printing of the same. All within reach were given an opportunity to join in the donations; in fact, the circular issued August 28, 1899, strongly pleaded for donations and financial aid. We hope there will be no criticism of this course, nor fault found on this account, but rather let all *rejoice* that a plan was devised which brought success, and rendered the book a possibility. It would be most *ungenerous* and *unmanly* not to feel grateful to all who have aided the work by donating funds and subscribing for books.

A SKETCH OF THE GRUBB ANCESTRY.

As we are not able, at this writing, to set forth the chivalry of the ancient European Talley family, on account of the lack of research among the archives and historical records across the Atlantic, we here give a *resume* of the Grubb ancestry ; so that, those of us who have descended on the maternal side from this illustrious family may draw inspiration and profit therefrom, while we await the unearthing of the emblems armorial of the Talley family, or the discovery of the true current of *their* royal blood in distant lands.

It appears that the Grubb ancestry dates back to 1127, in Denmark. Those of that name then held high positions in the government of that nation ; and were the possessors of coats-of-arms and other insignia of nobility. They were very near to the throne in ancient Denmark, being related to King Christian IV by a collateral marriage. Some of the Grubbs passed, at an early day, from Denmark over to England, and from them have descended the Grubb family of England, and later of America.

The American Grubbs trace their recent ancestry back to Henry Grubbe, Esq., of Wiltshire, England. He died in 1581. Some of his descendants have held high positions in the Army and Navy of England, as well as in Parliament, Henry Grubbe being himself a member in that body, representing Devizes, Wiltshire, 14 Elizabeth, in 1571. Thomas, the son of Henry, died February 2, 1617. Thomas M. A., of Oxford University, and rector of Cranfield, was the second son of Thomas, Esq., and was born 1581, at Potterne, Wiltshire. John, Esq., of Bedfordshire, second son of Rev. Thomas, was born 1610, and died in 1667. He being an adherent of the Church of England in Cromwell's time, removed for safety to a remote corner of Cornwall, and there he married Helen Vivian.

The emigrant, John Grubb, who came to America just before the landing of Penn, was a son of John and Helen (Vivian) Grubb, of Cornwall, England. He was born in 1652, and came to America in 1677. He married Frances Vane. She was of English descent. He died in 1708 and is buried at St. Martin's P. E. Church at Marcus Hook, Pa. The children of the marriage of John and Frances Grubb were, 1. Emanuel, 2. John, 3. Charity, 4. Phebe, 5. Joseph, 6. Henry, 7. Samuel, 8. Nathaniel, and 9. Peter.

The Talleys have intermarried with descendants of John, Emanuel and Joseph, and perhaps with descendants of other children of John the emigrant. Joseph was the father of Hannah Grubb, who intermarried with William Talley about 1735. From this marriage have descended possibly two-thirds of the Talleys named in our *Genealogical Register.* Thomas, the son of William and Hannah (Grubb) Talley, married Hannah Grubb, a supposed descendant of John Grubb, second.

For a more extended and complete history of the ancient Grubb family in Europe, we refer to the sketch of Judge Ignatius C. Grubb's life in the " Biographical and Genealogical History of Delaware," vol. 1, pg. 231. The Talleys who have descended from the Grubb line are of noble birth, and should feel under lasting obligations to Judge Grubb for his most thorough work in tracing the ancestry back to so remote a period ; and in permitting the same to be recorded for the benefit of ALL who may take interest therein.

GENERAL WILLIAM COOPER TALLEY.

WILLIAM COOPER TALLEY, son of Rev. Lewis S. and Priscilla (Clark) Talley, was born December 11, 1831, on his father's farm (later the home of Lewis Zebley), at Talley's Corner, Brandywine Hundred, Del. His father died in 1847, and his mother in 1850, as shown by their tombstones at Bethel Cemetery. He attended the Forwood School when a boy, it being close to his home. The Forwood School House was memorable for one thing at least. A debating society was organized there many years ago. Among the active debaters were William Cooper Talley and Powell Clayton, now Ambassador to Mexico, each of whom in the Civil War rose to the rank of Brigadier General. These brigadiers were related by John Clayton and Rev. Lewis S. Talley each marrying a daughter of George Clark. There was also a slight relationship by Sarah (Foulk) Clayton, the grandmother of Powell Clayton, being the daughter of Sarah (Talley) Foulk. Cooper Talley and Powell Clayton were of necessity on opposites sides in the debates, but during the Civil War they were on the same side, battling for their country, one in the far West and the other in the East. They each succeeded well in shedding new lustre on their family names.

William Cooper Talley graduated in 1853 at Professor Sudler's Academy at Wilmington, Del. The professor was a graduate at West Point and a fine military tactician. Under his teaching young Talley perhaps received the military impulse which later developed into the brave soldier of the Civil War.

After his graduation he took a prospecting trip through the West, but finally decided to locate at Media, Pa. Here he began the reading of law, and at the same time, with other parties, published the *Upland Union*, a Democratic newspaper issued at Media. Talley was a strong Douglas man, and his associates were equally as strong for Breckenridge. The want of harmony caused Mr. Talley to withdraw from the paper. Being solicited by a committee from Norristown, Pa., he purchased the *National Democrat* of that city, and advocated the election of Douglas.

Lincoln being elected, the war followed. The brave young man from Brandywine Hundred, with the military spirit already kindled at the Wilmington Academy, could not resist the call to arms. He raised a company, unsheathed his sword, and gallantly fought for his country and his convictions.

Upon his return home, at the expiration of his three years, he became Deputy Collector of Internal Revenue for the Seventh District of Pennsylvania, and later received the appointment of Collector. When his office expired he again took up journalism, and published the *Delaware County Democrat*, at Chester, Pa. While editing this paper, in 1874, he was elected on the Democratic ticket to the Pennsylvania Legislature, and served until the close of the session in 1876. During two sessions of this term he was Chairman of the Ways and Means Committee, and a member of the Centennial Committee. He assisted in arranging for the Centennial grounds, and for a State Building. Meeting with financial reverses, he retired from politics and disposed of his paper; and in 1877 took a position in the Printing Department at Washington, D. C., in the proof room of the *Congressional Record*. He now leads a quiet and honorable life in that city.

We extract the following from a sketch of General Talley's military life, furnished by O. B. Talley, of Sioux City, Iowa :

' When the first shot was fired on Fort Sumter he sold his newspaper at a sacrifice and organized a company at his home in Delaware County, Pa. The company became Co. F of the 1st Regiment of the Pennsylvania Reserve Corps. In 1861 the company was mustered in, subject to the call of the President. The call came during the first Bull Run fight, and he soon joined the Army of the Potomac. At the Battle of Antietam he was given the command of his regiment by General Warren, the Corps Commander. He received his Colonel's Commission Nov. 2, 1862. At the Battle of Spottsylvania C. H. he commanded the 1st Brigade of the 5th Corps, Crawford commanding the division. He was, upon recommendation of General Crawford, Breveted Brigadier General for gallant and meritorious action at Antietam, Fredericksburg, Gettysburg, the Wilderness, Spottsylvania and other engagements. He was mustered out with his brigade at Philadelphia, June 13, 1864.'

'Steine in his *History of the Army of the Potomac* in substance says of him : 'Col. William Cooper Talley, in command of the 1st Regiment of the Reserves at the Battle of Fredericksburg, was on the right. In this charge, which was longer and equally as brilliant and daring as the famous Pickett's charge at Gettysburg, or MacDonald's at Wagram, the command was exposed to a heavy artillery fire from the front and the flanks. Colonel Talley was a young officer of unpretending manner and not ambitious for promotion. C. H. Ingram, of Talley's regiment, said that he looked at the Colonel as his regiment reached the slope to make the charge on the works ; that Colonel Talley was one of the coolest men that he ever saw in action. He guarded his right against surprise while he led the charge in front.'

'Bates in his *History of the Pennsylvania Volunteers* in substance says : 'In the Battle of Fredericksburg the 1st Regiment of Pennsylvania Reserves, under command of Colonel Talley, moved in a steady line across an open plain under a heavy enfilading artillery fire, and charged with resistless energy, crossing the railroad and ditches, and driving the enemy two hundred yards beyond the entrenchment. He was compelled to retire for want of reinforcements, after having opened the way to victory. He led his regiment with great gallantry and aided in gaining the signal advantage of the battle. If this successful assault had been followed up, a victory would have been gained instead of a defeat which filled the land with gloom.'

O. B. Talley, in closing his sketch, says :

"It has been my good fortune to know General Talley in his home life in Washington. During three years of my service as clerk to a committee of the lower branch of the National Legislature, I spent many pleasant evenings with the General. He is a grand old man, full of years and of glory, unassuming and generous. Those of his family whom I have met are fit descendants of such a sire. Our family has reason to be proud of him, and the coming generations may well emulate the example he has set before them."

ELIZA A. TALLEY,   GEORGE W. TALLEY,
JOHN TALLEY,   HANNAH (TALLEY) WELDIN.

These four persons were the children of Thomas and
Mary (Weldin) Talley. Thomas was a man mentally and
physically strong, and joined his lot in life with Mary Weldin,
a woman remarkable for her fine physical endowments and
strength of character. They were perfect strangers in blood
to each other. From these conditions we have presented the
four children named above, remarkable for their size, strength,
longevity and mental development. It is rare to find a family
of four, and all worthy of the historian's pen. Here are
suggested questions for our earnest consideration.

The subjects of this sketch received the ordinary District School education of the day, which was limited often on
account of the lack of ability in the teacher, and the lack of
funds to continue the school. These children easily digested
whatever in an educational way was presented to them,
whether at school or out rubbing against the activities of the
world. The lack of book learning was supplemented with
natural endowments, which carried them through life successfully, even in the day of the "higher education."

ELIZA A. TALLEY was born March 8, 1806. She
never married, not, however, on account of the want of opportunity, for it is well known that many sought her hand in
marriage. She was the idol of her parents; this, no doubt,
was the cause of her remaining single.

She spun the wool as long as spinning was in vogue,
and knit the stockings that warmed the feet of many of her
relatives, and of many outside of her family. This was rarely
done for hire, but out of the purest kindness and charity.
She was of a remarkably cheerful and hopeful disposition,
yet did she live only in the real substantial atmosphere of life,
caring not for its lighter pleasures. With *her*, "life was real,
life was earnest." She was tall and slender, and a remarkable

walker. Many times did she walk to the night meetings at Bethel Church, a distance, from her home, of six miles. In her younger days a horse was rarely used by her.

Having no family, she was often found among her relatives and neighbors, a true and faithful Samaritan, giving aid and consolation, and wise counsel, when and where it was needed. Although a ready adviser, she was no intermeddler in the affairs of others. She rarely saw anything but good in the people she knew and discussed. This virtue was remarkably developed in her. Only a few have an "aunt Eliza." This one was known far and near in her neighborhood.

She strove to live up to her Christian teachings. Her loyalty and devotion to the Methodist Church were really remarkable. Her religious zeal was not of the spasmodic order, but born of the intellect. Hence, day by day always the same. Aunt Eliza passed away at the ripe age of 85 years, mourned by all, leaving a void difficult to fill.

GEORGE W. TALLEY was born February 8, 1808. As soon as he was competent he began business on his own account, although he still resided under the parental roof. He did not marry until 30 years of age. In the year 1838, he married Lavinia Beeson, a pretty girl of 18 years of age. She was small of stature, and of rare good judgment. She was of English descent, and of the colonial family of Beesons, who lived south of the Philadelphia Turnpike, near the Wilmington City line. She was a model wife, and a solicitous and ever watchful mother.

Soon after their marriage they took up their abode on that portion of his father's farm which lay adjacent to the mill property of Henry Webster. While carrying on a general farming business, he engaged especially in buying, selling and fattening cattle. This naturally led him in the direction of the Cherry Island Marsh, for his good judgment soon told him that bushes and rolling stones did not produce fat cattle, while the fine white clover of the marshes did.

He began to buy marsh land shortly after his marriage, and was, in 1840, taxed on the marsh books as the owner of 8 acres. From this time the acreage increased almost annually until in after life he owned about 225 acres of these marsh lands. This included the historic old Cherry Island or Cooper's Island, of the days of the Dutch and Swedes. This property is still in the Talley family, and it is said that it was the site of the first ship-building plant along the Delaware. On these marshes before and during the Civil War, George W. Talley fed more than one hundred head of fine steers at one time.

Haying was a vast industry on the marsh, and with this Talley family it began in June, and lasted until the ground was white with autumn's frost. There was hay in barns, hay in stacks almost everywhere, and too often loads of hay and the oxen all in the ditch at sun down, and four miles from home. It took a little of everything to make up a full round season of haying on the " old Island." One term of this kind of schooling oftentimes would equal one year at the boarding school. It was practical education, with much stress on the word " practical." These were days when oxen were more plentiful than horses, and doubly as trying on one's temper.

Still, 'midst it all, the Talley world moved slowly on. George W. Talley added to his lands, farms and tracts on the highlands of Brandywine Hundred, and finished by building a row of brick houses at the corner of La Mott Street and Vandiver Avenue in Wilmington, Del. He owned at one time about 325 acres, all of which either lay within the city's limits or not far from it. One peculiar circumstance connected with his land dealings was that, although a great land-buyer, he scarcely ever sold, except to a railroad company, or to be used for some public purpose.

He, with such able men as Jacob S. Weldin, Lewis Weldin, William Todd and many others, organized the Mt. Pleasant M. E. Church Society, at the old school house of the same name, and assisted in the building of the present church near Quarryville. He continued to be a leading member here until his decease. He held the office of Church Trustee for years, was a Director of the Cherry Island Marsh Company, and a School Director. These were the only offices held by him. He had no taste for politics, although he was a true patriot, and a lover of his country. He kept well posted on public affairs, being a great newspaper reader, and had excellent judgment on National matters. When the call of his country seemed to demand it, he consented that his two older sons might join the great Union Army of 1861 to 1865.

He was a man of powerful build, and never used stimulants nor tobacco. He demonstrated his ability to carry on large undertakings, as did William Talley of old. He prized money only for the good he could do with it. He was economical, yet had the idea of public improvement so firmly implanted in him that large sums were given to bridges, railroads, and other public improvements. He, although a member of Mt. Pleasant Church, was at the same time one of the Board of Trustees that erected the Brandywine M. E. Church, and gave more to the building fund of the latter than he could well afford.

When the National Dredging Company, some years ago, filled with dredged mud a large tract in Cherry Island, George W. Talley and his life-long friend, Isaac S. Elliott, donated to the city of Wilmington a strip of ground one hundred feet wide, extending from Brandywine Creek to the Delaware River, for the bed of Fourth Street. He fostered all public improvements, and opposed none. It afforded him *pleasure* to see the building of railroads, even when they came through his own land. His exterior might at times to some appear rugged and unpolished, yet beneath this exterior was a fully developed manhood, and a heart as tender as a child's. He reared and educated a family of ten children, and left at his decease lands that at public executors' sale brought a very handsome sum of money. One tract, consisting of but eleven acres and a large mansion, located on the Philadelphia Turnpike, east of the Riverview Cemetery, was laid out into building lots by the executors and called " Maplewood." This alone brought the sum of $20,000.

George W. Talley acquired substantially all of his property by his own energy, industry and indomitable will. Truly is "a workman known by his chips." Here again have we the proof of the adage, that greatness is inherited and not acquired in the schools. In the spring of 1888, the subject of our sketch made a visit of pleasure to Florida, and shortly after his arrival there, was stricken with pneumonia, and to quote his language, he was "a thousand miles from home, and sick." He was brought home, but survived but a few days, and passed away in his 81st year, at his home on the Shellpot. In life he was strong in body, strong in character, and strong in his attachment to his family.

"Lives of great men all remind us,
We can make our lives sublime,
And departing leave behind us,
Footprints on the sands of time."

JOHN TALLEY was born November 15, 1813. He married Sarah A. Stidham in the early part of 1853, she having descended on the paternal side from one of the early Swedish families that settled at Christiana, about 1638. He did not marry until nearly 40 years of age, and never left the home of his birth, but when he married he took his wife to reside with his parents, who were quite in years, and needed his help in managing the farm, which was located near the Shellpot,

Soon after coming of age, or a little before, he, like most of the energetic young men who resided close to the Delaware River, provided himself with net and boat, and in early springtime engaged in shad fishing on the river. This business gave both enjoyment and excitement, while it at the same time very signally increased the account at bank, for shad fresh from the Delaware commanded no small price. Many a farm in the vicinity of the river was paid for by this lucrative business of fishing.

As John Talley resided at home while fishing, his outlay was small, and the profits of the season were loaned at interest, and became the foundation of his present fortune, which to-day amounts to no meagre sum. He is considered by his neighbors to be a man of "full and plenty." He is the owner of many mortgages, and his income from interest is much more than the profits from the farm.

He has had large experience in loaning money, and knows a good thing at sight. He is remarkably keen in a business transaction, and his judgment is quick and reliable.

Even now, at the age of 86 years, he attends to his many financial transactions. He is quite a temperate man, caring nothing for intoxicants.

At his father's death he purchased the home farm of 60 acres from the other heirs. This farm, although not extensive, has been conducted in a most neat and careful manner. Thus demonstrating that, had his living depended on agriculture, he would have been not only an extensive but an exceedingly prosperous farmer. He chose a more profitable business for his main occupation. Being a Talley, he also drifted into Cherry Island, and owns several acres there.

He, like his brother, George W. Talley, inherited a strong muscular system, it having been said of him in his youth that he scarcely knew his strength. Born and reared as he was without the proper advantages of schools, his career has been one of wonderful success. He is fond of amusement, and is quite companionable. He has a keen sense of humor, and enjoys a joke, even when about himself.

He keeps in close touch with all public questions, and is rarely found on the wrong side. He is firm in his convictions, and is not easily swayed from his opinions. He usually casts his vote at important elections, yet has never sought office or dallied with politics.

Rigidly honest himself, he despises dishonesty in every form. He will long be remembered for his strength, courage, endurance and material prosperity.

HANNAH TALLEY was born July 25, 1816. She married, in 1845, Jacob R. Weldin, who was born June 12, 1821. He was the son of Isaac and Hannah (Tussey) Weldin. Isaac was the son of Jacob, Jacob was the son of Isaac, and Isaac was the son of Jacob Weldin, who came to America about 1700.

Jacob, upon the death of his father, purchased the homestead from the other heirs, and he and his wife Hannah (Talley) Weldin began farming on the 40-acre place, adding to the small profits of the farm many dollars made annually by shad fishing on the Delaware River. The services of his wife now became very important in the matter of finding a good market for the catch of fish. Jacob R. Weldin was always fond of the sea, having sailed in his youth in the coasting trade from Boston to Southern ports. He was accidentally thrown overboard several times into the ocean, but was always rescued by others of his crew. In after life he never lost his attachment for the ocean, but made annual visits to the shore to enjoy the old sights, and to take a dip into the briny waves.

Hannah (Talley) Weldin was the youngest child of her parents, and was of a very jovial disposition, and quite a favorite with the young people of her day. Jacob and Hannah after marriage were very hospitable, and enjoyed the company of their friends and neighbors. They were both of exceeding good temper, and all business about the farm and home moved along smoothly and in perfect unison. It was not long before the profits from fishing and from the little farm began to accumulate, and money was on hand to loan.

Jacob soon began to long for larger fields to conquer. The opportunity came about 1861. The very large but impoverished farm of Albanus C. Logan, consisting of 220 acres, one mile from Wilmington, and called "Chestnut Hill," located near the Blue Ball estate, was offered for sale, at about $75.00 per acre. The price named seemed small, but the farm looked large and dilapidated. Mr. Weldin being cautious, and as a wise man, he advised with his friends, and finally made the purchase, and settled down to business, as an active, thrifty farmer. As he looked back in after years, he said that he had nothing to regret on account of the purchase. He lived to see this extensive level tract of land, under his good management, produce abundance of hay, grain and other products usual to a large farm. It was later turned into a dairy farm, and the milk product was retailed in Wilmington. He, too, found out that high lands needed the succor of the marsh lands. He gradually acquired land in Cherry Island, until at his death he owned 50 acres there. He was a man much interested in public improvement, and was glad to see the coming of railroads, and the building of good highways, bridges and similar improvements.

He was for many years a Director in the Cherry Island

Marsh Company, and gave much of his time to the affairs of the company. He was for over twenty years Treasurer of Mt. Pleasant M. E. Church. He and his wife could be seen almost every Sunday driving a distance of three miles behind a well fed, active horse, to the church of their choice. They were consistent and generous in their church work. Many times did Jacob R. Weldin advance the minister's salary, and run the chance as to being repaid. Jacob and Hannah lived an honorable and harmonious life, and from this came a full measure of prosperity and happiness. The combining by marriage of two such minds as those of Jacob and Hannah Weldin, could not result otherwise than in the greatest of success. They both were stout and of full stature. They were robust in body, and noble in character, and consequently were fitted for large undertakings. Being very plain people, they naturally detested all shams and false pretenses.

Jacob R. Weldin died after a short illness, on December 24, 1891, and his wife, in a very short time, on January 5, 1892, followed him. They rest peacefully at Newark Union Cemetery, kindly remembered by the whole community.

J. HENDERSON TALLEY is the son of Rev. John Talley and his second wife, Ann (Henderson) Talley. He descended by his maternal line from Col. Major Henderson, of Revolutionary fame, who resided at Dividing Creek, Cumberland County, N. J. Henderson Talley is a person of learning and of considerable research. He has been associated with educational matters the greater part of his active life. He taught school for a number of years in Brandywine Hundred, and in this way became widely known among the people of the hundred. Later he was engaged in farming, but now, at the age of 75 years, leads a retired life at West Chester, Pa. He and his wife on December 30, 1896, celebrated their "golden wedding," many relatives and friends being present. He has always taken great interest in the family history, and has collected much valuable *data*.

His mother having died, leaving him a child, he was largely reared by his stepmother, Ann (Hollingsworth) Talley.

Fortunately she was a woman of rare attainments and of wealth. She was the daughter of Col. Henry Hollingsworth, of Maryland, who led his regiment in a skirmish with the British in Maryland during the War with that nation. Ann H. Talley was prominent in business affairs, and conducted a plantation of 500 acres in Cecil County, Md., at the same time she resided in Delaware, as the wife of Rev. John Talley. She was a strong advocate of temperance, and a great religious worker. It is said that she was one of the most able women that ever resided in the "Old Hundred." She was a powerful platform speaker, and possibly excelled her very able husband in this line of work. She was the owner of slaves by inheritance, but upon her marriage with John Talley she set them all free. J. Henderson Talley says of her, that "she was a good woman, and to her I owe in a great measure what I have been and what I am."

There is considerable talent in the descendants of J. Henderson Talley. A grandson, Rev. Francis M. Dowlin, graduated at the High School at West Chester, and was awarded a *gold medal* for oratory. He is now passing through his graduating year at Dickinson College, Pa., and has an appointment under the Philadelphia Conference at Washington Borough, Lancaster County, Pa.

WILLIAM D. TALLEY (*138*), the son of Adam Talley, resided when first married on the westerly corner of the Kellam and Foulk Roads, at Talley's Corner. He was then engaged in the blacksmith and wheelwright business. His eyesight becoming impaired, he went into farming, at first on the farm devised to him by his father at Talley's Corner. Later he removed to Maryland, and there conducted the farming business. He afterwards removed to Delaware County, Pa., and resided for years at the village of Trainor. He and his wife, Elizabeth (Bullock) Talley, reared a large family. William D. Talley was a man of fine intellect and of fine character, and was devoted to the Methodist Church, and lived and died within its fold. He was a class leader for a number of years. He was buried at Bethel Cemetery, in Brandywine Hundred, November, 1882. He was one of the descendants of Thomas Talley (who died in 1818); and was in his early life a part of the congregation of the old Bethel Church ; and was highly respected by those who came in contact with him.

THOMAS G. RAWSON (*282*) is the son of Warren and Jemima (Cartmell) Rawson, who were married at Brandy-wine Village, Del., in 1810. There were six children from this marriage. Three died in youth, and three survived, viz : Regina, born August 26, 1815 ; Thomas G., born January 9, 1823 ; and William, born April 1, 1825. The husband, War-ren Rawson, died suddenly in Wilmington, June 25, 1825, at the age of 40 years. Mrs. Rawson was left with one son scarcely two and a half years old and a baby less than two months old, and with little means at hand. Warren was buried at the Baptist Church Cemetery on King Street, Wil-mington. Jemima died August 31, 1846, and was buried at the Newark Union Cemetery, Brandywine Hundred. The son Thomas was then left in poverty, with nothing but pluck and energy as his fortune.

Captain William Rawson, a mariner and an English-man, married, April 14, 1781, Lydia, the widow of Peter Woolbough ; her maiden name was Morton. This marriage is recorded at the Swedes' Church, Wilmington, Del. War-ren Rawson was a son of William and Lydia Rawson, and was a ship carpenter at Wilmington. He became acquainted with his future wife by being a boarder at the house of her mother, Susanna Cartmell, widow of tall Thomas Cart-mell, who resided before his death above Quarryville, Del. Susanna was a daughter of David and Catharine Talley, of one of the older generations of Brandywine Hundred Talleys. Thomas and Susanna Cartmell had four children. Thomas Cartmell died in 1804 at his home at Quarryville.

In 1846 Thomas G. Rawson began work at the Baldwin Locomotive Works at Philadelphia, and later became very successful in fitting up the '' connecting rods'' of engines. In 1859 the work was '' farmed out,'' and Mr. Rawson took charge of the '' connecting rod'' branch of the business, with men and apprentices under him. Through skillful management he made money rapidly for himself and also for the firm.

He remained with this firm twenty-three years, and when he retired, in 1869, he had become one of their most valuable men. He retired with a competency, which has been very largely increased by fortunate investments. He has always led a most abstemious life, using neither stimulants nor tobacco. He has been for fifty years a member of the Tenth Baptist Church at Philadelphia, also has been a member of Penn Lodge, I. O. O. F., of the same city, for fifty-five years.

We are pleased to record Thomas G. Rawson as one of the honest, able and wealthy members of the David Talley branch of our family.

THOMAS W. JOHNSON (*613*) was born at Johnson's Corner, Delaware County, Pa., January 7, 1833, being the son of Eliza Ann and William Johnson. The Johnson ancestry, so far as it is known, dates back to a time previous to the Revolutionary contest, when one emigrated from Scotland to America, married here, and having a family of small children, enlisted in the Continental army and fell at the battle of White Plains.

Robert, his youngest son, was "bound" in Christiana Hundred, Del., to a man named Brown. What became of the other children is, as yet, a profound mystery. Robert married, in 1794, Margaret Webster, sister of Clark Webster. The names of their children and their marriages were as follows, viz: William to Eliza A. Talley; Robert to Mary Talley; John to Brandling Clark; David to Sarah Barnet; Harriett to Harman Talley; Anna to James Grubb Hanby; Margaret to Samuel Hance; and Mary to Anthony Bigger Carey, first, and David Gilbert, second. One son (Thomas) never married.

William Johnson in 1832 came into possession of the farm of 190 acres at Johnson's Corner. The farm is now owned by Thomas W. Johnson, the only son of William and Eliza A. Johnson. Felspar was accidentally found on this farm as early as 1848. This was the earliest discovery of felspar on the east side of the Brandywine.

Samuel Stockton was the first manufacturer of artificial teeth in America. He was succeeded in this business by S. S. White, of Philadelphia. About 1848 Mr. White, who had been on a visit to the Dixon Quarries in Christiana Hundred, stopped, on his homeward trip, at the house of his relative, William Johnson, of Concord Township, Pa. He told Mr. Johnson of the purpose of his visit to the Dixon Quarries, and showed him a sample of felspar. Mr. Johnson said, "Why, there is plenty of that kind of rock down along my run." He took a grubbing hoe and went to the run, and was soon back with a basketful of the white rock. Mr. White soon thereafter contracted with Mr. Johnson for all the felspar then known to be on the farm.

Thus began the felspar business of the great Brandy-wine Summit Quarries. The beginning was made near the spring in the easterly part of the "Camp Meeting Woods." Teeth made from this rock were exhibited at the great Expositions in London and in Paris, at each of which they were awarded the premium. Thousands of tons of this rock, since 1850, have been shipped to Trenton, N. J., and to East Liverpool, Ohio, for pottery uses. The finer portion is selected at the quarry for the manufacture of teeth. This higher grade is sold at $30 per ton in Philadelphia and in other places.

It is scarcely necessary to say that the famous "Brandywine Summit Camp Meeting Grounds" are a part of this farm. The Camp Meeting began here about 1866, and increased in size and in importance year by year, until a few years ago the association became incorporated, and many permanent wooden cottages are to be found here. These cottages are occupied weeks before the Camp Meeting proper begins, by families from Wilmington and elsewhere. Year after year many find recreation, rest and comfort in this beautiful grove.

Thomas W. Johnson attended the Union School of Concord Township until he was seventeen years old. He next spent one term at Pine Grove Select School, near West Chester; then a term at Norristown. He closed his school days at the Charlotteville (New York) Methodist Seminary.

At the age of twenty he began teaching school at Mt.

Pleasant, in Brandywine Hundred. He next taught one year at Brandywine Village. Then came the very successful term of three years at the Shellpot School. He was especially proud of his record at this last school, and was much interested in his geometry class. He introduced many studies here that belonged to the boarding rather than to the district school. He was very earnest in whatever he undertook, even in playing ball at the noon hour.

He married Sarah Poole, in March, 1857, taught about one year longer, then, at the earnest solicitation of his father, moved to the home farm. This moving business brought health and wealth; but some profession, possibly the law, was deprived of what might have been a very able member. His mental and physical energy equipped him for almost any position in life.

In his youth he was a *school* boy, in early manhood a *school* teacher, and in after years a *school* trustee, having served on the official board of his township for thirty years. What is still more remarkable, seven of his nine children became, for a time, school teachers.

Mr. Johnson is very strongly in favor of the temperance cause, and is an advocate of the higher order of politics. He is also quite public spirited, and fondly cherishes the hope that he may see a trolley line running between Wilmington and West Chester, along the Wilmington and Great Valley Turnpike.

Mr. Johnson and his very genial companion have reared a large and interesting family, six of whom are married and occupy prominent positions in life. Truly may it be said, that the fine old mansion at Johnson's Corner has shed a healthful influence over the affairs of Concord Township.

ELIZA J. TALLEY (**500**) married, February 22, 1866, George W. Weldin, who was born November 7, 1840. George was the son of George and Beulah Weldin; George, the father, was the son of Jacob, Jacob was the son of Isaac, and Isaac was the son of Jacob Weldin the first. The last named Jacob landed in this country about 1700.

George W. Weldin's career has been so interwoven

with the Talley family that it is not out of place to mention him in this book. Being a staunch Methodist from boyhood, he was, of necessity, thrown much in the society of the Talleys, and finally married a Talley. Mr. Weldin, although a most successful farmer, is best known by his temperance and religious work. Temperance and religion are "hand and hand" with each other, hence George W. Weldin, being a consistent churchman, could not be other than a great temperance worker.

He has always been passionately fond of music, and he and his very interesting family, when in good tune, are able alone to give a very entertaining concert. He is also a local preacher in the church, and fills many appointments in the absence of the minister in charge. He is earnest, conscientious and faithful in all church labor, and is not a dry-weather Christian, but equally energetic in sunshine or in storm.

He was a patriot in the dark days of 1861. Having a widowed mother to support, he could not join the three-years' men, but joined the nine-months' regiment, and drilled at nights and worked at home during the day. They were "minute men"—men ready to go on a minute's warning. The momentous time came in the midst of the cherry season. George W. Weldin was over at neighbor Miller's, assisting in cherry picking, and well up towards the top of a huge tree, with a basket partly filled with cherries, when suddenly a member of his regiment was seen coming up from Wilmington at a full "double quick," calling out as he ran, "Come on, George—come on ! We are ordered out !"

The patriotic George slid, jumped or fell down the tree—no one at this day seems to know definitely which. Over across fields he ran, with his neighbor's cherries in his hand. These he unconsciously threw down somewhere about his mother's house ; and in less than one hour had joined his regiment in Wilmington, three miles from his home. Putnam left his plow in the middle of the field, and has been immortalized in history ever since. George took his neighbor's cherries to his own home, and no one, not even Mr. Miller, has given him praise for it.

Cherries or no cherries, he went to do his duty at Fort Delaware, and assisted in guarding ten thousand Confederate prisoners ; and stood ready to perform any service that his country might place upon him. George W. Weldin never knew anything else than to do his duty, and to go wherever it called him.

JOHN SMITH TALLEY (*468*), is the first son of George W. and Lavinia (Beeson) Talley. He was born in Brandywine Hundred, Del., near what is now known as Shellpot Park, on May 23, 1840. He married Mary E. Beeson, January 17, 1867. She was reared near his early home, and was the daughter of Edward and Leah (Weldin) Beeson. His father being a man of great energy and activity, and John being the eldest son, he was thrown, at an early age, into the work about the farm, often filling a man's place.

His early education was obtained at the Shellpot District School, but mostly during the winter months. At the age of seventeen he passed a four-months' term at Barton's School, at Village Green, Delaware County, Pa. The next two winters he spent at the Upland Normal School, at Upland, Pa. The following winter he took a six-months' term at the Fort Edward Institute, on the Upper Hudson. He was accompanied here by William A. Talley, Daniel S. Ferguson and George L. Cloud, from Delaware. He returned from school in the spring of 1861, and finished Thomas W. Johnson's last term of teaching at the Shellpot School. He taught the same school for one year longer, and a spring term at Mt. Pleasant School in 1862.

In July, 1862, he made due preparation for another term at Fort Edward, with a view of entering Yale College possibly a little later on. In the early part of August he was arranging his trunk preparatory to his departure for the school on the Hudson. The war then assuming such vast proportions, he concluded that it would be better to assist in settling the war, and to get his education afterwards. He, with many other young men of his hundred, joined the First Delaware Battery, a select company of 150 men, under the command of Captain Benjamin Nields, of Wilmington. He

remained in the army until the close of the war, and was discharged in Arkansas, and formally mustered out early in July,
1865, at Wilmington.

He entered the battery as a private, was made Sergeant, and soon was promoted to Orderly Sergeant. During
the last year of the war he was commissioned Second Lieutenant. Perhaps no soldier served more faithfully than did
he. An incident may be cited : During the New York riots
of 1863, the battery was ordered there to assist in preserving
peace. Returning to Washington by the P. W. & B. R. R.,
they made a short stop at the Wilmington depot, to permit
relatives and friends to have a short visit with them. A great
temptation was thus held out for the soldier to linger awhile
with loved ones. But John Smith Talley, William A. Talley,
and scarcely a dozen more, were on hand promptly when the
train arrived in Washington, while many remained over until
morning at Wilmington. General Barry, in command at
Washington, gave immediate orders, that as soon as sufficient
men arrived in camp to care for the horses and guns, that the
faithful few should have a furlough for 48 hours.

After the war John Smith Talley took a prospecting
trip in the West, and located at Litchfield, Ill. He engaged in
the drug business, and did the largest trade in this line in the
town. Being progressive he did not permit the store to absorb
all his time, but in odd moments he was out among the enter-
prising men devising ways and means to extend the industries
of the city. In this way he engaged with many others in
sinking a coal shaft near the city line. As the coal business
enlarged, the drug business was crowded out, and the store
was sold. He was fortunate in associating with men of business foresight, for the company soon purchased mines and
coal lands in the great bituminous coal region, between Terre
Haute and Greencastle, Indiana.

The subject of this sketch seeing the vast prospects of
the Indiana fields, decided to locate at Terre Haute, and be in
the "midst of the fray." He moved there in 1877, and
assisted in the organization of the Coal Bluff Mining Company
of Indiana, with headquarters at Terre Haute. He soon
became the leading spirit in the company, and through his

energy its business has extended almost all over the Northern and Northwestern parts of the United States. He manages coal mines at Perth and Pratt, also the celebrated Block coal mines at Clay City. The bituminous mines at Fontanet, and Coal Bluff in Vigo County, are of vast magnitude. In these mines are used the great mining machines of the Jeffrey and the Whitcomb Mining Machine Companies. These machines are operated hundreds of feet under ground by power from air compressors on the surface. The annual output of coal amounts to 750,000 tons. There are employed about these mines 1000 men. The companies control about 1500 acres of land, much of which is underlaid with coal.

He owns 100 acres of building lots at Muncie, Indiana, and jointly with his brother, George A. Talley, owns two tracts in Delaware; one being 107 acres in Cherry Island Marsh, Wilmington, the other a farm on the Edgemoor Road, Brandywine Hundred.

The amount of his railroad travel is simply enormous. No distance appears too great when business or duty is at the far end. He is prompt in meeting his engagements, having acquired this faculty from army life, and from meeting trains.

He is President of the Mine Operators' Association of the State of Indiana, and always advises a conciliatory course towards the laborer. He is a Director of the Terre Haute Trust Company; a Trustee of the Young Men's Christian Association; a member of the Indiana Division of the Loyal Legion; a Master Mason; and a very active supporter of the Methodist Church. He has recently been appointed a lay delegate, from the State of Indiana, to the General Conference of his Church, which is to sit in Chicago in 1900.

His energy may be judged of when we find him President of the following named corporations: The Coal Bluff Mining Co., The Western Indiana Mining Co., The Standard Block Coal Co., The Chicago and Indiana Block Coal Co., The Surbaugh Drill and Tool Co., The Indiana Powder Co., and The Independent Powder Co. He seems to be as profuse in corporation matters as was William Talley of old, with his many farms more than a century ago, along the Foulk Road.

John Smith Talley is as generous as he has been pros-

perous. Thousands of dollars are donated by him to churches
and other charitable uses. Whatever he is to-day he has
become through his own industry, and from his progressive
ideas, in spite of his education having been curtailed three
years by the war. He was prompt and firm as a soldier, and
since has been prompt and firm in business. He *sometimes*
filled a man's place in boyhood, but in later years he has filled
it *always*.

HANNAH TALLEY (*454*) married John M. C.
Prince, October 9, 1862. She is the daughter of Lewis and
Elizabeth (Zebley) Talley. Hannah was born March 12, 1841,
on her father's farm along the Foulk Road. John M. C.
Prince is the son of Adam and Charlotte (Hanby) Prince.
Adam was the son of John and Sara Prince, and was born
July 2, 1800. Adam had a brother named Isaiah, born
March 12, 1797. John, the father of Adam, was the son of
Adam, and was born November 5, 1760. The last named
Adam was the first settler in Brandywine Hundred, of the
Prince (Prentz) name. Adam, who was born in 1800, had
two half-brothers, John and Abner. It is stated that they
were both doctors and died in early manhood.

The Prince family is an old and respected one. They
have continuously resided on the present farm of 100 acres,
adjoining Carpenter's Station, on the B. and O. R. R., since
1762. At this date the greater portion of this land was purchased from Edward Cloud, the son of John Cloud, John
being the son of Jeremiah Cloud. This is a fine dairy farm,
but has other and greater value as sites for country homes, it
being elevated and decidedly healthful.

The present Prince family have always been considered
as having a large account at bank, in addition to their lands,
and there is no doubt but what they realize much more income
from the money at interest than they do from the farm.

Adam Prince (of later years) died on July 7, 1878,
leaving his farm by will to his son John ; also leaving to the
Trustees of Bethel Church the sum of $500, to assist in pay-
ing off the debts of the church. His widow still survives, at
the age of 87 years.

Hannah (Talley) Prince was musical in very early girlhood, being one of the "musical" Lewis Talley family. Her voice was *contralto*, while her sister Mary's was *soprano*. Lewis Talley and his family, a few years ago, were able to give a fine concert without other assistance. Hannah still aids in the choir at Bethel Church and finds great enjoyment in this work. She has been a member of this church since fourteen years of age, and her purse strings are easily untied when the church is in need of funds. She gives liberally and cheerfully, and is broad-minded and hospitable.

REV. JOHN T. SIMMONS (*663*) is the son of Margaret (Talley) Simmons and John Simmons. They resided in Delaware until 1836, when they moved to Ohio. John T. Simmons entered the Methodist ministry in Ohio. In 1855 he went to reside in Iowa, and then united with the Iowa Conference. He joined the 28th Iowa Regiment during the Civil War, became its Chaplain, and served with his regiment the full three-years' term. He was in the siege of Vicksburg, in the Red River campaign, and with Sheridan in the Shenandoah Valley ; and was in thirteen different engagements.

In 1852 he married Martha Arganbright, of Ohio. In 1894 he married his second wife, Jennie S. Bryant, of Birmingham, Iowa. He is quite an able minister, having filled some of the best appointments in the Iowa Conference. He has served two terms as Presiding Elder, and was a delegate to the General Conference of his church, in 1872. On his paternal side he descends from the Simmons family, who lived near the Brandywine many years ago. On the maternal side he comes from the Talley and the Grubb lines. Although miles distant from the old Talley haunts, he still has a lingering affection for the sturdy pioneers who centuries ago dwelt here. He is willing to do his part in preserving his ancestry.

THOMAS LEA TALLEY (*167*) was the son of Curtis Talley, and also a grandson of William Talley, on the Brandywine, and was born in 1812, the year of his grandfather's death. He was remarkably strong and agile in his younger days, although not so large in stature as was his brother, Eli B. Talley. He was a man of honor and of excellent judgment, and was many times selected by the Courts to fill positions requiring both ability and clear judgment. He held many local offices, and discharged the duties thereof faithfully, and never avoided the performance of a public duty, although not in any sense an office seeker. He was Collector of Internal Revenue after the Civil War. Thomas Lea Talley was a leader in his party without being offensively such. His leaning was towards the Methodist Church. He died in May, 1882, and was interred at the Bethel M. E. Cemetery. Being exceedingly kind to his family, he was always ready to lend a helping hand. No generation is likely to be overcrowded with men of the ability of Thomas Lea Talley.

SAMUEL M. TALLEY (*132*) was born December 27, 1815, and married Sarah Aldred Day, the daughter of Joseph Day, in 1840. Samuel was born on his father's homestead, in Brandywine Hundred, southeast of Perry's Hotel, and was educated partly at the old " Talley School House." He was very apt at school and was prompt in everything he undertook. He studied far into the night by the glow of the "tallow dip." When his mother concluded that he needed sleep more than he did to solve a particularly difficult problem, she would take away the light. Often the boy was so intent on his study that he would linger awhile, stirring the coals on the hearth for *more light.*

Samuel, being a good mathematician, studied surveying with Isaac Grubb, and did some work laying out lands. He taught school three winters at Forwood's School House. He built his future home in 1841, and moved to it in the fall of that year. His father dying in 1839, the 100-acre farm was divided, 50 acres passing to each of the sons, Hezekiah and Samuel M. Samuel M. Talley held many small offices. He was a member of the Board of Trustees that erected the *New* Bethel M. E. Church, and gave largely to the building fund.

DR. JAMES ELY TALLEY (*909*) was born July 22, 1864, near Kennett Square, Chester County, Pa. He attended the public schools of Chester and Delaware counties, and spent two years at the Millersville State Normal School. In 1883 he entered the Ann Arbor, Michigan, High School, and being graduated there in 1885, he entered the University of Michigan in the fall of the same year. He pursued the studies required for the degree of Bachelor of Arts, elected biological and chemical work with the study of medicine in view, and spent the summer of 1888 in European study and travel. Receiving his A. B. in 1889, in the same fall he entered the Medical Department of the University of Pennsylvania, and was graduated with the class of 1892. After serving as resident physician for more than two years at the Presbyterian, Children's and Philadelphia Hospitals and the Infirmary for Nervous Diseases, he settled in Philadelphia, where he has been ever since in active practice of his profession.

THOMAS MILLER TALLEY (**450**). son of Lewis Talley the singer, was a remarkably bright lad in his youth. His eyes were weak from birth. As soon as he was of proper age he attended school, but soon his eyes began to fail, and when about fourteen years old he became entirely blind ; and ever since he has gone through life in darkness. Although the world is *dark* to him, yet is his intellect *bright* and his feelings most buoyant.

He is happy, not on account of his condition, but in his good feelings for the world about him. He is most industrious, and can pick cherries from the tree, load hay in the field, and work with carpenter tools. Being decidedly musical, he can play almost all ordinary musical instruments. He goes where necessary upon the highways, not with a horse, but on foot, and mostly unattended. He has walked miles to church after night, and across railroad tracks, with nothing to assist him but his staff, and his implicit confidence that the whole world about him is his friend, and will not harm him. His memory is his daily register of events, and rarely fails him.

NELSON L. TALLEY (**522**), the son of John R. and Eliza Talley, was born April 7, 1852. He married Lavania Simons, daughter of Charles Simons, Sr., November 13, 1873. His father died in 1890, and was buried at Mt. Pleasant Cemetery. He left his farm, by will, to his son Nelson, the latter to pay certain legacies specified therein. In 1891 Nelson moved to this farm, the home of his birth, and at once began the improvement of the same. He spent about $2000 in the rebuilding of the house. He doubled the capacity of the barn and other outbuildings, and had an artesian well bored to the depth of 106 feet, which was fitted up with a windmill.

After this he began the betterment of the land, and in a short time he had 30 acres of his 56-acre farm in fine condition for the raising of garden crops. The hay-fields were not neglected, but were so fertilized that often a crop of four tons of new-made hay have been cut to the acre. Figuratively speaking, the desert was made to blossom as the rose. Fine vegetables from these gardens are wholesaled at Chester and Wilmington ; and retailed from his stand in the Eighth Street Market at Wilmington, which he has occupied for over twelve years, and also from his stand at Sixth and King Streets, which he has occupied for twenty years.

During the winter and spring he has in use in his hot-bed gardens about one thousand sashes. Water-pipes have been laid from the water-supply tank through these gardens, and lateral pipes have at intervals been branched off and adjusted with hydrant attachments, much the same as a water-works system in a small town. The hot-beds are thus irrigated, and early vegetables are raised according to the most modern system. About ten men and boys are engaged in these gardens through most of the year. Ten head of horses are in use on this farm. Mr. Talley, being up to date in his line of business, uses modern machinery and appliances, and his work is done by system. He is a moral as well as a working man. Six days' labor, and then one for rest and religious devotion, is his motto. This rule is religiously adhered to by him, and never violated unless on account of some overpowering necessity. He joined the Methodist Society at the Newark Union Church fourteen years ago. He is a steward as well as a local preacher in that church. His donations to the church are exceedingly liberal.

It can be truthfully said that Mr. Talley is an industrious, thrifty, religious and progressive man. This comprehends all, and constitutes complete manhood.

REV. JAMES WALTER TALLEY (*1236*), the son of James Wilson and Margaret E. Talley, was born August 22, 1871. He connected himself with the Methodist Church when fifteen years old, and first felt a call to the ministry the following year.

He attended the public school until seventeen years old. During the last four years of this period—having had such teachers as Harvey Whiteman, now a lawyer in Wilmington, Del., and Miss Lizzie Bigger, who afterwards taught and studied in Germany—he was kept in advance of the regular classes and pursued some studies not regularly taught in the public schools. In 1890 he attended "The Select School" in Wilmington of which Miss Rachel Bigger was principal. In the school year of 1891–1892 he was a student in the Wilmington Conference Academy, Dover, Del. Later, he spent one year in Drew Theological Seminary, Madison, N. J. After this he took up a Correspondence Course with a University in Chicago, Ill., where he received the degree of Master of Arts.

James Walter Talley was received on trial by the Wilmington Conference of the Methodist Episcopal Church, March, 1897, and was admitted into full membership in that body, March, 1899. He now holds an appointment under this Conference at Bozman, Maryland. He is deserving of great credit for his energy in preparing himself for his chosen work.

ELI BALDWIN TALLEY (*162*) was a man of magnificent presence. He was more than six feet tall, and large proportionately in breadth of shoulders. He was a man of marked natural ability and excellent judgment, and, like his body, his heart was large and generous, as is so often the case with men of generous physical attributes. Having lived among his neighbors of Brandywine Hundred all his life, he was highly respected by them, and his counsel and advice were freely sought and as freely given.

Mr. Talley was always interested in everything per-
taining to his native hundred, and being a leader in his party,
was ever active in local politics. He never was an office
holder, in the ordinary acceptance of the term, although he
held many small offices of trust within the gift of his neighbors. His domestic relations were extremely pleasant and
cordial. In fact, through his whole life he was kind, generous and true.

HENRY GRUBB (*777*) is the fourth son of Joseph
and Ann Grubb, and was born February 10, 1846. He was
reared on a farm and received a limited education in the common schools of Putnam County, Ind. At the age of sixteen
he enlisted in the Twenty-third Regiment Indiana Volunteers,
or better known as the First Regiment Indiana Heavy Artillery. He was under the command of Generals Butler, Banks
and Canby, in the Department of the Gulf. It is claimed that
he was the youngest soldier who enlisted in Parke County,
Ind. He served his full term of three years, and returned
home in 1865.

He entered the Waveland Academy and received a fair
education, and afterwards taught school for nine years in
Parke County. On March 28, 1875, he married Euphony E.
Harney, the daughter of John M. Harney. To this union
five children were born. The eldest daughter died in infancy.
The remaining children are, Miram M., Carrie, Marion H.
and Clellie A.

In 1882 he was elected County Surveyor of Parke
County, and has served as Deputy Surveyor for many years
since. He also engaged in the lumber and stave business. In
1895 he manufactured the staves for the largest oak cask in
the world. It is thirty feet long, and was manufactured in
Calhoun County, Miss. This cask will be on exhibition at
the World's Fair at Paris in 1900.

Mr. Grubb is also engaged in farming, and has a farm
of 250 acres. He attended the Grand Army Reunion at
Philadelphia, Pa., in 1899, and while visiting among his relatives on the highlands of Delaware, he accidentally came in
contact with the Talley History. He at once placed himself

in the way to secure a book, and in other ways demonstrated his kindness and generosity. Manly ideas and principles accompany Mr. Grubb even when he is hundreds of miles from home.

ROBERT TALLEY (*452*) was born August 29, 1837. His parents were Lewis and Elizabeth (Zebley) Talley. Robert was deformed from birth in one limb, and although using crutches, he worked about his father's farm until he was fifteen years old. Samuel Hewes, a shoemaker of Chelsea, was coming home from Wilmington, by way of the Foulk Road, with a load of leather, and found the Lonkum Run so much swollen by freshet that there was danger in crossing it. He remained over night at the house of neighbor Lewis Talley. During the evening Lewis asked Mr. Hewes how he thought Robert would do for a shoemaker. The reply was that he could soon tell if the boy would come to his place and stay awhile. Robert went with Mr. Hewes, and ever after he has "stuck to his last." He served four years in learning his trade.

When the war broke out in 1861, Robert, being compelled to shoulder his crutches, could not shoulder the musket. He, being at this time a full-fledged "shoebuilder," served his country by making shoes. While his brother and thousands of other young men were serving the Nation in the field, Robert kept "pegging away" at home. He made shoes for Col. Henry McComb and other government contractors, and turned out more than five hundred pairs a year by hand. The government furnished the upper leather, cut out ready for use, and the sole leather was weighed out in the roll. Robert's business was to put the soles on these shoes at sixty cents a pair. Many times were shoes condemned by the contractors, but Robert does not remember that any were turned back to him bearing the big letter "C" stamped on the sole. He continued this government work until peace was declared.

He married Emily Beeson, daughter of Robinson and Rebecca (Talley) Beeson, March 8, 1866, and ever since he has resided in the country. There he has found peace, plenty and happiness. Robert does whatever his hand findeth to do. He, in addition to his shoe business, repairs clocks, having learned this trade from Jesse Kendall. He also puts in and repairs pumps for those needing such work in his neighborhood. He, although afflicted with lameness, has "hoed his own row" in life, and "kept the wolf from the door," and has a fund "laid away for a rainy day."

He has been a member of the Bethel M. E. Church for thirty-four years, on the official board for twenty-six years, and has acted for many years as secretary to the Board of Stewards. He is musical and plays the organ at the church when needed. He has served his State in various ways in holding elections. He has been clerk and voters' assistant, and now holds an appointment as Assistant Register under the Governor's commission for two years. Robert is bright, industrious and thrifty. Although afflicted and not possessed of *broad acres*, it is difficult to find one with a broader smile of contentment, or one who meets the issues of life more cheerfully and philosophically than he.

JAMES WILSON TALLEY (**527**), son of Nelson L. and Rachel Ann (Wilson) Talley, resides in Brandywine Hundred, about one-half a mile west of the Newark Union Church. He resides on and owns a well-cultivated farm of about 50 acres. He is engaged in general farming, but prides himself in raising fine fruits and vegetables. When driving past his farm, one cannot help admiring his neat home and the well-kept grounds surrounding it. Mr. Talley is a modest man, not caring to have his many virtues brought before the public in a sketch. But his liberality in supporting our book, and his kindly and encouraging manner, entitle him to a word of commendation at our hands.

It is proper to state here that J. Wilson Talley is a prosperous man, a kind parent, and a most excellent neighbor. He has been a member of Bethel M. E. Church for years, and is Treasurer of the Board of Stewards of that church. His son, James Walter Talley, is a minister in the Wilmington M. E. Conference. Mr. Talley and his wife, Margaret (Cartmell) Talley, conduct affairs very smoothly about this model home.

LEWIS F. TALLEY (**455**) was born March 26,

1843, and married, February 15, 1870, Mary Miller, daughter
of George L. and Jane Miller. He lives on the homestead,
late of his father, Lewis Talley. This land was purchased by
William Talley of old, in 1760, from the Pennsylvania Land
Company, and was part of the great Rockland Manor owned
by William Penn. This tract has never been out of the Talley
name, but has been continuously occupied by the Talleys since
1760. Prior to this last date they were known as vacant lands.

Associated with the possession of these lands are the
records, deeds and other valuable papers which established
many important matters connected with our genealogy. These
papers seem to have been transmitted from William to
Thomas, and from Thomas to Adam, and from Adam to
Lewis. This home must ever remain historic on account of
it being the depository of these all-important papers.

Lewis F. Talley now owns this tract of 60 acres, also
the house and a few acres occupied by his mother along the
Grubb Road. These lands are well set with small fruits, and
also with many cherry, pear and apple trees. As this fruit
must be marketed, he raises fine vegetables to give variety to
his salable products. He is a liberal supporter of the Bethel
M. E. Church, where he and his family attend. He has served
his School District in an official way for six years. The
musical talent of his father has descended to the son's children. They sing and play without apparent effort, it being
as natural for them to be musical as it is for the brook to
babble over its pebbly bed.

Mr. Talley has the distinction of having been appointed
by the Legislature of his State a Road Commissioner, by act
passed March 30, 1895. This act overthrew all prior modes
of caring for the roads of his hundred. He held under this
appointment until 1896. In this year he was, on account of
good and faithful services, elected by the people for the term
ending 1900.

He is true to the interests of his hundred, and carries
the respect of all about him, whether they be merely neighbors, or those interested in his official career. He was educated at the Forwood School, and has not retrograded since,
but is of the kind that grows and improves as experience

widens and opportunity unfolds itself. Lewis prefers to be known only as a *plain American citizen*. What a depth of meaning in these few simple words!

HENRY C. TALLEY (**519**) was born February 1, 1844, and married Anna Mary Mousley, the daughter of George K. and Ann Eliza Mousley, November 7, 1867. Henry learned the mason trade at an early age, and worked at it, by times, for several years. Before and after marriage he followed in the footsteps of his father, and fished for shad in the Delaware River. This was the real start in accumulating the funds to buy the farm. He recollects that in one year one thousand dollars was the result of three months on the river. It was not always thus, however.

He purchased of Jacob Jefferis the farm of 40 acres in Brandywine Hundred known as "The Hezekiah Talley Farm." This land was purchased many years ago by William Talley, father of Hezekiah. At the death of the latter, his brother, Samuel M. Talley, purchased this land, and afterwards sold it to Jefferis, and Jefferis sold it to Henry C. Talley. Henry moved to this farm in 1872.

In the great storm of 1878 Henry had the misfortune of having his barn partly blown down. This was discouraging to one who was struggling to pay for the recently-purchased home. His father kindly assisted him, and soon the barn was again erected. He has been able since to make many substantial improvements and to clear the land of all debt. He, like many others, raises large quantities of small fruits and fine vegetables for the Wilmington market. In this line he is greatly aided by his wife, who is a good marketer and exceedingly kind and hospitable.

He has served on the official board at the Point Breeze School for a number of years. He has been a member of the M. E. Church for thirty-five years, and has been Treasurer of the Board of Trustees of Bethel Church for about sixteen years. He most generously aids the church in a financial way, and even borrowed money at six per cent. interest a few years ago to help discharge the debt on the handsome new Bethel Church. Things have changed since, and perhaps

Henry could be the lender instead of the borrower, at the present time.

He is most prompt in the payment of all bills. A second demand is never allowed to be made. He is not an office seeker, but votes when it is necessary to elect good and true men to office. He is exceedingly temperate in all things, excepting in work, and has reared a prosperous family, and possesses a fine reputation among his neighbors. Correct living and prosperity are often found hand in hand. This is abundantly shown in the life work of Henry C. Talley.

THOMAS SMITH TALLEY (*495*) was the son of Penrose R. and Edith (Smith) Talley, of Brandywine Hundred, Del. He was born before daylight of the morning of November 13, 1833. This was the morning of the "falling stars." A physician was procured from Wilmington to attend Mrs. Talley, and as he drove along the stars were falling in all directions. It was so alarming that the physician instructed the family to say nothing of the event to his patient, who had no knowledge of the strange phenomenon. The child and its mother passed through this *phenominal* period without any injurious results so far as is known. This child became a very lively lad, and a man of great activity and usefulness. He married Sarah Elizabeth Hanby, March 13, 1862, she being a daughter of William and Sarah Ann (Pierce) Hanby. William was a son of William and Sarah Elizabeth (Webster) Hanby, the last named William being a son of Richard. This family of Hanbys resided on the farm northeast of Hanby's School House in Brandywine Hundred. Camp meeting was held in the woods on this farm for three different seasons.

William Hanby, the father of Mrs. Talley, had the following brothers and sisters: John, George, Richard, Clark, Margaret, Fannie, Isabella, Sarah and Susan. The first three brothers mentioned moved to the West, possibly to Ohio. William remained on the home farm and died there, and was buried at the Siloam M. E. Cemetery, he being connected with that church.

Thomas S. Talley, upon his marriage, moved to one of his father's farms about a mile west of Booth's Corner, Delaware County, Pa. This farm consisted of 52 acres, and was purchased of Joseph Larkin. Thomas and his wife were both exceedingly industrious, and it was not long before this home became one of prosperity, as well as of happiness. They raised large quantities of fine apples and peaches, and realized handsome sums for the same in the market. The consequence was, that new outbuildings and additions to the house were erected, and money was also in bank to loan. He many times requested his father to sell him the farm, but the answer was that it was time enough for him to get it when he, the father, was done with it.

Thomas S. Talley died in 1890, and survived his father eleven years. The father died in 1879, and devised the farm mentioned to Thomas, he paying some small sums on other accounts. Thomas now became the full owner of the farm that he had been the acting owner of for years. His industry did not abate on account of the devise to him of the farm. He did his hauling usually in the winter, and it is said that for one week he never saw his home in daylight. Overwork led to consumption, which caused his death.

He was a man of strict integrity, and a member of Bethel M. E. Church for thirty-five years, also a member of the Board of Stewards. He rarely missed a Sunday at church, unless through sickness. He gave the sum of $700 towards the building of the new Bethel Church, and aided it in many other ways. Thomas was both zealous in home and in church work, and was manly in all things.

WILLIAM A. TALLEY (*451*) was born April 2, 1836, in Brandywine Hundred, Del. He first attended the Forwood District School in 1843, Milton S. Barlow being his teacher. He went to school here during the winter terms until he was twenty years old. His school days ended with a term at Ft. Edward, on the Hudson, in New York. On March 29, 1857, he engaged, as foreman, with Jacob Zebley, on one of the DuPont farms near the Delaware River, and remained there until August 7, 1862.

In the early part of the latter month several young men from Brandywine Hundred (including Charles W. and John

Smith Talley) gave their names as members of the First Delaware Light Artillery.   William A. concluded that duty called
as loudly for him as it did for the others.   He at once heeded
the call, and joined this battery, as he says, "in our country's
darkest days."   The company took quarters in George W.
Weldin's woods in Brandywine Hundred.   William was here
promoted to Corporal.   The company moved to Camp Barry,
at Washington, D. C., December 21, 1862.   Here they drilled
and made ready for service.   In the spring they moved to
Suffolk, Va., and while there had two engagements with
General Longstreet's forces, and made a raid to the Black-
water River.

In the summer of 1863, they shipped by water from
Washington to New York City, to assist in quelling the draft
riots.   They returned to Washington, and in mid-winter shipped from Baltimore on the "Arago" for New Orleans.   They
arrived there safely and camped in the Tivola Circle in the
Crescent City.   About March 1, 1864, they were ordered to
join Franklin's Division, and prepare for Banks' Red River
Campaign.   The Delaware Battery was on this raid engaged in
the battles of Cane River, Sabine Cross Roads, Monsuriaville,
and Pleasant Hill.   At the latter place the Union Army was re-
inforced by A. J. Smith's Corps of 10,000 men, and the enemy
were driven back.   The Union Army moved down to Alexandria, and remained long enough to permit Colonel Bailey to
dam the river, and release the gunboats which were above the
rapids.   The enemy getting below our army cut off the supplies, and the men were compelled to subsist on boiled field
corn for several days.

The Union Army moved on down the river, and while
crossing the Atchafalaya River at Simmesport on a bridge of
boats placed side by side, with planks extending from one to
the other, they were attacked by Marmaduke's forces.   The
Delaware boys had some very active and exciting fighting at
Yellow Bayou, a place close by.   This battery did very effective work here, and soon silenced the enemy's guns.   At this
battle Sergeant Vernon's horse was killed by a shell.   The
Union Army shortly arrived at Morganzia, on the Mississippi.
Here the battery remained until December 21, 1864, when

they moved to Du Vall's Bluff, Ark. William A. was here promoted to Sergeant and placed in command of a gun. Here the company was discharged, June 25, and were mustered out at Wilmington, Del., July 3, 1865.

This was one of the lucky companies, and although in fifteen engagements, not a man received a scratch from the enemy's guns. Some of the wheels and a few splinters were knocked off some of the caissons, and one horse was killed. Another remarkable fact is that this company traveled, on railroads and on vessels at sea, almost from one end of the country to the other, and not a fatal accident occurred. A terrible catastrophe was averted, however. In 1863 the battery was shipped from Washington to New York by vessels. A part of the men were sent on a dilapidated river ferry-boat. As soon as she struck the surf at the mouth of the Chesapeake Bay the whole forward deck broke loose from the bottom, and all on board seemed destined to a watery grave. Fortunately, the "old tub" struggled back to land, and the soldiers were saved.

On March 27, 1866, being a free man once more, William A. Talley began farming on a small place which he had purchased from William L. Wilson. After a few years this farm was sold, and a larger one purchased, upon which he now resides. He is grateful for his success, and says, "by Divine help and good health I have been successful enough to procure a good home." He has held a few offices, such as School Director for many years and Assessor for four years. He was the Census Enumerator in East Brandywine Hundred for 1890, was Manager for the Mill Creek Mutual Fire Insurance Company for his hundred for a number of years, and is also Master of the Pomona Grange of New Castle County, Del. He joined the Bethel M. E. Church, under the ministry of Henry R. Calloway, in 1855, and aids the church in a substantial manner, being one of the large contributors to the fund for the building of the new church. He leads the choir, and engages in other departments of church work, and has been a part of the official board of this church for twenty years. He feels that he has been successful in his business life, and attributes this result to a wise and kind

Providence that rules over all. He has been taught this doctrine for years in the church, and this is his faith and his hope.

CHARLES W. TALLEY (*469*) was born on his father's farm, one mile from Wilmington, in Brandywine Hundred, on September 25, 1842. He was educated at the District School, and at the Normal School at Millersville, Pa. He married Sarah Jane Perkins, daughter of Christine and Julia Ann (Pierce) Perkins, of Holly Oak, Del. In 1862 he joined the First Delaware Light Artillery, in company with his brother, John Smith Talley, and William A. Talley. He became Corporal, but after his brother's promotion to Orderly Sergeant he stepped to the position of Sergeant, in charge of a gun. He went with his company through to the finish in June, 1865, and was honorably discharged. He was in every engagement with his comrades, and did his duty faithfully. The services of this battery are fully detailed in the sketch of William A. Talley's life, given on another page.

When the war closed he became Superintendent of the Wilmington City Railway, which was then in its infancy and under the management of Joshua T. Heald. He was very successful in this line, and voluntarily resigned his position, and engaged in the saw-mill business. He was elected to the Wilmington City Council, and was a valuable member in that body. In 1883 he became Manager of the Diamond Match Company's immense lumbering plant at Ontonagon, on the Upper Michigan Peninsula, and remained there for several years. In 1890 he returned to Wilmington, and with Alvin R. Morrison formed the Delaware Construction Company; he and Mr. Morrison owning the stock of the company.

The Delaware Construction Company at this time did considerable important work, including the erection of bridges, among which were the Seventh Street Bridge, which crosses the Brandywine Creek near its mouth, and the fine Washington Street Iron Bridge, leading from Wilmington into Brandywine Hundred.

Under most severe affliction of himself and two other members of his family, he was compelled in 1898 to retire from business and spend the winter in Denver. The surviving

children of the family are Ella M., Charles P. and Herbert.
Charles W. Talley now resides at Terre Haute, Ind., leading
a quiet life.

WILLIAM TATNALL TALLEY (*180*), son of Har-
man and Rebecca (Grubb) Talley, was born May 7, 1808, in
Brandywine Hundred, Del. He was married December 23,
1835, at Philadelphia, to Anna Mary Elliott, the daughter of
J. Cloud Elliott, of Elliott's Hill, in the same hundred. In
May, 1836, they, with others of his father's family, moved to
Ohio. William Tatnall Talley and his young wife settled on
a farm eighteen miles south of Zanesville, in Muskingum
County. Here they lived for almost fifty years. Five children
were born of this marriage, four sons and a daughter. Two
sons died in infancy, and on March 4, 1857, William Cloud
Talley, a son 18 years of age, also passed away. He was a
youth of remarkable literary tendencies. It is said that his
writings, when a mere boy, were noted for their depth of
thought and beauty of expression.

In 1861 the only remaining and eldest son, E. Hillis
Talley, under a commission from the Governor of Ohio, raised
a company, which became Company " D " of the 78th Ohio
Volunteer Infantry. They encamped near Zanesville in the
fall of that year, and in February, 1862, they were ordered to
active service in the direction of Fort Donaldson. It is said
that they arrived, not in time for the battle, but to take part
in the rejoicing over the victory just won. Young Captain
Talley had been tenderly reared, and the hardships of soldier
life soon made inroads on his delicate constitution. Just
before the battle of Pittsburg Landing he was stricken with
fever. It was difficult at that time to get a furlough, and his
Colonel advised him to go home without one ; but he responded that he would sooner stay and take the *chance* of
recovery than to violate a law to *insure* it. He remained, and
passed away in the hospital at Savannah, Tenn., April 4,
1862. He was a favorite with both officers and men. His
remains were brought North and laid at rest beside his brother,
William Cloud Talley, in the county of his birth, and within
sight of his once happy home. The only surviving child,

E. Jennie E. Talley, was married October 11, 1876, to Samuel
M. Rutledge, and moved to his beautiful home on the Muskingum River, nine miles from Zanesville. They have two
children, William Cloud and George Armstrong Rutledge.

William Tatnall Talley was a remarkably large and fine-
looking man. He was successful in life, and not only acquired
a competency in worldly effects, but had some to spare in
entertainment of friends and prominent men of his vicinity.
He was very highly respected, and exerted considerable influence in State and County affairs. He was hospitable to the
itinerant minister, and many found shelter and comfort under
his roof. He and his wife were life-long members of the
M. E. Church, and died in the faith ; he on May 15, 1885,
and she on July 20, 1886. After her decease a very touching
poem, bearing date November 15, 1885, was discovered in her
album. It was in her handwriting, and was supposed to have
been composed by her, expressing her grief at the sad loss of
her husband. A few stanzas are here given :—

      *   *   *   *   *

"Oh ! how he soothed my saddened heart,
   And calmly lulled my fears;
Well may I say we shared our joys,
   And wept each other's tears.
Thus do I sit and feed my grief
   With memories of the past,
'Till naught in earth can give relief,
   And tears are falling fast.

I cannot fully understand
   Why thus my tears should flow,
But what I know not here on earth,
   I shall hereafter know.
Oh, what is all this world to me !
   'Tis filled with sin and care ;
Now all my treasures are in heaven,
   O ! I would fain be there.

Yet, would I wait thy bidding, Lord,
   To leave this house of clay,
And calmly resting on thy word,
   Pursue my lonely way.

Trusting that when life's work is done,
With him I'll join to swell
That glorious, that triumphant song,
Which echoes no farewell."

JACOB ATWOOD WELDIN (*486*) is the son of
Jacob R. and Hannah (Talley) Weldin. He was born on his
father's farm in Brandywine Hundred, Del., on January 31,
1855. He married Clara V. Talley, daughter of Lewis and
Elizabeth (Zebley) Talley, in 1879. Clara was born on February 12, 1858, and died August 3, 1895. She was quite
musical and was an excellent singer.

J. Atwood Weldin attended the public schools in
Brandywine Hundred, and finished his education at Professor
Reynolds' Academy, at Wilmington, Del. He remained with
his father on the extensive farm called "Chestnut Hill," near
the Blue Ball Hotel, on the Concord Turnpike, until he married, in 1879. He then moved to the smaller farm formerly
the homestead of his father, and which adjoined the larger
place. Here he was convenient to aid his father in operating
his farm, either with advice or labor, as circumstances demanded.

Upon the death of his parents, about seven years ago,
he moved to his father's late residence. Here he has since
resided, as successor to a most worthy sire. Upon the division
of his father's estate he procured the fine, old and commodious mansion, with all the surrounding barns and outbuildings, together with 100 acres of the land adjoining. These
buildings and this land constitute one of the excellent farming
plants of Brandywine Hundred. Ever since this farm was
purchased, about 1861, by Jacob R. Weldin, it has been a
home of thrift and prosperity.

J. Atwood Weldin has inherited a large and finely developed physical form, the natural result of being the child of
Jacob R. and Hannah Weldin. He uses his powers for the
good of himself and others of his community, and belongs
to and holds official position in all such beneficial societies as
The Grange, the Order of United Workmen, and Knights
of Pythias. He has been for years a Director of the
Cherry Island Marsh Company. He is Treasurer of the Board

of Trustees of the Mt. Pleasant M. E. Church of his hundred, having succeeded his father in this position of trust. He liberally supports the church, and is regular in his attendance at service. Owning a tract of land along the Delaware River, in Cherry Island, he much desires to see the city of Wilmington doing business on its true and natural "River Front." He has imbibed the spirit of public improvement, and is proud to see the developments around and about him of steam and trolley railroads, of good highways, and similar beneficial institutions. He is always ready and willing to perform his part in all efforts which tend to the betterment of the great world about him, and is a good and useful citizen.

CURTIS M. TALLEY (*523*) was born February 17, 1843, near Talley's Corner, on the Foulk Road. He married Anna Mary Miller, daughter of Martin and Ann Miller, on March 7, 1867.

In 1860 Peter Talley, his father, then owning a homestead of 30 acres near Forwood's School House, purchased of Lewis Weldin, the farm, now the home of Curtis M., consisting of 60 acres. Mr. Weldin bought this place at Sheriff's sale, it being sold as the land of Henry Frank. The fences and buildings thereon were in a ruinous state. Curtis and his father built, substantially, all of the buildings now on the farm. Curtis, when married, moved to this place. Then the uprooting business began in earnest. Fields were cleared, orchards and small fruit were set out.

He is an expert in fruit growing. His orchard near his home is a leafy bower, an overhanging mass of plum, pear and apple trees, amidst which are strawberries, raspberries and blackberries; everything in luxuriance. Here are also to be found the quince, the peach, and the cherry.

In this year of 1899, his row of smokehouse apple trees are a remarkable sight. Each one is almost a perfect dome in shape, with the fruit as evenly and regularly set on the branches as if placed there by human hands. These thrifty orchards are not a matter of mere chance. The spraying machine has performed an important part here; and book-learning has supplemented active experience. Science is important even in farming.

Fully understanding the grafting of trees, he has successfully grafted an apple branch into a pear stock. He failed in grafting a pear branch into the shade maple, as the sap of the maple overflowed and drowned the graft.

In addition to fruit, he raises general crops of farm products ; and old corn is always to be found in his crib. He has occupied a stall in the Eighth Street Market, at Wilmington, for over twenty years, and raises for this trade the finest and newest sorts of vegetables, and has them in perfection. He is *the* cider-maker of Brandywine Hundred, having purchased a very modern press, which has a capacity of thirty-five bushels of apples at one press. He has made as many as one hundred and fifty barrels of cider in one year, and always has vinegar in his storehouse ; one barrel contains vinegar twenty years old.

He supports the church, and has served fifteen years on the official board of the Forwood School District. It is said that the Tax Collector never came twice for his tax. He inherited a strong constitution, and uses it most industriously. He owns 90 acres of land in two farms. These he acquired and holds largely through his progressive industry, his integrity and fair dealing.

ISAAC N. GRUBB (*634*) is the son of Adam and Julian (Talley) Grubb. His mother was a daughter of Harman and Priscilla (Foulk) Talley. Harman married, as his second wife, Rebecca Grubb, a sister to Adam above named. By this arrangement Isaac N. Grubb's grandfather became his uncle by marrying his aunt Rebecca, and Adam Grubb's father-in-law (Harman Talley) became his brother-in-law.

Samuel Grubb, Isaac N. Grubb's*grandfather, was a first-cousin to Hannah Grubb, who married William Talley, the grandfather of Harman Talley. Hannah (Grubb) Talley then was the great-grandmother of Julian (Talley) Grubb. From this we deduce the fact that Adam Grubb and his wife Julian were third-cousins *once removed ;* and that Harman Talley and his wife Rebecca were full third-cousins. We need,

* Great

then, no apology for inserting a sketch of Isaac N. Grubb in this Talley Record.

Isaac N. Grubb's ancestry in America runs in this way : John first was the father of John second, John second was the father of Samuel, Samuel was the father of Isaac, Isaac was the father of Adam, and the latter was the father of Isaac N. Grubb. The subject of this sketch resides on the farm which was first owned by his great-great-grandfather, John second. His great-grandfather Samuel, his grandfather Isaac, and his father Adam, were all born on this spot. On this farm *he* was also born. It is said that it never has passed by deed since the patent from Penn, but has continuously passed from father to son by will. The old stone colonial mansion (the Grubb home), it is stated, was built in 1787, and is finished inside with fine paneled work. This house shows very little injury from age or from the elements. Three different shingle roofs have been placed upon it. The first roof was put on with nails made by hand at the smith-shop.

His grandfather Isaac, on September 11, 1777, the day of the battle of Brandywine, set out at the easterly corner of the house a catalpa tree. It is still living, although the wind has taken away its top. This tree measures eighteen and a half feet in girth, two feet above the ground. Another tree, remarkable, not for its girth, but for its shapely top and over-towering and beautifully spreading branches, is an English walnut, fully seventy-five years old. This tree in one year has produced thirteen bushels of nuts.

Mr. Grubb has in his possession two heirlooms which he justly prizes highly. One is his " grandfather's clock," a tall eight-day clock, purchased by Isaac Grubb, his grand-father, in 1778. It cost £14, as is shown on the old account book. This is a remarkable clock. It tells the day of the month, and to all appearances it is as good as the day it was made. It keeps time accurately at the present date. The other heirloom is a very old Bible, which was printed in London in 1738 by John Baskett, Printer to the King. It is stated on the title page that it is the New Testament of our Lord, translated from the Greek, and diligently compared with former translations, and commanded to be read in the churches. There is in this Bible a very valuable register of deaths and important events happening in the neighborhood about one hundred years ago.

Mr. Grubb has filled many important offices. He was elected to the Levy Court of his county in 1884. He was chosen President of the Board in 1886, and acted as presiding officer until 1890. His office of Commissioner expired 1892. During his eight years of service in the court many important bridges were constructed, in all of which matters he took very active part. The Market Street Bridge over the Brandywine was rebuilt; the Third Street Bridge over the Christiana was rebuilt, and was the second drawbridge in the United States to be operated by electricity. Then came, in regular order, the acceptance of the donation to the county of the Seventh Street Bridge across the Brandywine, and lastly, the procuring of the erection of the Washington Street Bridge, which has become the great viaduct leading from Wilmington into Brandywine Hundred. Mr. Grubb was quick to perceive what his constituents needed, and took most energetic steps to procure it for them.

Isaac N. Grubb is living a quiet life on his farm of 100 acres on the old Grubb Road. He is genial and hospitable, and enjoys the entertaining of his friends and neighbors. Like his ancestors of old, he is a man of strong character and of great influence in his neighborhood.

WILLIAM W. TALLEY (*576*) is the son of Thomas Lea and Mary Ann (Hanby) Talley. He was born in Brandywine Hundred, not far from the "Old Talley School House," on October 5, 1845. He married R. Emma Baker, daughter of Dilworth and Hannah Baker, of Chester County, Pa., on April 26, 1870. In the spring of 1871, just one year after his marriage, he moved to his father's home farm of 135 acres, along the Naaman's Creek Road. He purchased this farm in 1880, and for several years he and his energetic companion carried on business here with industry, economy and great success. The work of the farm becoming too severe for them, they concluded to rent it and to take life more easily. He purchased the very nice, new home, late of William Talley, son of Eli B. Talley, located on the Concord Turnpike at Talleyville, Brandywine Hundred, and moved there a few years ago.

William's industrious habits would not permit him to live in idleness, so he continued his milk business in the city of Wilmington, which he had carried on for many years while on the farm. He is strictly a *business* man and a *home* man. These qualities usually bring success, and Mr. Talley's good judgment led him to adopt this course in life.

He is of a genial disposition and is respected by those whom he meets in business or otherwise. He is not a church member, yet he inclines to the Methodist Church. Although now fifty-four years old, he is very youthful in appearance. It has been well said of him that he never "engages in any political schemes." He, however, votes at important elections, and has the interests of his country at heart. He has shown a kindly interest in our efforts to preserve our family's ancestry. He is, all in all, one of our very excellent citizens.

BENJAMIN F. TALLEY (*409*), son of Adam G. and Sarah (Aldred) Talley, was born in Delaware, and now resides at Mt. Ayr, Ringgold County, Iowa. He taught school for sixteen winters in Iowa, working on his farm in summer. In 1888 he was elected Recorder of Deeds for his county, and served in this capacity for three terms. Having gained a large amount of valuable information while Recorder, he concluded to open an abstract and real estate office at Mt. Ayr, the place of his residence. In 1895 he and his sons, Lloyd and Adam C. Talley, purchased the abstract books and business of an old firm at Mt. Ayr, and put out the sign, "B. F. Talley & Sons." They do a general Real Estate and Abstract business, and stand high in the business world of Ringgold County. Their abstract work is well known for its neatness, accuracy and completeness.

Lloyd Talley, the son, is County Surveyor of his county, while his brother, Adam C. Talley, is editor of *The Southwest News*, at Greenfield, Mo., being an experienced newspaper man. Another son, Ambrose E. Talley, is a minister of the Methodist Church, in the Des Moines Conference.

Still another son, Gilbert H. Talley, is City Editor of *The Ringgold County Record*, at Mt. Ayr.

Many of the descendants of Adam G. Talley are holding positions of prominence in the educational, religious and business world. In addition to those above noticed of Benjamin F. Talley's family, we may mention : Martha A. Stahl, Professor of Latin and History, Simpson College, Indianola, Iowa ; W. Sherman Stahl, Attorney-at-Law, Chicago, Ill. ; and Catharine J. Stahl, a Missionary in India. The latter is the *heroine*, who, during an earthquake at Darjeeling, India, in October, 1899, saved many of the Mission children by her coolness and bravery, announcement of the fact being made at the time through the public press of our country.

Adam G. Talley moved with his family from Delaware to Thornsville, Perry County, Ohio, April 1842 ; from Ohio to Hamilton County, Indiana, October, 1850 ; and from Indiana to Ringgold County, Iowa, June, 1856. He took with him to Iowa all of his children except Catharine R. Ford, who continued to reside in Indiana with her family until her decease. The family, with the exceptions mentioned above, are engaged in agricultural pursuits, and are distinctively religious, almost all being members of the Methodist Church. This is a remarkably large family, and have furnished the only representatives of the tenth generation. They may well feel proud of their numbers, their high position in life, and their influence for good.

WILLIAM TWADDELL TALLEY (*185*) was born May 6, 1817, on his father's farm, and on which he has ever since resided. This spot is in full view of the historic Brandywine Creek, and is in the extreme western corner of Brandywine Hundred, close against the Pennsylvania line. William Talley, his grandfather, bought this land in 1807, and upon his death it passed to Elihu Talley, father of William T. Talley. The latter inherited this and other lands from his father, but by his thrift he has been able to add acres to his estate, so that it now runs well up to 300 acres.

The subject of this sketch, having inherited a vigorous constitution, has been one of the workingmen of our family.

Now, at the ripe age of 82 years, he is active, and moves about almost as in youth. He aids in the work, and advises about all matters connected with the management of the farm. He has had little time to gossip about hotels or smithshops, but always finds something useful for his mind and hands to engage in.

We are told that years ago he made a large amount of money in the timber and wood trade, selling these products in Wilmington, Chester and West Chester. He has even hauled timber and lumber with team to Philadelphia. For years he was Manager of the Mill Creek Fire Insurance Company for his hundred. He was elected Road Commissioner for one term, but has had very slight ambition to occupy places of public trust. Although generally voting at elections, he does not care to linger about the polls.

He and his wife, for a number of years, have been members of the Brandywine Baptist Church, and are very much attached to the church of their choice. In order to encourage the building of a chapel near his home, he donated an acre of ground for this worthy purpose, and aided in other ways, to the end that there has been erected on the edge of his farm, close by the State line, a cozy little church, with a seating capacity for about two hundred persons. This, in honor of its most generous benefactor, has been named the " Talley Chapel."

William T. Talley, on November 16, 1843, married Elizabeth Heyburn, of Birmingham Township, Delaware County, Pa. The children of this marriage are, Elihu Dallas, Sarah Ann, John Heyburn and Letitia B. They all reside at home except John Heyburn Talley, who resides near Perry's Hotel, on the Concord Turnpike, where he conducts a farm, keeps a store, and performs the duties of Postmaster.

William T. Talley received his education at the District School, but he has been able to do much better by his children, and has educated them at the Boarding or Select Schools of Chester County, Pa. Elihu, the son, has been for several years Treasurer of Pomona Grange, of New Castle County, and was a charter member of the West Brandywine Grange. The whole family are courteous, intelligent and very much respected. They are willing to devote time and money to religious work, or to any commendable, social or charitable enterprise. They therefore stand high in the estimation of those residing in their vicinity.

SALLIE EDNA DOWLIN (*1447*), a grand-daughter of J. Henderson Talley, married Rev. Joseph Lawton Guernsey, June 21, 1899. He is the only son of Elizabeth W. and Prof. A. B. Guernsey, and was born at the Fort Edward Institute, N. Y., January 31, 1874. He joined the Methodist Church at the age of fourteen years, and decided to enter the ministry. He was educated at the public schools of Bridgeport, Conn., and at Dickinson College, Carlisle, Pa. The year before entering college he was pastor of the M. E. Church at South Wilton, Conn. ; and at the present time is pastor of the M. E. Church at Long Hill, in the same State.

JOHN BOOTH (*511*) was born on the original Talley tract, July 15, 1843. He married Margaret A. Phillips, December 20, 1866. This family has preserved several valuable historic deeds and other important *data*. They hold in their possession the oldest Talley deed known to be in existence.

John Booth, on August 31, 1864, enlisted in Company B, of the 203d Pa. Vol. Infantry. The regiment was organized in the early part of September, 1864, and on the 22d of that month started for the front, and were before Petersburg on September 27. They were attached to the Second Division of the Tenth Corps, and were engaged at the battle of Chapin's Farm the day they landed, and here had one killed and six wounded. On December 7 they shipped under General Butler for Fort Fisher, on the Cape Fear River, in North Carolina. They landed on December 25, with a view of attacking the fort. The attack was not made, and the troops were by General Butler ordered back to the James River, in Virginia.

On January 2, 1865, General Terry was placed in command of a second expedition. It was only a few days until they were again in front of the fort. They landed January 14, and, in conjunction with the fleet, began an attack upon the stronghold. The 203d Pennsylvania Regiment was attached to Ames' Division, and this division was selected to make the assault. This Regiment made the attack in the face of bullets and grape-shot, and was fearfully cut up. It was one of the first to enter the fortification, and fought hand to hand with the enemy, nearly all of its officers being either killed or wounded. In this fearful struggle the regiment lost forty-six men killed and one hundred and forty-five wounded. Inside the fort were nine different traverses to be taken. The fighting continued from three o'clock in the afternoon until midnight, when the last traverse was taken, and the Stars and Stripes were thrown to the breeze.

John Booth and Theodore Smith (another descendant of the Talley family) rushed with their comrades over the numerous breastworks, and aided in gaining this glorious victory. The action of this raw regiment, recruited in September, 1864, and in January, 1865, found charging with all the vigor and coolness of veterans, is a glorious record for the American Volunteer. The regiment rested until February 21, when they aided in taking Wilmington, N. C. They then marched to the interior, and made a junction with General Sherman's Army. They were afterwards detailed for guard duty at Raleigh, and were discharged at that place, June 22, 1865.

JOHN THOMAS TALLEY (*481*) is the son of John and Sarah A. (Stidham) Talley, and was born January 10, 1862. On November 21, 1891, he married Lillie O. Mayne, a daughter of William and Rebecca Ann Mayne, who reside in Wilmington, Del. Upon his marriage he built a comfortable brick residence in East Lake Park, Wilmington, and there began housekeeping. His mother dying in 1893, the next year he sold his home in Wilmington and moved to his father's homestead in Brandywine Hundred. At his father's request he took charge of the farm, and managed the same on his own account. He has conducted this farm in a very orderly and successful manner ever since. He attends strictly to business, and is very honorable in his dealings.

For about five years he has been Treasurer of the Cherry Island Marsh Company, and performs his work in this line with satisfaction to all concerned. He is a young man, yet he is painstaking, conscientious, genial, and of excellent habits. Having made a proper start in life, he may well hope for success and prosperity all along the way.

JOSEPH M. PIERCE (*513*) married Susanna T. Barlow, daughter of Malachi Barlow. Mr. Pierce is the son of Joseph and Sarah (Talley) Pierce. His mother was born January 27, 1809, and was twenty-seven years old on January 27, 1836 ; on this day Joseph M., her son, was born. Joseph, the son, was not only born on January 27, but he was married on January 27, 1863, when he was twenty-seven years old.

He learned the carpenter's trade in Wilmington. The first work done by him as a contracting carpenter, was the building of a barn for his uncle, Penrose R. Talley, of Talley's Corner. The barn now stands on the farm of the late Charles Talley, son of Penrose. Mr. Pierce being accustomed to fine work in the city, worked out the lumber for this barn almost as smoothly and exactly as if it were a city mansion. Both he and his uncle were proud when the barn was raised and everything matched so nicely.

Mr. Pierce served as Tax Collector of his hundred for two years, also for a like term as Trustee of the Poor, and is a member of the Grange. He has been a member of Bethel M. E. Church for thirty-five years, and was a Trustee and a member of the building committee when the new church was erected, and was the contractor for the carpenter work on this fine edifice. He has been a class leader in this church, and cheerfully aids it in a financial way.

ABNER P. TALLEY (*574*) married first, Sarah J. Graves ; and second, Hannah Mary Harkins. This family is remarkable on account of the number of its children. There were twenty-five children born of this father by virtue of the two marriages ; eleven by the first, and fourteen by the second. We often read in the newspapers of prolific families, not knowing whether it be truth or fiction. Here we have the facts, and anyone may read the name of each child in its proper place in the list. Two of the first eleven died in infancy, and the remaining nine all married. Abner P., Jr., and Hannah B., of the second line, have followed the example set by their older brothers and sisters, and are each now the head of a family.

The descendants of this father are not only numerous, but active and prosperous. Those who have married have made a good start in life, each launching into business with independence and a determination to succeed. This family has shown its loyalty to the Talley cause, and have subscribed for ten books. What other family can excel this one in the number of books taken?

If there is *strength* in union, there surely must be *great power* in numbers working in unison. Who, then, can forecast the *power* of this great family for good in the years that lie before them? We no doubt speak the sentiment of all of the Talleys when we wish the parents and this extensive family prosperity, harmony and happiness far into the future.

JOSEPH BEESON TALLEY (*475*) was born and reared on his father's farm in Brandywine Hundred, near Wilmington. He was the ninth child of a family of ten children. After attending the District School, he completed his education at Professor Reynolds' Academy in Wilmington. On January 28, 1877, he married Hannah Mary Blackwell, and began farming on one of his father's places, and resided in the old mansion on the Philadelphia Turnpike at Maplewood, close by the Riverview Cemetery. He continued farming until a few years after his wife's death, in 1882. His health not being good, he visited relatives at Chicago and Terre Haute. After his return from the West, he assisted his father in managing his business until the latter's decease, in 1888.

He married as his second wife Sarah J. Lodge, April 4, 1889. She is the daughter and only child of Isaac W. and Mary Jane (Hanby) Lodge, of Holly Oak, Del. In 1890 he moved to the farm of his father-in-law, and continued there until 1894. His health again failing, he quit farming, and built a store and residence on the Philadelphia Turnpike, at Holly Oak. Here he began the developing of the business of a general store, being greatly aided by his active and energetic wife. He at once became Postmaster, for a post office is an inseparable adjunct to the rural store. Mr. Talley has been very obliging, always bringing into his store such a selected line of goods as is demanded by his many customers.

The steam railroad accommodations were excellent at Holly Oak, but in 1899 the great Wilmington, Chester and Philadelphia Trolley line was put into operation, and gave fresh impetus to the already very thriving suburban river town. The building of many handsome residences on the beautiful hill slopes all reflect rays of prosperity in the direction of the store. Joseph B. does not object either to the building up of the town or the extending of his business.

He is a property owner with others of his name in Cherry Island Marsh, and was for some years the Treasurer of the corporation. He is a member and a supporter of the Mt. Pleasant M. E. Church, being a member of the Board of Trustees, also of the Board of Stewards. He is conscientious and prompt in his dealings, and is deserving of the success he has attained.

HENRY IRVING TALLEY (*814*) was born at Philadelphia in 1854. In the year 1869, and when fifteen years of age, he entered the Railroad and Telegraph service, and has been connected with different companies in the East, West, South, Southwest and Northwest, sometimes as operator and at other times as manager of office, until the year 1887. At this date he engaged in the typewriter business, and is still occupied in this line. During the year 1896 he traveled in Europe, visiting the following countries : England, Ireland, Wales, Scotland, Belgium, Switzerland, Austria, Bavaria, and Northern and Southern Germany.

In June, 1898, he designed a six-turreted Monitor of twenty-two guns—twelve in the main battery and ten in the secondary battery. The Monitor is of an entirely original pattern. The design was sent to the Government at Washington, he receiving in reply several letters of acknowledgment, signed by the highest officials in the Navy Department. His plans have been filed by the officials for future reference.

He is one of the vigorous helpers in getting *data* and subscribers for our *Talley History*, and is solicitous to know all about the Talley family of old.

CURTIS TALLEY (*554*), son of Eli Baldwin Talley, died September 18, 1851, aged 22 years and 10 months. He was a member of Star of Bethel Lodge of I. O. of O. F., of Delaware. Upon his decease a beautiful poem was composed by Milton S. Barlow. Two stanzas are given below :—

> Friendships throne! how pure and fervent
>   Was thy worship at her shrine,
> Friend of man!—of God the servant,
>   Love and truth in thee did shine:
> Loved by thee our faithful Brother
>   We have been and hope to be—
> Vain the wish, for soon another
>   Quenched thy light—'tis dark with thee,
>
> Dark with thee?—no: thy Creator,
>   All whose creatures and whose laws
> Thou didst love, will give thee greater
>   Light than earth's, as earth withdraws
> To thy God thy immortal spirit
>   Back, we give in filial trust
> Thy cold clay—we grieve to bear it
>   To its chamber—"dust to dust."

THOMAS TALLEY WELDIN (*487*), son of Jacob R. and Hannah (Talley) Weldin, married Emma M. Naylor, daughter of Isaac and Phebe Naylor, late of Brandywine Hundred, Del. Thomas T. Weldin attended the District School, and Reynolds' Select School in Wilmington, and finished his education with a six-months' term at the Millersville State Normal School in Pennsylvania. He made his home with his parents until after his marriage. Soon after this event he moved to his new home at the intersection of the Foulk Road and the Concord Turnpike. He thus remained close to his parents, assisting them in conducting matters about the farm until their decease, about seven years ago.

Upon a division of his father's estate he received about 100 acres of the fine Chestnut Hill farm, and several acres of the River Front land in Cherry Island Marsh. There are also included in his property list several brick houses in Wilmington. After acquiring his land, he immediately erected near his house an excellent barn, with all necessary appliances. He thus placed himself in a way to do business, and has succeeded finely in his undertaking. He finds some spare time to devote to the public affairs of his hundred, and has satisfactorily filled the office of Trustee of the Poor for several years. He is a member of the Order of United Workmen, and a member of Dupont Lodge, No. 29, A. F. A. M. He, like his brother, J. Atwood Weldin, has inherited a fine physique, and is able to carry out what he undertakes. He is liberal in donations to worthy objects, and does not fail when the church calls for aid. The family attends the Mt. Pleasant M. E. Church, Mrs. Weldin taking an active part in the singing.

Thomas T. Weldin favors public improvement, and is quick to see the value of his land for farm use and its value for building purposes. The city of Wilmington is reaching out in his direction, and he needs no one to notify him of the fact. He is a man of integrity and good business judgment.

JULIA L. and PAUL TALLEY, children of Charles W. and Sarah Jane Talley, died within two weeks of each other at Denver, Colo., and as a small tribute to their memory this sketch is prepared.

The daughter, Julia L., was an earnest and devoted member of Trinity P. E. Church in Wilmington, to become later, when the family removed to Philadelphia, a member of St. Matthias' Church. Not ever strong, she was debarred from doing as much charitable and church work as was always her desire ; but she was ever a faithful attendant at both church and Sunday school. It is not vouchsafed to every one to do great and noble deeds, but those who are faithful to the little duties of life, who make the world brighter for their having lived in it, and to whom can be applied the words, " She hath done what she could," have neither lived nor died in vain.

Paul Talley was a young man of brilliant attainments and of much promise. He was graduated at the Wilmington High School, class of 1894, and on this occasion received the Latin Prize. Having decided artistic talent, he turned to architecture as being a most congenial occupation, and in the fall of 1894 he entered the University of Pennsylvania, taking up the four-years' course in Architecture. At the end of two years he was, on account of ill-health, advised not to prosecute his studies longer. In the autumn of 1898 the family left Philadelphia for Denver, in search of health. Paul and Julia did not long survive, both dying in June, 1899. Their remains were brought from Denver to Wilmington, and were, in sadness, buried June 23rd beside their brother, Stillman J. Talley, in the family lot in the Wilmington and Brandywine Cemetery. 'Gone not into darkness, but into a clearer day than our poor twilight-dawn on earth.'

NATHANIEL BOOTH (**509**) is the son of Nathaniel and Charity (Talley) Booth. In August, 1855, Nathaniel, Jr., sixteen years of age, and his brother, Enoch, twenty-four, shipped from New Bedford, Mass., on a full rigged ship called the "Navy," on a whaling voyage around the world. They sailed across the Atlantic, and when leaving the Cape Verde Islands, Enoch was stricken with yellow fever; and, within a few days he died, and was buried at sea off the west coast of Africa. The vessel sailed around Good Hope, and turning north visited New Zealand, Van Dieman's Land, Australia, most of the Polynesian Islands, the Philippines, and the Japan Islands. In June, 1856, they passed through Behring Strait into the Arctic Ocean, and spent the summer in whaling, north of Siberia. Nathaniel and five others got lost in a fog while away from the ship. They had to spend some time with the Esquimaux before they could find their way back.

At the farthest point reached by the ship there were but two hours of night in summer. Here, for the first time, Nathaniel says, he saw the phenomenon of the "Mock Sun." He says he could see two distinct suns, one above the other. This was not visible below the 68th degree of north latitude. The vessel could not remain in this Northern Ocean longer than the first of October, or it would be frozen up fast until spring. They always journeyed southward for the winter. Once, as they sailed south through the straits, the wind being ahead, they had to tack ; and as they "beat" to the westward they could hear the roaring of the surf on the Siberian coast. When they "went about" and sailed to the eastward they could hear the dashing of the waves on the Alaskan coast. They thus visited both continents in a comparatively short space of time.

While in the Esquimaux country, and having a craving for fresh meat, they traded a piece of calico to the natives for a scrub bullock, which had hair on it several inches long. These hardy whalers knew well how to prepare it for the culinary department. It made an exceedingly palatable stew, and was a welcome treat to those who had so long subsisted on fish and salt provisions.

Nathaniel informs us that the largest whales inhabit the Arctic regions ; one very large species, called the Bow Head whale, is found only in the North. The latter are so very large that one will often produce as many as sixty barrels of oil. Nathaniel being young when on this trip, his eyes were wide open to everything new and exciting. He still keeps his whaling voyage fresh in memory. He changed ships at Honolula, and returned home by way of Cape Horn, and landed on Long Island, New York, in 1858, having experienced three years of dangerous and exciting life on all of the oceans of the world. Here ends the first important period of Nathaniel's life.

The second period began when, on October 1, 1861, he enlisted in Company "F" of the 97th Reg., Pa. Vol., Colonel Guss commanding. This regiment was recruited in Chester and Delaware Counties. They camped at West Chester November 12, 1861, went to Washington, and passed down to Fortress Monroe. They joined the Tenth Corps, and went to Port Royal, S. C., and then to Florida. They afterward moved to Charleston, S. C., and joined in the attack there. This expedition did not succeed. A second attempt was made in April, 1863, with Gillmore commanding. The 97th Regiment landed on Folly Island, marched up and passed over to Morris

Island. This regiment had plenty of fighting about Charleston, and lost several men there. They assisted in the capture of Fort Wagner.

A large Parrot gun was placed on logs in a marsh several miles from Charleston, for the purpose of shelling the city. This gun was called the "Swamp Angel," but by the men it was dubbed the "Marsh Hen." Nathaniel was detailed to help take ammunition to this monster in the swamp. The gunner in charge was a German. He said to Nathaniel that, "ven dish old hen cackles, she vill lay an egg in Charleston." She did not stop with laying one egg, but kept on until several were laid in one day.

The regiment, after some other work in the South, returned to Virginia and rejoined the Tenth Corps, under General Butler. They moved up to Bermuda Hundred, and had continuous service in that vicinity. The regiment made a dashing charge, May 18, 1864, and gained some lost ground, but lost nineteen killed and thirty-eight wounded. In a desperate charge on May 19th, they had three officers and forty-four men killed, and eight officers and one hundred and twenty-one men wounded. They were present before Petersburg at the time of the famous mine explosion. They were engaged about Petersburg from May, 1864, until their discharge in October following. This was a crack regiment, and went into service fifteen hundred strong, and had a band of twenty pieces. Only a few stood in line to be mustered out at the end of their three-years' term.

An interesting episode occurred as the men lay in trenches about Petersburg. Men, by turns, were detailed to carry soup from camp to the men at the front. Nathaniel was detailed for this work on September 3, 1864, the day of the celebration of the fall of Atlanta. As he came across the open country with a huge bucket of soup in each hand, cannonading began everywhere along the Union lines. He, having no knowledge of the order, concluded that a terrific battle was raging along the whole front. This was the only time that Nathaniel was frightened during the three years of active service. He felt strong when with his comrades and armed with his gun, but trembled when he found himself *alone* and armed only with *soup*. He fully realized that *soup* might be a fair diet to "fight on," yet it was a very inferior weapon to fight *with*. Fortune smiled on the *brave*, and Nathaniel passed through the whole three-years' term of continuous conflict without a scar and with only one fright.

THOMAS TALLEY (*152*) was born November 11, 1810, and died August 13, 1899, in his 89th year. He married Elizabeth Bird, May 31, 1849, she being a daughter of Joseph and Rebecca Bird. Thomas Talley owned at his death 100 acres of land at Talley's Corner, on the Foulk Road, in Brandywine Hundred. His constitution was remarkably strong, never having failed him, until he approached the fourscore mile-stone of life. When a young man he visited Ohio, but did not remain long, concluding to settle near his birthplace, in Delaware.

His only surviving daughter, Leah, married Thomas Booth, of Booth's Corner, Delaware County, Pa. Their two children are Thomas A. and Laura E. The latter is a school teacher in her home county, and the former is a student in the Medical Department of the University of Virginia.

WESLEY TALLEY (*174*) was born January 12, 1812. He taught school for many years at the Rockland School on the Brandywine. In later life he removed to Wilmington, and became identified with the business men of that city. Here he was respected for his promptness and correct business habits. He held many positions of trust, and at his decease was the Treasurer of the School Board. He was most abstemious and correct in his daily life, and was, above all, gentlemanly and urbane to those with whom he had intercourse. It is said of him that in whatever position placed, he was always worthy of the confidence reposed in him.

Wesley Talley had natural mental endowments, which were cultivated by study and application, and all of which were ever nourished by elevated moral principles. He passed from life with the respect of all, and will be kindly remembered by those who knew him.

MABEL TALLEY (*1116*) is the daughter of George
A. and Julia Emma (Perkins) Talley, and was born in Chicago, Ill., June 20, 1879. She has a literary turn of mind,
and has written many short stories, some of which have
found their way into public print. She has aided much in
collecting material for the Talley Book, and for this purpose
has accompanied her father in almost numberless trips with
horse and buggy through Brandywine Hundred, and many
parts of Delaware County, Pa. Page after page of manu-
script has been copied by her and her mother, and they have
acted as audience when the copy was being rehearsed, before
forwarding it to the printer. All of the members of this
family of three have performed important work on this family
book.

ISAAC JONES TALLEY (*237*) married Eliza Grubb,
of the Grubb family of Brandywine Hundred. He was born
in 1814, near the Foulk Road, in Delaware, his parents being
Mary and Harman Talley. He went West many years ago,
and was a prominent man at Madison, Ind. He engaged in
"steamboating" on the Ohio and other Western rivers, and
became quite wealthy, in one instance making a large sum
by the rise in the price of wheat, which he had fortunately
purchased. His business being largely on the Ohio and
Mississippi Rivers, and the war coming on, he was thrown
into the midst of its activities. He used his boats in the
Government service, and made many hairbreadth escapes.

During the Red River campaign he owned one-third
interest in the City Belle, a large steamer, and was her captain. The boat was employed as a transport to carry troops
and supplies up the Red River to relieve Banks' Army.
When about twenty-two miles below Alexandria, the City
Belle was fired on by the Confederates, who were concealed
on the shore. Many soldiers and officers on board were
killed, being at the time unarmed and with nothing to protect
themselves. The vessel was burned, and Captain Isaac Jones
Talley was made prisoner, and carried to a Texas prison,
where he was held until the close of the war. Here he suf-
fered starvation to such an extent that he was reduced to a
mere skeleton, although a very robust man when taken pris-

oner. His emaciated condition is shown by a photograph taken after his release. His sister, Mrs. Mary Jane Pyle, of Booth's Corner, Delaware County, Pa., is in possession of letters written by him to his mother in 1865, which very graphically describe the destruction of the City Belle, and the hardships in the Texas prison.

Although everything had been lost by the war, he, at the age of fifty-one years, with true Talley courage and energy, was soon engaged at his old business on the river and nobly battling to retrieve his fortune. He again succeeded, and left at his death, in 1873, several thousands of dollars to his family. Very few of the numerous Talley family were aware of the existence of this plucky Delaware Talley, when he was steaming his boat into the jaws of death on the Red River, or when, after the war, he, alone and single handed, was fighting the battles of life all over again, and was wooing Dame Fortune, up and down and over the shoals of the winding Western rivers. A new and glorious page is here added to the Talley History, and Isaac Jones Talley is the hero.

MISCELLANY.

SOUTHERN TALLEYS.

We have been able to get a few disconnected names of the Talleys in Virginia. They are here given for the assistance of those who may be willing to take up the task of connecting the two families of the North and the South. We believe that the Talley family of the South have had persons of decided ability in their ranks. Several of the older members of the Virginia line resided in Hanover County, one of the great battles of the Civil War in that section having been fought on "Talley's Farm." Obadiah Talley was one of the very early Talleys in Virginia, although he may not have been the emigrant Talley in that State. We find that Alexander, Elkanah, Thomas, William and Ezekiel Talley lived at some period in this county. Alexander Washington Talley and Herbert Washington, his son, reside at Petersburg, Va., and are dentists. There is also a storekeeper in the same city named Chestine Talley.

The following Talley names were taken from the Richmond Directory for 1898, by Thomas S. Robinson, in the interest of the *Talley Book*, viz: Alvin, a driver ; Ann P., widow of Zackariah ; Charles H., a policeman ; Daniel D., secretary to the Dean of the Medical College ; Edward, a locomotive engineer ; Elizabeth M., widow of Nathaniel ; Ezekiel S., a carpenter ; Frank, a hoseman ; Gatewood, Jr., a blacksmith ; George S., a stenographer ; George T., a farmer ; James A., a salesman ; John F., a book-keeper ; John L., a tipstave for the Supreme Court ; John W., an engineer ; Malinda ; Mary E., a dressmaker ; Mollie J. ; Nathaniel ; Nathaniel, Jr. ; Richard A., a book-keeper ; Robert B. ; Robert H., stenographer ; Robert W. ; Waddey W. ; Walker R. ; William T. ; and Williamson, an insurance agent.

Sarah Archer Talley published a book of poems. She resided at Richmond, and died there about 1859. Allen W. Talley is cashier of a bank at Lynchburg, Va. Rev. Nicholas Talley was a minister of the M. E. Church, South. He was born in Richmond, Va., May 2, 1791, and died May 10, 1873, at the age of 82 years. For many successive sessions he was a delegate to the General Conference of his church.

We take the following from a Genealogy entitled "The Cabells and Their Kindred":

Pauline Preston married Dr. William Talley, who went from Cumberland County, Va., to Wentzville, Mo. He was a son of William Talley by his wife Fannie Daniels, a sister of Judge William Daniels the elder, and daughter of William Daniels, an ensign in the Revolutionary War. Dr. William and Pauline Talley had two sons—Dr. William Talley, Jr., who married his first-cousin, Lucy Talley; and Joseph Talley. Aurinthia Preston married Joseph A. Talley, brother of Dr. William Talley. He lived at Wentzville also, and had one child, Lucy Talley, who married Dr. William Talley, Jr.

There are, it is stated, a great number of Talleys in Tennessee, and in Mississippi. South Carolina was also, in the early day, a home of the Talleys. It has been stated to us that recently a monument was unveiled at Columbia, S. C., which had been erected in memory of a Doctor Talley, a man of great prominence.

In a book of the Grant family, just issued, it is stated that William Nathaniel Talley, born at Fredericks Hall, Va., August 4, 1857, married, on January 20, 1880, Caroline H. Tompkins, who is a grand-daughter of Rachel Maria Grant, who descended with General U. S. Grant from Noah Grant, their common ancestor. It is said that Rachel Maria Grant taught the future President his alphabet. William Nathaniel Talley is the son of Samuel Cole Talley and Emma Cole Talley, of Virginia. He is Superintendent of the K. and C. R. R. R., of West Virginia, and resides at Montrose, in that State.

It has been found in the records at Washington, that John Talley was a member of Washington's Dragoons in the Revolutionary War.

A LETTER.

The following is an extract from a letter written by Isaac Jones Talley to his mother, dated "Madison, (Ind.,) July 31, 1865":

"Dear Mother:

"It has been a long time since you heard from me. I have got home again. I suppose you heard of my capture on Red River, on the 3d of May, 1864. I was a prisoner of war for thirteen months. I was at Camp Ford, Texas, Smith County.

"Mother, I tell you what we had to eat: One pint of corn, or corn meal, per day, three quarters of a pound of beef per day and salt, and that was for eight long months; and in winter time one pint of corn or meal and one pound of bacon for six of us a day. Only think, the one-sixth of a pound of bacon and a pint of meal, or corn in its place. I lost forty-three pounds of flesh while in prison. When captured I owned one-third of the steamer "City Belle," and had on board the 120th Ohio Volunteers, commanded by Colonel Spegal. He was killed. Colonel Mudd, of the 3d Illinois Cavalry, and Colonel Basnett, of the colored regiment, were killed; and there were only about thirty-five colored troops on board, and some of the 19th Kentucky Volunteers, making in all 900. There were a great many killed on board. Mother, I was captured twenty-two miles below Alexandria, Louisiana. The rebels burned the boat and all we had, which cost us nearly $24,000. I owned one-third of it." * * * * "I carried the musket a short time, and then took charge of the steamer "Caroline," which I built in 1862, and sold her in 1863, and bought the "City Belle," which I was captured on." * * *

"Remember me to Aunt Hannah and her family; also excuse me for being so neglectful and disobedient. May health be your lot in your old age! and write to me at Madison, Indiana."

THE FOURTH STREET BRIDGE.

This drawbridge spans the Brandywine River near its mouth, at the westerly end of Fourth Street, in Cherry Island Marsh, Wilmington. It was largely through the instigation of the Talley family that this bridge was constructed. They owned land in Cherry Island, between the city proper and the Delaware River. The city also, through the generosity of George W. Talley and Isaac S. Elliott, was the owner of Fourth Street, one hundred feet wide, extending from the Brandywine River eastward to the Delaware. The citizens of Wilmington were careless as to whether this street was brought into use or not; also as to whether or not this river front property should remain an undeveloped and foreign district of the city. The marsh owners reasoned thus : We are *in* the city, yet *not* in. If *in*, let us prepare a way to go in and out at pleasure.

An act authorizing the Directors of the Cherry Island Marsh Company to erect a bridge across the Brandywine River, at the point mentioned above, was prepared by George A. Talley, and its passage by the Legislature of the State of Delaware was secured on April 27, 1891. The act authorized the building of the bridge by private subscriptions. It provided that the bridge, when it was completed for public travel, should be conveyed and donated to the County of New Castle by the Marsh Directors, and should thereafter be taken charge of as a county bridge by the Levy Court of the county.

The Marsh Directors by formal power of attorney authorized and empowered George A. Talley to procure the donations of money for the purpose mentioned in the act, and to contract with the Delaware Construction Company for the erection of the bridge. Every dollar of the money used in the erection of this bridge was obtained by private donations, the public having no part in the matter until the bridge was turned over to the county as a completed structure. The attorney above named procured all of the subscriptions, and the Marsh Directors, viz : Jacob R. Weldin, Charles W. Talley, William Sellers, Isaac S. Elliott and Thomas J. Talley, met and adopted the plans for the bridge, and approved of the site selected for the same.

A contract was made by the attorney with Charles W. Talley and Alvin R. Morrison (the members of the Delaware Construction Company) for the building of the bridge. The bridge was completed, according to contract, on April 23, 1892, and was, by two separate deeds, made under the hands and seals of the Directors of the Marsh Company, conveyed and donated to the County of New Castle as and for a public bridge forever. The following members of the Talley family were subscribers to the fund, viz : John Smith Talley, Charles W. Talley, George A. Talley, Thomas J. Talley, Joseph B. Talley, Jacob R. Weldin and John Talley, Sr.

The bridge was thrown open to public travel on April

26, 1892, this being the time of its acceptance by the Levy Court. The bridge was a substantial wooden structure, and has served its purpose from 1892 until the present time. It is the connecting link which unites the Fourth Street of the meadow with a street on the westerly side of the Brandywine. It has served a dual purpose : it has let the City people out, and, at the same time, has let these Marsh people in.

A most terrific onslaught was made by a few prominent citizens of Wilmington against the acceptance of the bridge by the Levy Court. The battle waged furiously, both outside and inside of the court room. The right, however, at last prevailed, and the bridge earned its well-deserved victory. The Talley Marsh owners were in the forefront of this contest, and were aided by the influence of their Talley friends, and many others in the "Old Hundred," as well as in the city of Wilmington : petitions by the yard being signed by these friends. Many men of prominence gave friendly aid, among them being Hon. Thos. F. Bayard. The much-abused bridge at last caught the popular ear, and almost every one was happy to join the River-Front Army. The day of conflict has ended, and all now tread in harmony the great road to the River.

This bridge has opened up the vast tract of one thousand acres of land, which lies within the city, and occupies, substantially, the whole Delaware River frontage of the city. Many acres of this meadow have been filled by pumping in mud from the rivers. A project is now on foot for the filling of larger tracts with mud from the Delaware channel. This tract is destined, in the near future, to become the dock yards and wharfing front of Wilmington.

THE CHURCH.

The Talley family, so far as we have found, have been friendly to the church, and largely are members and supporters of it. We find the early ones in America attending the

BETHEL M. E. CHURCH.

St. Martin's P. E. Church at Marcus Hook, and the St. John's at Concord, both in Delaware County, Pa. Their church affiliations may have much to do in demonstrating their nationality. They being so distinctively Protestant, one may well conclude that they were either French Huguenots, or were reared in the free and Protestant atmosphere of romantic Wales. The family of the present day (and those before us) have believed in a church free from the restraints and dominations of worldly powers, and in which the Divine power alone was supposed to rule. They, in colonial days, worshiped with the Episcopal Church, but when Methodism came into the "Old Hundred" they allied themselves with that denomination. The Bethel Church was the first Methodist Church in the northern part of Delaware, and was established somewhere near the site of the present church. Robert Cloud donated the land in 1780, and his sons, Robert and Adam, became the first Methodist ministers in that section. The pioneer church was built of logs; the second was of stone; and the third, and last, of serpentine stone and of brick.

The picture on another page represents the present edifice, which was kindly photographed by Leonard C. Talley ; the photo-engraved plate being furnished by other descendants of Lewis Talley, the singer. The picture has been inserted not as a claim that the Church belongs to the Talley family, but merely to present the home church of the upper Brandywine Hundred Talleys, to the view of others of our name residing in distant parts of the country. This church to-day stands as the representative of the early log church, and thus represents the birth-place of Talley Methodism. Our whole family, from East to West, should ever remember with pride and affection this rural sanctuary, and the sacred home of the departed which adjoins it.

AN ANECDOTE.

We have the following, reported by O. B. Talley, of Sioux City, Iowa : His uncle, Henry N. Talley, of Batavia, Ohio, was in 1848 on a visit to his relatives at Hagerstown,

Md., he then being a young man. While on this visit he received a letter, dated June 8, 1848, from his young friend, P. B. Swing, of Batavia, and who in later life was Judge of the United States Court in Ohio. This letter is now in the possession of Frank F. Talley, of New Richmond, Ohio, who is a son of Henry N. Talley. It contains the following: " We have an officer of the army here who has taken a fancy to all the girls in town, and is towing them on all occasions. I think if you were here you might clip his feathers, but the rest of us boys are all afraid of him and dare not interfere." The officer referred to was Lieutenant U. S. Grant, who was born in Cleremont County, Ohio, not many miles from Batavia. He was fresh from the fields of glory in Mexico, being home on a leave of absence. The troubles of the Batavia boys were, however, but for a moment, for Lieutenant Grant married Julia B. Dent, on August 22d of the same year.

A CORRECTION.

Since writing Chapters VIII and IX, at pages 36, 37, ante, some additional information has been obtained. It appears in the Swedes' record at Wilmington, that a William Talley married Judith Fitzsimmons, November 4, 1768, one day before William Talley, on the Brandywine, married Dinah Stilley. We now, by a deed in the possession of Elihu Talley, son of Eli B. Talley, find that William and Judith Talley conveyed to Eli Baldwin 50 acres of the 175 acres of land bought by Samuel Talley first, from the Pennsylvania Land Company ; and by another deed it is shown that this William purchased these 50 acres from Samuel Talley first, and that William was the nephew of Samuel. William, who married Dinah Stilley, was also a nephew. Samuel having two nephews named William, one would of necessity be the son of David Talley. We conclude then that William, who married Judith Fitzsimmons, was the son of David Talley, one of the three sons of Thomas of old.

THE ISAAC JONES TALLEY FAMILY.

George L. Talley (798) married Emma Gertrude Norman, December 14, 1872. A daughter was born of this

Charles Maurice and Norman Donham, children of George L. and Dora Rebecca Talley, of Cincinnati, Ohio, and grandchildren of Isaac Jones Talley.

marriage, but lived only a short time. The mother only survived her marriage about two years. George L. Talley married as his second wife, Dora Rebecca Donham, January 17, 1883. She is of Scotch-Irish lineage. It is said that some of her ancestors, at one time, were usurpers of the throne of England. They fled to Spain for safety. The children of this marriage are ; Lulu Ethel, born Jan'y 15, 1884 ; Clyde Edgar, born Sept. 12, 1885, died in 1887 ; Charles Maurice, born July 9, 1891 ; and Norman Donham, born Aug. 31, 1893. George L. Talley is a member of various secret and other societies, is an ardent Republican in politics, and has been connected with the Post Office Department at Cincinnati, Ohio, for about twelve years. He was born June 6, 1850 ; his brother, Isaac Elbie Talley, was born March 28, 1856 ; and his sister, Emma J. Talley, was born July 3, 1847.

Emma J. Talley (797) married Watson N. Brown. They reside at Steubenville, Ohio. Their children were : A daughter who died at the age of 2 years, and George E., a son, died at the age of 13 years.

TALLEYS WHO HOLD FEDERAL OFFICES.

A. B. Talley, Postmaster, Wattacoo, S. C.

Chas. E. Talley, Postmaster, Brokenburg, Spottsylvania, Va.

D. N. Talley, Postmaster, Trussville, Jefferson Co., Ala.

George R. Talley, Postal Clerk, New York to Pittsburg.

John H. Talley, Postmaster, Brandywine Hundred, Del.

John S. Talley, Postal Clerk, Macon, Ga., to Palatka, Fla.

Joseph B. Talley, Postmaster, Holly Oak, Del.

Joshua W. Talley, Postmaster, Ioka, Keokuk, Iowa.

L. F. Talley, Postmaster, New Berlinville, Pa.

Mary E. Talley, Postmaster, Curlew, Va.

W. D. Talley, Postmaster, Grady, Ala.

Wm. E. Talley, Clerk in Post Office, Philadelphia, Pa.

Wm. R. Talley, Postmaster, Crimora Station, Va.

J. N. Talley, Clerk to District Attorney, Macon, Ga.

John G. Talley, Storekeeper and Gauger, Int. Rev. Service, Clark's Hill, S. C.

William Cooper Talley, Government Printing Office, Washington, D. C.

GEOGRAPHICAL NAMES.

A list of Geographical names formed from our family name :

Talley, a town in Carmarthen County, Wales.
Talley Road Station, in the same county, Wales.
Talley Post Office, Cumberland County, Va.
Talley Post Office, Jackson County, Ala.
Talley Post Office, Oconee County, S. C,
Talley Post Office, Marshall County, Tenn.
Talley Covey Post Office, Allegheny County, Pa.
Talleysville Post Office, New Kent County, Va.
Talleyville Post Office, New Castle County, Del.
Talley's Point, in Maryland, on the Chesapeake, near Bay Ridge.

SOLDIERS OF 1861.

A register of the soldiers of the Civil War, so far as information has been received :

Col. William Cooper Talley, 1st Regiment Pa. Reserves, Brevet Brigadier General.
Chaplain John T. Simmons, 28th Iowa Volunteers.
Capt. E. Hillis Talley, Co. " D," 78th Ohio Volunteers.
Lieut. John Smith Talley, 1st Delaware Battery.
Sergt. Chas. W. Talley, 1st Delaware Battery.
Sergt. Wm. A. Talley, 1st Delaware Battery.
Nathaniel Booth, 97th Pennsylvania Vol.
John Booth, 203d Pennsylvania Vol.
Theodore Smith, 203d Pennsylvania Vol.
Nelson T. Himes, 4th Pennsylvania Reserves.
Wm. S. Himes, 68th Pennsylvania Vol.
Sergt. Wellington G. Lloyd, 1st Delaware Reg.
Geo. L. Lloyd, 91st Pennsylvania Vol.
Edward Talley, 5th Maryland Reg.
Adam Clark Talley, Co. " I," 4th Delaware Reg.
Chas. A. Thompson, 91st Pennsylvania Vol.
Wm. T. Thompson, Co. " I," 97th Pa. Vol.
Gideon G. Thompson, 26th Pa., 1st and 99th Pa. Vol., afterwards.

John C. Talley, 3d Delaware Reg., Co. " F."
John Bullock.
William H. Hanby, Co. "A," 1st Del. Cavalry.
Adam Talley Hanby.
Robert S. Johnson, 8th Pa. Cavalry ; also in 198th
Pennsylvania Vol.
Jesse L. Talley, in a Delaware Reg.
Benj. Keller, Iowa.
Henry Grubb, 23d Indiana Reg.
Isaac A. Talley, Iowa.
James K. Polk Bullock, 62d Ohio Vol.
Isaac Jones Talley. In the West.
Nelson S. Talley, 197th Pennsylvania Vol.

Captain E. Hillis Talley died in the hospital from
typhoid fever at Savannah, Tenn. Wellington G. Lloyd
was wounded at the battle of Gettysburg, July 2, 1863, and
lay on the field for several days without the proper attendance.
He was removed to Tilton Hospital at Wilmington, Del., and
there expired on July 29, 1864, and was buried at the Mt.
Pleasant M. E. burying-ground in Brandywine Hundred.

Edward Talley was wounded at the battle of Petersburg, on July 11, 1864, and died on July 21 of the same year.
He was also interred at the Mt. Pleasant burying-ground.

Adam Clark Talley died from fever in a hospital in
Virginia.

George L. Lloyd served in several battles with his regiment, but being a seaman by occupation, he was transferred
to the navy. While in the land service, it is said that he had
a very lucky escape. A ball passed through his coat sleeve,
one passed through his canteen, and still another passed
through his hat. Escaping the dangers of the war, he engaged as captain of a vessel on the great lakes, and was lost
in a storm, with his crew, on Lake Superior, Nov. 19, 1886.

INCIDENTS.

It may be that William Talley the emigrant landed at
Upland (Chester), Pa., at or near where the Penn Landing
Stone is now located. From here he took a westward course,

stopping for a time on the east bank of Chichester Creek, Delaware County, then known as Chester County, Pa. Here he wooed and married Mrs. Elinor Johnson (Jansen), the widow of Jan Jansen, who, it has been claimed, was Vice-Governor Jan Jansen of the Dutch Colony on the Delaware.

William, after spending his honeymoon, passed on to Foulk's Corner, in Rockland Manor, and there located. His descendants moved on gradually westward, until one, William Talley, a great-grandson, met the Brandywine torrents; here he stopped. This William had a son, Rev. John Talley, and John had a son, James Zebley Talley. The latter, in early manhood, gravitated back to Chester, Pa., and for many years resided within two hundred feet of this historic landing-place, and here he passed away.

William Talley the Great had a son Thomas, Thomas had a son Adam, and Adam had a son William D. Talley. William D. resided, after marriage, at Talley's Corner, in Brandywine Hundred; later he moved to Maryland; still later he moved to Delaware County, Pa., and for years lived east of Chichester Creek, on the same tract that Elinor Jansen resided on at the time of her marriage to William Talley the emigrant. William D. Talley died at this place.

William Talley the Great was a member of the St. Martin's Church at Marcus Hook, in Delaware County, Pa.; so were his sons Thomas and William, and his brother Samuel, members there. The only discovered record that shows their relation to this church was found at the home of Benjamin Johnson, who now occupies almost the identical spot on which stood the residence of Jan Jansen of old.

These are merely incidents, and perhaps of some interest as matters of history.

SCHOOLS.

The Talley School House is located on the Naaman's Creek Road, a short distance east of Perry's Hotel, in Brandywine Hundred. The land on which it stands was donated by Curtis Talley by deed dated in 1806, and recorded in Book H³, page 81, at Wilmington. The deed recites that Curtis and Mary Talley his wife, 'In consideration of the esteem which

THE TALLEY SCHOOL HOUSE.

Photographed by W. Arthur Green.

they bear to their neighbors and in regard for the education of children and also in consideration of fifty cents,' etc., sold and conveyed (the tract of land on which the school house was afterwards erected) to Amer Talley, Jesse Plankenton and Joseph Talley, as trustees, for school purposes, and upon which a school house was thereafter to be erected. This deed provides that in case a dispute arises as to the use of the property, it shall be decided by the Legislature of Delaware. Many of the early Talleys were educated at this place. Rev. John Talley and Rev. Curtis Talley both taught at this school. It was used for church purposes for many years after it ceased to be used as a school. This time-honored building is almost a total wreck, as can be seen by the cut on another page.

The Talleys, although not all possessed of a collegiate education, are and have been much interested in educational matters. It is exceedingly rare to find a family with a list of teachers equal to the one here given. This is only a *partial* list, as no doubt many belong herein of whom the proper information has not been obtained. The known list is as follows :—

53.	Rev. John Talley.	174.	Wesley Talley.
165.	Rev. Curtis Talley.	971.	Ida Green.
205.	J. Henderson Talley.	805.	J. Jackson Peirce.
409.	Benjamin F. Talley,	868.	George W. Phillips.
1004.	Martha Stahl.	1181.	Winifred F. Weldin.
1003.	Catharine J. Stahl.	1382.	Mattie W. Johnson.
468.	J. Smith Talley.	1376.	Harriet E. Johnson.
470.	George A. Talley.	1375.	Mary Eva Johnson.
473.	Ella Talley.	1378.	Maggie A. Johnson.
1121.	Mary L. Robinson.	1380.	Sallie E. Johnson.
777.	Henry Grubb.	1377.	Lottie T. Johnson.
624.	William W. Johnson.	1383.	Thos. W. Johnson, Jr.
613.	Thos. W. Johnson.	761.	Matilda B. Walter.
456.	Elizabeth J. Talley.	918.	Hanna R. Lenderman.
132.	Samuel M. Talley.	1198.	Laura E. Booth.
1161.	Penrose R. Talley.	370.	Harman H. Talley.

We gather from this record of teachers that the Talleys were an intelligent class, and did not hide their light under a bushel, but were willing to impart what information they had obtained, to others of their neighborhood. The Church and the Public School are all-important factors in the processes of building up a community and of introducing civilization. In this way are the germs of morality and enlightenment implanted in the home, and the seeds of good government sown in the nation.

CONCLUSION.

The allotted space having been more than filled, our work in this behalf must of necessity come to a close. The searching for our ancestry and genealogy at the early stages brought pleasure and created enthusiasm. As the months passed, the enthusiasm increased instead of diminishing. In pursuing our labors we have passed over all of the hills and through all of the valleys that were along the way. Our work being one largely of friendship, we have no disposition to indulge in odious comparisons of the merits of our family with others. Some may believe it presumptuous for us to issue this book ; but after months of careful application and study, we are wholly unable to find in ethical culture or from the Science of Propriety the *true line* of greatness at which the historian's pen may begin, or the exact point below at which it must be dried and laid aside. Must a subject rise to the eminence of a Napoleon, a Washington, or a Lincoln, before his virtues may be recorded even in a family history ? Should not this delicate question be left to the decision of those who choose to preserve their history in this way?

Having begun this labor with nothing but the best of motives, we have pursued it earnestly and faithfully to the end. The work having passed our scrutiny and judgment, it must now be handed over to the final arbiters—our many kind and indulgent friends—and later, may we hope, to a charitable and generous posterity.

November 15, 1899.

INDEX.

INDEX

HEADS OF FAMILIES IN THE GENEALOGY.

www.ingramcontent.com/pod-product-compliance
Lightning Source LLC
Chambersburg PA
CBHW030355270326
41926CB00009B/1115